American Indian Literature,

Environmental Justice, and Ecocriticism

American Indian Literature, Environmental Justice, and Ecocriticism

THE MIDDLE PLACE

Joni Adamson

THE UNIVERSITY OF ARIZONA PRESS

TUCSON

First Printing
The University of Arizona Press
© 2001 The Arizona Board of Regents
All rights reserved

06   05   04   03   02   01   6   5   4   3   2   1

Library of Congress Cataloging-in-Publication Data
Adamson, Joni, 1958–
American Indian literature, environmental justice, and
ecocriticism : the middle place / Joni Adamson.
p. cm.
Includes bibliographical references (p.   ) and index.
ISBN 0-8165-1791-6 (alk. paper)
ISBN 0-8165-1792-4 (pbk. : alk. paper)
1. American literature—Indian authors—History and criticism.
2. Environmental justice—United States.   3. Environmental
protection in literature.   4. Wilderness areas in literature.
5. Ecology in literature.   6. Indians in literature.   7. Nature
in literature.   I. Title.
PS153.152 A33 2001
810.9′355—dc21   00-010360

British Library Cataloguing-in-Publication Data
A catalogue record for this book is available from the British Library.

For Alice Richards Poole

grandmother, sister, friend

Contents

Acknowledgments

Many people provided invaluable help, advice, and support while I was completing this book. The initial idea was sparked in the 1992 "Poetics and Politics" seminar conducted by Larry Evers and Ofelia Zepeda, which brought twelve American Indian writers to the University of Arizona campus. I am particularly grateful for the opportunity the seminar gave me to interact closely with Joy Harjo, Simon Ortiz, Leslie Marmon Silko, and Ofelia Zepeda.

I am grateful to Barbara Babcock, Larry Evers, and Susan Hardy Aiken, who played key roles in helping me structure my project in its initial stages. Patrick Murphy's early and generous support of my work has always been and continues to be very important to me. I thank him for his insightful suggestions for revision on the first and second drafts of the manuscript. I would also like to thank Annette Kolodny for asking difficult questions that led me to rethink parts of my argument, especially on Silko's *Almanac of the Dead*. Kent Ryden's groundbreaking scholarship on the invisible landscape and on the links between nature, culture, and work has been central to my thinking on these issues, and the book has benefitted from his comments on chapters one through three. Diane Freund brought her novelist's sensibility and creative insights to bear on every page of this book. Her unstinting kindness, generosity, and support kept me from dropping the ball, even when the pulls of writing, teaching, administrating, and parenting seemed too great. Kathleen Donovan provided not only useful comments on the manuscript but a space in her South Dakota home for a summer writing retreat. As we walked by the lake with our dogs, watching and listening to the white pelicans, she helped me break through many a writer's block.

I am also indebted to John Krueckeberg, Mary Lee Sheldon, Jennifer Ellis, June Harris, and Ruth Claros-Kartchner for their meticulous reading and helpful comments; to Carl Etsitty for giving me insight into the Dinéh Alliance and for explaining how water contamination and air pollution affect the Diné living at Black Mesa; to Pat Moreno for helping me research the lawsuits brought by the Dinéh Alliance against Peabody Western Coal; and to the Association for the Study of Literature and the Environment, whose publications and conferences provided me with a supportive scholarly community. I would also like to thank the University Foundation of Sierra Vista for generously supporting my research and writing with a summer grant.

Conversations and correspondence with friends and colleagues helped stimulate my thinking about specific issues raised in the book. I am particularly grateful to Awiakta, Gloria Bird, Claudia Sadowski-Smith, Rachel Stein, and Adam Sweeting. Many thanks as well to the Sierra Vista campus students whose insights enliven this study—particularly Robbie Pock and Martha McGrath. I would also like to thank University of Arizona Press editor Patti Hartmann for her patience and warmth, and Annie Barva for her excellent, thorough copyediting.

For teaching me while they thought they were being taught, I thank the many American Indian students with whom I have worked. I regret being able to name only a few. I thank Michelle Tsosie and Alexandra Tsosie for giving me much insight into what it means to live near Black Mesa, the world's largest open-pit coal mine. I am grateful to Lynette Antone, Melanie Bautista, Debra Cachora, Valentino Carlos, Sherwin Curley, Winnifred Garcia, Kim Jesus, Lynnia Kidde, Patrick Lewis, Clayton Nez, Monica Nuvampsa, Gwen Salt, and Jocelyn Salt for teaching me much about their cultures and for allowing me to share some of their important insights and some of our experiences together.

I was not alone in my trips to Arizona reservations. Adrienne King accompanied me on each of my trips to Tohono O'odham high schools during the 1996 school year. I greatly value her broad knowledge of the social and environmental issues that face American Indians, her activist commitment to working for balanced and positive changes in American Indian communities, and her inexhaustible sense of humor. Gerald Dawaventiwa, Raho Ortiz, Daryl Begaye, and Nikki Chavez have been wonderfully informative and helpful guides on my trips to the communities, high schools, hospitals, historical sites, and sacred places on both the Tohono O'odham and White Mountain Apache Reservations. Roxanne Begay, Garrett Holm, and Celeste Mills accompanied me as teaching assistants to Tohono O'odham high schools and contributed greatly to my understanding of life on and off the reservation.

My experiences in the classroom with students of diverse cultural backgrounds were made possible because of the generous support and encouragement of Debbi Nalwood, Karen Begaye, and Josie Gin at the University of Arizona's Native American Resource Center; Claudia Nelson at the American Indian Studies Office of Community Development; Linda Don and Jonathan Robles at the University Medical Center's Minority Medical Education (Med-Start) Office; Lois Patricio at Tohono O'odham High School; Marietta Martin at Baboquivari High School; and Tom Miller, Tilly Warnock, and Marvin Diogenes of the University of Arizona Composition Program. My heartfelt thanks goes to each of these incredibly dedicated teachers, counselors, and administrators.

Holly Sanchez, the truest of friends, provided my children with a home away from home when I needed quiet time to write and constantly buoyed me with her love and support. My children—Brittany, Nicholas, and Derek—tolerated my forty-hour days with great patience and understanding. I thank them for the music recitals, skating tournaments, and wrestling matches that provided me with time to relax, admire them, and remember the things that really matter. Finally, for his unfailing encouragement, unselfish support, and constant love, my deepest gratitude and thanks go to my husband and friend of more than twenty years, Cole Clarke.

Several chapters were revised extensively from previously published essays, and I would like to acknowledge those original publications. "Cultural Critique and Local Pedagogy: A Reading of Louise Erdrich's *Tracks*" originally appeared as "Why Bears Are Good to Think and Theory Doesn't Have to Be Murder: Transformation and Oral Tradition in Louise Erdrich's *Tracks,*" *Studies in American Indian Literatures* 4, no. 1 (spring 1992): 28–48. Parts of "Simon Ortiz's *Fight Back*: Environmental Justice, Transformative Ecocriticism, and the Middle Place" and "A Place to See: Self-Representation and Resistance in Leslie Marmon

Silko's *Almanac of the Dead*" appeared as "Toward an Ecology of Justice: Transformative Ecological Theory and Practice," in *Reading the Earth: New Directions in the Study of Literature and the Environment,* edited by Michael P. Branch, Rochelle Johnson, Daniel Patterson, and Scott Slovic, 9–17 (Moscow: University of Idaho Press, 1998).

Publishers and authors have generously given permission to use extended quotations from the following works. "Pulling Down the Clouds" and "The Man Who Drowned in the Irrigation Ditch" from *Ocean Power,* by Ofelia Zepeda. Copyright © 1995 Ofelia Zepeda. Reprinted by permission of the University of Arizona Press. "We Must Call a Meeting" and "Resurrection" from *In Mad Love and War,* by Joy Harjo. Copyright © 1990 Joy Harjo. Published by the Wesleyan University Press. Reprinted by permission of the author. "For Alva Benson and Those Who Have Learned to Speak" from *She Had Some Horses,* by Joy Harjo. Copyright © 1983 Joy Harjo. Published by Thunder Mouth Press. Reprinted by permission of the author. "My Father's Song," "Grand Canyon Christmas Eve 1969," "Mid America Prayer," "To Change in a Good Way," "Final Solutions: Jobs, Leaving," "That's the Place the Indians Talk About," "Mama and Daddy's Words," "We Have Been Told Many Things But We Know This to be True," "Returning It Back, You Will Go On," and "Bury Me With a Band" from *Woven Stone,* by Simon Ortiz. Copyright © Simon Ortiz. Published by the University of Arizona Press. Reprinted by permission of the author.

Introduction

Entering the Middle Place

Ecocritics should tell stories, should use narrative as a constant or intermittent strategy for literary analysis. The purpose is not to compete with the literature itself, but simply to illuminate and appreciate the context of reading—that is, to embrace the literary text as language that somehow contributes to our lives "out in the world."
—Scott Slovic, "Ecocriticism: Storytelling, Values, Communication, Contact"

I began writing this book in the mid-1990s while living on the edge of a saguaro and palo verde forest near the Tucson Mountains. Once home to the Tohono O'odham people and, before them, to the Hohokam, these small, saw-toothed mountains are now the location of some of the most rapidly growing housing developments in Tucson. On walks near my home, I have watched archaeologists, hired by the state of Arizona, hurriedly removing pottery shards and farming implements from ancient village sites slated to become golf courses for gated luxury communities. My walks along sandy arroyos also acquainted me with giant, 250-year-old saguaros, some with up to twenty perfectly symmetrical arms, some with arms akimbo, and some with arms that had curved around nearby saguaros for decades, maybe even for a century. Watching these old friends fall before bulldozers clearing land for strip malls and subdivisions, I became passionately converted to the environmental movement.

During the same period of time, I was also teaching composition courses for American Indian students at the University of Arizona and in Tohono O'odham high schools. In 1989, Arizona tribal leaders asked University of Arizona administrators to work more diligently at retention of American Indian students. In response, the directors of the Native American Resource Center and of the English Department's Composition Program decided to create a small freshmen composition class in which American Indian students could support one another academically and socially during their critical freshman year. Upon being invited to teach this course, I designed a curriculum that would take the students' backgrounds and experiences into account by focusing heavily but not exclusively on American Indian cultures and literatures. I taught this class for five years, and when the American Indian Studies Office of Community Development sponsored an outreach program offering composition courses to Tohono O'odham high school students, I began traveling to the Tohono O'odham Nation to teach classes there as well.

My classes brought me into contact with hundreds of American Indian students, and the discussions we had in those classes—about oral and written literatures, indigenous cultures, Anglo-American culture, history, politics, art, and ecology—made me think much more carefully about the insights and challenges that Native American literatures and cultures offer to the emerging culture of environmental concern and to the emerging field of ecological literary criticism, or *ecocriticism*. I was the instructor and had studied the ways Native American cultures and traditions are depicted in contemporary literature, but I did not share my student's Diné, Hopi, San Carlos Apache, Tohono O'odham, White Mountain Apache, or Yaqui cultures or their daily experiences on and off the reservation.[1]

Listening to them talk about their experiences and reading their essays, I was invited to see more from their multitribal perspectives than from the perspective of mainstream American culture and mainstream American environmentalism. For example, in a discussion of Leslie Marmon Silko's *Ceremony,* I might begin by drawing students' attention to Tayo's mystical connection to nature and his journey to wholeness, but my students would redirect our focus to the ways in which American Indians have been stereotyped for far too long by environmentalists and by others as the people with an ancient wisdom that alone can save the planet. Discussions of Tayo's symbolic battle with the "Destroyers" to save the earth were transformed into discussions of the novel's depiction of the literal radioactive poisoning of the Four Corners communities where many of the students live. Every time I wanted to discuss the abstract, aesthetically beautiful concept of "the earth in balance," they wanted to discuss the ways in which Tayo's mother represents the high rates of teenage pregnancy, the high rates of suicide, the high rates of alcohol abuse, and the high numbers of alcohol-related automobile accidents that occur in communities that have been racially marginalized and impoverished by the U.S. government's reservation system. Most importantly, they wanted to discuss the underlying reasons for such imbalances. In *Ceremony,* Silko's description of human relation to the land most certainly taps into the beauty and harmony of American Indian oral traditions, but she always has her eye on power inequities that have distinct and interconnected social and environmental consequences for impoverished people of color communities. My students made sure I noticed the contested terrain.

During the same six years that I was teaching American Indian students, several historical and literary events drew my attention again and again not to the "pristine" natural world celebrated by many mainstream American environmentalists and nature writers, but to the contested terrains where members of marginalized communities had begun mobilizing around issues of environmental degradation that affected their families, their neighbors, and the environments where their homes were located. In October 1991, the First National People of Color Environmental Leadership Summit convened in Washington, D.C., with more than three hundred grassroots environmental leaders from the United States, Canada, Central and South America, Puerto Rico, and the Marshall Islands participating. The purpose of the meeting was to bring together people of African, American Indian, Latino, and Asian descent to discuss their experiences with *environmental racism,* a term that entered into political discussion on the environment in 1987 when the United Church of Christ's Commission for Racial Justice (UCC-CRJ) published a report that found race to be the leading factor in the location of commercial hazardous waste facilities.

The UCC-CRJ report determined that people of color suffered a "disproportionate risk" to the health of their families and their environments: 60 percent of African Americans and Latinos, and more than 50

percent of Asian/Pacific Islanders and Native Americans were living in
areas with one or more uncontrolled toxic waste sites. In the report, the
Reverend Benjamin Chavis, then executive director of the ucc's Commission on Racial Justice, defined environmental racism as "racial discrimination in environmental policy-making and the enforcement of
regulations and laws, the deliberate targeting of people of color communities for toxic waste facilities, the official sanctioning of the life-
threatening presence of poisons and pollutants in our communities, and
history of excluding people of color from leadership in the environmental movement."[2] At the Environmental Summit, delegates took a stand
against environmental racism, drawing up seventeen Principles of Environmental Justice that profile a broad and deep political project to
pursue environmental justice and secure a "political, economic and cultural liberation that has been denied for over 500 years of colonization
and oppression, resulting in the poisoning of our communities and land
and the genocide of our peoples."[3]

In the same month that the People of Color Environmental Leadership Summit was meeting, Leslie Marmon Silko's *Almanac of the Dead*
appeared on bookstore shelves. Today, nearly a decade later, the novel
seems uncanny for having anticipated an event of major importance to
the emerging international environmental justice movement. The novel
revolves around a "people's army" that is gathering in the Mexican state
of Chiapas and calling for an end to human rights abuses and to unjust
expropriation of indigenous lands. Three years after publication of the
novel, on New Year's Day 1994, Silko's people's army seemed to jump
from the pages of fiction and materialize in the real world when rebels
of Mayan decent, calling themselves the Zapatistas, burst out of the rain
forest on the Mexico-Guatemala border and took over several towns in
Chiapas. From the first, the Zapatistas made it clear that they were not
fighting to preserve a pristine rain forest; rather, they were fighting
for the right to plan their own political, economic, and environmental
futures.

The Environmental Summit, *Almanac of the Dead,* the Zapatista rebellion, and the discussions taking place in my classes challenged all my
previous notions about the environmental movement and many of my
previous convictions about Native American literature. It has become
almost a truism in Native American Studies to observe that contemporary American Indian writers examine the relationship between hu-

mans and the land, but novels such as *Ceremony* and *Almanac of the Dead* are not set in the "pristine wilderness areas" celebrated by many mainstream American environmentalists and nature writers. They are set on reservations, in open-pit uranium mines, and in national and international borderlands. These novels question and confront our most popular assumptions about "nature" and "nature writing" by inviting us to take a hard look at the contested terrains where increasing numbers of poor and marginalized people are organizing around interrelated social and environmental problems.

Though Silko finished writing *Almanac of the Dead* many months before the People of Color Environmental Leadership Summit convened in Washington, D.C., her novel ends with an International Holistic Healers Conference that also seems to anticipate this event. The conference brings together Mayan members of the people's army, mainstream environmentalists, spiritual healers, affluent Anglos, working-class people of all races, computer experts, radical environmentalists, and small groups of tribal peoples working to save the lands on which they depend for survival. But Silko leaves the novel hanging on a dystopian note by making it clear that the cultural, philosophic, religious, racial, and economic differences of her characters are so great that their endeavor to work for a better world might fail. Therefore, if delegates to the convention are to be effective, they will need to come together, to engage in the hard work of discussion and debate, and to find some common ground on which to work for social and environmental change.

This book is about the struggle for that common ground. It is about the search to find ways to understand our cultural and historical differences and similarities sufficiently well that we might come together in the "middle place"—that contested terrain where interrelated social and environmental problems originate—to work for transformative change. It is written for everyone who is interested in working to make the world more livable, but it takes a special interest in how writers and literary and cultural critics might employ their talents and training in ways that will help us to understand and change the local, national, and global processes that give rise to social and ecological problems. The focus is on poetry, fiction, and prose written by American Indians, but the book is not meant to be an exhaustive or definitive look at American Indian literature. Rather, I examine a few representative texts in order to suggest that when we begin exploring the differences that shape diverse cultural and literary representations of nature, we reveal the challenge they present to mainstream American culture, environmentalism, and literature, and uncover the rich ground they offer us in which to root new, more multicultural conceptions of nature and the environment. In each of the chapters of this book, I suggest the possibilities that open up for writers, environmentalists, scholars, activists, and teachers when they incorporate multicultural perspectives and literatures into their study and practice.

To put a human face on the social and environmental justice issues raised by an analysis of Native American literature, some of my experiences teaching American Indian students find their way into the pages of this book. Including personal experiences in a book that purports to be a scholarly treatment of literary texts is contested terrain in itself, but my approach might be described as *narrative scholarship,* a term ecocritic Scott Slovic coined in a position paper delivered at the 1994 Western Literature Association Conference in Salt Lake City. Slovic challenged ecocritics to bring their scholarship down to earth by using narrative or storytelling as a "constant or intermittent strategy for literary analysis." The purpose, Slovic explained, is not to compete with the literature itself, but to encounter the "world and literature together, then report about the conjunctions."[4] Certainly ecocritics are not the only scholars to experiment with narrative scholarship or autobiographical criticism, as it has also been called. This increasingly accepted form of literary criticism owes much to the freedom of the essay tradition in general, to the second-wave feminist tenet that the personal is the political, and to the essays of such multicultural writers as Gloria Anzaldúa, Skip Gates, and Houston Baker, who connect their personal experiences to the literary texts they are discussing. Narrative scholarship is based on the notion that life experiences shape and define the critic as a person and cannot be discarded when the critic enters into a piece of writing. Initially, in writing the first chapters of the book, I attempted to maintain the standard, detached voice that is the convention in most literary criticism, but my experiences on and off the reservation with my students and their families, friends, and teachers so shaped and refined my understanding of the texts I was analyzing that I repeatedly found myself writing about them and decided at last to include them. In a sense, I am entering a middle place between scholarship and experience, and reporting on the conjunctions.

In chapter one, I describe my experience driving through the Sonoran Desert to reach the Tohono O'odham high schools where I taught composition. On "the road to San Simon," I began to understand how the cultures and histories of those whose identity has been construed as "Other" imagine new stories that offer us the materials for a more inclusive environmentalism and a more multicultural ecocriticism.

In chapter two, I juxtapose Edward Abbey's *Desert Solitaire* with the struggle for the environment that is currently being waged by Diné and Hopi people at Black Mesa, Arizona. I examine how mainstream conceptions of "wilderness" and "nature" create blind spots in the environmental movement that excuse us from thinking seriously about the consequences of our everyday activities in culture; I also explore why an ecocriticism that focuses solely on works that strictly separate nature from culture hold little promise for activating concrete social and environmental change.

In chapter three, a reading of Simon Ortiz's *Fight Back: For the Sake of the People, For the Sake of the Land,* I examine why we must develop more multiculturally inclusive concepts of nature, justice, and place that are rooted not only in deep, reciprocal relationships to the natural world, but in our diverse cultural histories, in our different relationships to colonial oppression, and in the consequences of race and class marginalization. I argue that writers, critics, and activists who wish to help us find answers to our most difficult social and environmental questions must come home from the wilderness, take a hard look at the middle place where culture emerges from nature, then work to reveal the broad socioecological forces that exploit humans, nonhumans, and their environments.

In chapter four, I argue that working for transformative social change will take more than the incorporation of multicultural literatures and perspectives into the college curriculum. It will take the committed practice of a *local pedagogy* that is informed by a better understanding of local people, cultures, histories, and geographies. In a reading of Louise Erdrich's *Tracks,* I illustrate how multicultural writers are using fiction to make the tools of cultural critique accessible to a wide audience of readers both inside and outside the academy, and discuss how this kind of reading might be employed in the practice of a transformative local pedagogy.

In chapter five, I focus on the poetry of Joy Harjo to examine how

American Indian writers are imagining a more expressive "land-based language" born of English and tribal languages, and capable of conveying a sense of a world in which nature and culture as well as event and place are not separate. I argue that for those who no longer speak the languages of their ancestors, there is no other recourse but to proceed with the search for a language in which to speak of the values by which individuals and communities might organize and regulate their lives morally and ethically in relation to each other and to the places they inhabit.

Chapters six and seven are devoted to an in-depth study of *Almanac of the Dead.* In chapter six, I set the novel into the context of the Zapatista uprising and the recent controversy over the accuracy of Nobel laureate Rigoberta Menchú's autobiographical narrative, *I, Rigoberta Menchú,* in order to examine why the issue of self-representation is key to the emerging international environmental justice movement. Focusing on Silko's four powerful women characters—Yoeme, Lecha, Zeta, and Angelita—I examine why characters in the literature of environmental justice must be persons of action who are not only capable of representing themselves but also prepared to fight for their survival and enter into dialogue and debate over what it means to "protect indigenous peoples" and "save nature."

In chapter seven, I focus on Silko's critique of Euro-American forms of "nature talk," those modernist and colonial philosophies of unlimited progress and unchecked development that rely for their authority on privileged Western scientific notions of objective truth and control of nature, and that sanction the sacrifice of people and their surrounding environments, thereby constituting the philosophical bases of contemporary environmental racism. In this final chapter, by drawing some connections between the wide-sweeping panorama of violence depicted in *Almanac of the Dead* and the recent high school massacres that have taken place all across the United States, I make some observations about how Native American oral traditions and cultures offer us models for communities in which we might more justly govern the relations and generate the practices of humans in the environment.

My hope for the book as a whole is that it will expand the parameters of what is currently considered environmental literature and provide an orientation to literature that is more theoretically, multiculturally, and ecologically informed.

American Indian Literature,

Environmental Justice, and Ecocriticism

CHAPTER 1

The Road to San Simon

Toward a Multicultural Ecocriticism

If, as environmental philosophers contend, Western metaphysics and ethics need revision before we can address today's environmental problems, then environmental crisis involves a crisis of the imagination the amelioration of which depends on finding better ways of imagining nature and humanity's relation to it.
—Lawrence Buell, *The Environmental Imagination*

Imagine an escape. Imagine that your own shadow on the wall is a perfect door. Imagine a song stronger than penicillin. Imagine a spring with water that mends broken bones. Imagine a drum which wraps itself around your heart. Imagine a story that puts wood in the fireplace.
—Sherman Alexie, "Imagining the Reservation,"
The Lone Ranger and Tonto Fistfight in Heaven

A Living Landscape

Adrienne King stood outside the carpool office waiting for me in the April sunshine. She waved when she saw me, and we walked together into the office to sign for the car that we would take to the Tohono O'odham Nation, where we were teaching a course in composition to two different groups of high school students.[1] All semester, we had been assigned to the oldest vehicles, but that day we pulled out of the garage in a new Chevrolet Cavalier. Because we had less than two hours to stop for sandwiches, drive south through Tucson on the interstate, turn west onto State Highway 86, and drive sixty miles to Sells, the capital of the Tohono O'odham Nation, we felt particularly lucky: a new car meant that we could travel fifty-five miles per hour without the unsettling shakes and rattles of the older cars.

Despite the relative proximity of the reservation to the Tucson campus, the Tohono O'odham are one of the most underrepresented groups in the state at the University of Arizona. Though the number of Tohono O'odham entering colleges and universities is steadily increasing, the ideological conflict of choosing between the values, traditions, and philosophies of their cultural heritages and those of mainstream America still leads many students to drop out, sometimes before the end of their freshman year.[2] To address this concern, the American Indian Studies Office of Community Development, in consultation with Tohono O'odham tribal council members and educators, created a program to reach out to high school students in their critical junior and senior years. The aim of the program—and of the composition course that I designed for it—was to recruit more Tohono O'odham students into the university and work toward retention by teaching them the reading and writing skills they needed to be academically successful in college *before* they arrived for their freshman year.

I had met my teaching assistant for the program, Adrienne King, five years earlier in a Freshman Composition course for Native American students that I was teaching at the University of Arizona. Even then, she stood out as a person with a strong sense of her own identity. On the first day of class, she proudly articulated each of the tribes in her genealogy, telling me that she was of Diné, Ottawa, and Delaware descent, and that one day she would become a lawyer and work to improve the lives of American Indian peoples. I could see that she was conscientiously collecting the tools she would need to help her reach a destination she already imagined. This imagined future motivated her to work diligently to improve her writing skills over the course of the year she was my student. When the class ended, we continued to meet often to discuss her political science classes, shop for clothes for her summer internship at the White House in Washington, D.C., and, after she graduated, to talk about the courses she was taking to earn her master's degree in American Indian studies.

Our Tohono O'odham students responded warmly to Adrienne both academically and personally. She had grown up in Tucson but spent most of her summers with her Diné grandmother in the village of Many Farms on the Navajo Nation. As a result, she and the students had much to talk about and often spent class time comparing the similarities and differences of their respective reservations and discussing the prob-

lems faced daily by the people who live there. But our class conversations were not always serious. The students could find the humorous
side of nearly every issue that concerned the reservation—the "rez," as
they called it—and they liked to tease Adrienne and me, so there was
always much laughing and joking going on in our classes.

Of course, the purpose of the course was to teach composition, a skill
not every student was convinced was necessary to his or her future.
When students asked Adrienne candidly if she thought writing was
important for American Indian students, she told them about the time
she wrote to the 3M Company to complain about a defective roll of
Scotch Tape: the company responded by sending her so many boxes of
tape, Post-it notes, and pens that she had no need for school supplies for
the next three years. She used this story to illustrate the power of writing
and told students she planned to use her skills as a writer and eventually
as a lawyer to effect changes on the reservation.

Adrienne and I traveled to Tohono O'odham schools many times, but
our last trip of the spring 1996 semester held great significance because
on that day I realized that the road I had been traveling each week was
leading me to think more carefully about the connections between environmental issues and social issues, and inviting me to make com-
parisons between conventional American nature writing and American
Indian literature. Local Tucsonans call Highway 86 "Ajo Way" because
it stretches across the Tohono O'odham Nation and leads to Ajo, one of
Arizona's small copper-mining towns. Following this road, we crossed
the bridge that spans the dry bed of the Río Santa Cruz, a river that once
flowed year-round. But since the 1940s, the city of Tucson has been
pumping so much groundwater to meet the demands of its population
that the water table has dropped dramatically, and the river and its
towering canopy of cottonwoods have disappeared. Regardless, Tucson's population is still growing, and we drove through one red tile–
roofed housing development after the other on our way out of town.

We always looked forward to the section of Ajo Way that traverses
the Tucson Mountains and passes the tiny town of Three Points because
one has the sense of moving from a highly urbanized world into a more
natural one. The road narrows to two lanes, only an occasional house
dots the landscape, and the desert vegetation becomes more lush and
varied. The winter rains had been heavy that year, so a kaleidoscope of
spring colors added to our sense of entry into another world. Purple owl

clover carpeted both sides of Ajo Way and fields of Mexican gold poppies and orange desert mariposa splashed color across the desert floor. Delicate yellow blossoms dotted the abundant creosote bushes, and green buds were just beginning to emerge at the tops of the giant saguaros' up-stretched arms. In another month or so, these buds would burst into waxy, white flowers and in July ripen into a sweet, ruby-red fruit that the Tohono O'odham make into a ceremonial wine. I could see why the Yaqui, one of the tribes of this region, describe the desert as an "enchanted flower world." Once or twice, I had to remind myself that we were not tourists out sight-seeing for the day and that I needed to drive a little faster so we would not be late for our class at Baboquivari High School.

Near Baboquivari Peak, which is visible at every point of the sixty-mile journey from Tucson to Sells, we crossed the border of the rez and entered the Tohono O'odham Nation. *Baboquivari* is an English version of a Spanish attempt at rendering the original O'odham name, *waw kiwulk,* or "Constricted Hill," words that imaginatively describe the craggy pillar of granite that reaches one thousand feet above the main ridge of the peak.[3] But because of the many stories students had told me about this peak, I knew it was much more to the Tohono O'odham than a dramatic geographical feature of the landscape. To use the words of Creek poet Joy Harjo, it is one element of a landscape that is alive with story, "alive with personality, breathing. Alive with names, alive with events."[4] Perhaps if I had traveled to the Sonoran Desert as a tourist only, passing through but not speaking to the people who inhabit the Tohono O'odham Nation, I might never have become aware of this living landscape. But in class discussions and in their written work, my students drew my attention again and again to an invisible layer of meaning and significance that blankets the physical landscape and binds Tohono O'odham myth and history and culture to this beautiful, arid land.

Baboquivari is sacred to the Tohono O'odham, students told me, because I'itoi, the creator of the Desert People, lives in a cave near the top of the peak. A few students had made the challenging climb to the cave and left offerings of feathers, ribbons, candy, and even a basketball. It is said that I'itoi comes out of his cave to mingle with human beings only when his help is desperately needed. One of the stories about such an occasion concerns a whalelike monster called the *nehbig,* which emerged from a vast lake near the village of Quito Wa:k, far to the southwest of Baboquivari in what is today Sonora, Mexico, and started sucking people, even whole villages, down its throat every time it breathed. I'itoi came to the people's rescue by mortally wounding the monster, which thrashed its body so violently during its dying agony that all the water splashed out of the lake. This story, which explains why there is no water in the now arid landscape surrounding Quito Wa:k, is just one of many traditional oral narratives that express the Tohono O'odham's deep understanding of the land and their relationship to it.[5]

Once I heard this story and others about I'itoi, I could not see Baboquivari Peak simply as the 7,730-foot plug of an ancient volcano; the mountain is I'itoi's home, and I thought about its significance each week as I drove toward Sells. I was learning the difference between what Kent Ryden calls the "cartographic" or "touristic imagination" of outsiders who come into a place with little prior knowledge of or thought about what they are going to see and the "mythic, legendary, historical, and personal imagination" of people who have lived for long periods of time in a place. The outsider and the insider may view the same piece of ground, but where one sees mountains and valleys, the other sees the "invisible landscape" of local and lived significance. The outsider follows a map's pattern of contours, symbols, and colors over geographical surface, but the insider annotates the map, tracing the invisible landscape "through mythic tales, labeling the land with the words and stories of their songs, sketching imaginative contours and dramatic peaks through repeating their traditional narratives." In fact, Ryden adds, "the meaning of a place for the people who live there is best captured by stories that they tell about it, about the elements that comprise it, and about the events that took place within its bounds."[6] Although words and stories are ill-suited for the precision of the cartographer's enterprise, they eloquently reveal the depth of a people's sense of the place in which they live.

When Adrienne and I arrived at Baboquivari High, which sits in the shadow of Baboquivari Peak, we stepped out of the car and into a landscape that holds not only mythic significance for the Tohono O'odham, but daily, lived significance for the high school students who grow up and go to school there. Checking in with the school's counselor before class, we learned that two of our students had won races at a track meet that week, one of the girls had scored eighteen points to help her team win a basketball game, and one student would miss class because he had to stay home and care for his ill grandmother. When the bell rang, we negotiated our way through halls crowded with students hurrying to their next class or talking with friends. Our classroom at the rear of the library had a large round table. When we arrived, a small group of juniors and seniors were sitting there, waiting for us. Two girls, members of the basketball team, were a couple of minutes late, but came in quietly and took their seats. Two weeks earlier, Adrienne and I had asked the students to write a personal response to one of the poems, essays, or short stories we had been reading for class. Their final essays were due that day, so the students spent much of the class period discussing their writing with each other. After collecting their essays, Adrienne and I returned to our car for the forty-mile trip to the small village of San Simon where we would meet with another group of students.

Encountering the Desert:
Terry Tempest Williams and Ofelia Zepeda

The saguaro forest through which we drove to reach San Simon is part of the 2.8 million acres that make up the Tohono O'odham Nation. Reservation lands sit adjacent to Organ Pipe Cactus National Monument, Cabeza Prieta National Wildlife Refuge, and the Barry Goldwater Air Force Range. Together, these four entities comprise one of the largest, primarily intact, arid ecosystems in the world. One million acres of this land have been congressionally designated as wilderness. Many first-time visitors, expecting only sand and spiny plants, are surprised to find so much green in a hot, dry place. More than one thousand species of plants grow in the region, and it is home to some rare and endangered animal species such as the Mexican rosy boa, the burrowing tree frog, the Sonoran pronghorn, and the bighorn sheep. Adrienne and I never saw a Mexican rosy boa, but from the car, even going fifty-five miles per hour, we saw lizards, some with iridescent splotches of blue or green, dart toward the road, think better of crossing, and scurry back into the dense underbrush. Zone-tailed hawks and turkey vultures soared the sky continually, and every week we laughed at a roadrunner or two in a great rush to cross the highway. Once, we saw what we thought was a mirage, a flash of water or light. A snake—probably a rattler and probably close to six feet long—shimmered across Ajo Way in a matter of seconds.

Many of America's best environmental writers—Joseph Wood Krutch, Edward Abbey, Charles Bowden, and Terry Tempest Williams—have written lyrical nonfiction prose about this unique region. Conscious of the ways in which urban populations such as Tucson's are spreading out into the desert, affecting rare plants and animals, and depleting the groundwater so severely that rivers are disappearing, these authors leave urban cityscapes to enter desert landscapes to ponder the meaning of wild places. There is the sense in many of their books and essays that the most important lands remain untouched by humans. In her essay "All That Is Hidden," included in *An Unspoken Hunger,* Terry Tempest Williams, well-known environmental writer and Naturalist-in-Residence at the Utah Museum of Natural History, enters Cabeza Prieta National Refuge with the desire to "get into beautiful country" and observe the elusive desert bighorn sheep.[7] Even though Williams is with her husband Brooke and ethnobotanist Gary Nabhan, she keeps herself separate and alert to the language of landscape as she wanders her "own path in solitude, meandering through mesquite, paloverde, ocotillo, and cholla" (117). In the animated postures of the giant saguaro, she reads the "secret narratives of desert country expressed through mime" and, in that way, hopes to be guided "toward bighorn" (117). All she finds are bones, but as she handles bleached ribs and vertebrae, her thoughts lead her back to a young ram she once saw kneeling in wet sand on the Colorado River. She muses that the mascot of her high school was the ram and wonders how she has found her way from the "pom-pom culture of Salt Lake City to this truly wild place" (119).

Williams's revery is shattered when bombs begin exploding at the nearby Barry Goldwater Air Force Range. Engaging in "military ornithology," she watches as A-10s and F-16s drop ordnance on the "live fire" area where the United States has trained pilots since the 1940s. She wonders what effects the terrifying cacophony of fire and shrapnel have on bighorn. Lying with her back to the earth, gazing up into the sky, she hears the language of rocks, plants, and animals, and voices their response to bombs. "Four jets screech above me, and every cell in my body contracts. I am reduced to an animal vulnerability. They can do with me what they wish: one button, I am dead. I am a random target with the cholla, ocotillo, lizards, and ants. In the company of orange-and-black-beaded gila monsters, I am expendable. No, it's worse than that—we do not exist" (123). Her physical connection to the earth of the Cabeza Prieta reveals the link between the "go-fight-win" culture of her high school and the "Desert Storm culture" of the United States: one reduces the ram to a stereotype and the other reduces desert lands and nonhuman species to expendable targets on a map.

The solitary Williams sees no bighorn that day, but does encounter a sheep carved into rock. Running her fingers over ancient petroglyphs— spirals, mazes, parallel lines, human figures, and bighorn, she muses on the ancient creators of the rock mural: "Who were these artists, these scribes? When were they here? And what did they witness? Time has so little meaning in the center of the desert" (124). Contemplating the petroglyphs further, Williams finds the meaning of her sojourn in the Cabeza Prieta in the etched eye of a stone bighorn: "The land holds a collective memory in the stillness of open spaces. Perhaps our only obligation is to listen and remember" (124). For her, then, the land is timeless, existing entirely apart from any need for human interpretation, but as essential to human existence as bread and water.

As I traveled to San Simon with Adrienne each week, I packed more than a lunch of sandwiches and sodas. I packed Williams's sensuous, detailed descriptions of the flora and fauna of the Cabeza Prieta. I often saw the landscape through the lens of her evocative words. Her essay raises questions about the values of a species that would choose to shatter "wild serenity . . . again and again" (124), and it made me more sensitive to the plight of saguaro and bighorn sheep. My own introduction to the petroglyphs was not solitary like hers, however; it invited me to imagine not "stillness" in the center of the desert, but the sound of human voices.

A short time before I began teaching in Tohono O'odham high schools, I traveled to Sells to meet with some of my future students. I wanted to get the "lay of the land" and a better sense of the needs of the students I would be teaching. Two students and an assistant principal met me at the high school and later took me on a tour of the hospital and on a short hike to see some ancient petroglyphs. At the school, we walked through rooms where Tohono O'odham students study Shakespeare, French, U.S. history, science, computers, and Tohono O'odham culture. Most of the school was relatively empty and quiet because it was summer break, but the gym was filled with noise, literally teeming with kids of all ages—even as young as five—who were shooting hoops at a basketball clinic. As we walked through the gym to get to the other side of the school, balls were flying everywhere, and we had to duck a couple of times.

After the school tour, my hosts took me on a drive through their village. I saw the houses where my students lived, and we stopped to talk with some of their sisters, nephews, parents, and friends. At the Indian Health Services Hospital, they took me through a large waiting room that did not have enough chairs to seat the many people seeking medical attention. The students told me that people needing to see a doctor waited for hours in that room. After a walk through the large dialysis unit and Physical Therapy Department, where the many Tohono O'odham who suffer from diabetes are treated, we gathered in a small conference room to talk to one of the doctors and a nurse about their experiences delivering Tohono O'odham babies, attending to the elderly, and treating car accident victims.

Later, we drove through the village of Topawa and turned off the pavement onto a dirt road that leads to the base of Baboquivari. We were headed to Picture Rock, an unusual outcropping that stands like a long, narrow wall, facing I'itoi's sacred home. As we walked the short distance to the outcropping, I pulled a few of the tiny, resinous leaves from a creosote bush and crushed them between my fingers. For many Tohono O'odham, the clean, desert-rain smell of creosote invokes a living landscape of mythic and sacred meaning: according to the Tohono O'odham creation story, creosote was the first plant to grow from the earth, and the mountains were formed from its resin. Scientists refer to the plant as *Larrea tridenta,* but ethnobotanist Gary Nabhan calls creosote the desert's "drugstore" because Tohono O'Odham uses for the plant extend from birth to death—treating the pains of childbirth, soothing the symptoms of colds, and lining the graves of the dead.[8]

The smell of creosote on my fingers always reminds me of Tohono O'odham writer Ofelia Zepeda's "Bury Me with a Band." In this poem, included in the collection *Ocean Power,* Zepeda's elderly mother tells her children that she wants a Tohono O'odham *waila* band—with its unique mix of fiddle, guitar, accordion, and saxophone—to play at her funeral. She says, "Bury me with a band."[9] Teasing her mother, Zepeda replies, "I don't think the grave will be big enough" (40). When Zepeda's mother passes away, a band plays while she is placed in a grave

lined with creosote so she can have "the smell of the desert with her, / to
remind her of home one last time" (40).

A professor of linguistics at the University of Arizona, Zepeda writes
lyrical poetry and prose about the clouds and rain and plants of the
Sonoran Desert; however, Zepeda's imaginative encounter with the desert is very different from Terry Tempest Williams's imaginative encounter. The people in Zepeda's landscape are connected to the "people
before them," the creators of the ancient petroglyphs scattered throughout the region. Like the "people before them," Zepeda's family and
neighbors still gauge their movements by the sun, especially in the
summer, when work must be planned around the heat and cool of the
day. They still participate in ritual dances to "[pull] down the clouds and
[fix] the earth" (5). Like the "people before them," they are deeply
affected by the smell of the rain, wet dirt, "the bark of mesquite and
other acacias. . . . It is all those things that give off an aroma only when
mixed by rain. It is all breathed in deeply" (2). The smell of summer
rains is associated with the harvest of saguaro fruit, which the Tohono
O'odham gather with long harvesting sticks from the tops of the giant
cactus, then make into ceremonial wine. In "Pulling Down the Clouds,"
a man smells rain, comforted in the knowledge that there is a storm
"somewhere out in the desert." Falling into a deep sleep, he "dreams of
women with harvesting sticks / raised towards the sky" (9–10).

Zepeda intends her poetry to "capture some of our collective memory" (4). But this is not the romantic, timeless "collective memory" about
which Terry Tempest Williams muses. Williams notes the "animated
gestures" of the saguaro but does not mention the people who harvest its
fruit. Williams wonders about the ancient creators of the petroglyphs
but notes that "time has so little meaning in the center of the desert" and
leaves those creators in a mystical past. The people in Zepeda's poetry
and prose feel their connection to the creators of the petroglyphs and
acknowledge the invisible landscape superimposed on the geographical
surface of the land, but they are not "timeless." The Tohono O'odham
have survived against great odds in their desert home, and Zepeda
places them in history, in the cotton fields, mines, urban areas, and
university campuses located throughout the vast region that they once
considered their homelands. In "The Man Who Drowned in the Irrigation Ditch," Zepeda recalls a time when she and her mother were
hurrying through a cotton field familiar because they had walked the

rows so many times to "thin out the growth" and "chop the weeds" (31). Approaching a ditch where a beloved elderly neighbor drowned, Zepeda remembers her mother's grief, made apparent by the way she wrung the towel she always carried. "This towel, a multipurpose kind of thing. / Women carry it to fan themselves, / to wipe sweat, to cover their heads and eyes from sunlight, to shoo away kids, dogs, flies" (31). Years later, Zepeda, moving easily through another familiar landscape—the university campus—shares a moment of laughter with a Tohono O'odham student. "I remember once a student of mine, out of habit, brought her towel with her / to summer school at the university. / Whenever we see each other on campus during a summer session we always / laugh about it" (31).

Still thinking about the creosote, rain, and people in Zepeda's poetry, I hiked with my student guides a short distance to the path that encircles Picture Rock, and we walked around the outcropping. On the west end, where the wall is flat and the surface smooth, we stopped. There, pecked into weathered, rust-colored rock, were several fading petroglyphs—circles, spirals, mazes, and what looked like stick-figure people. I sat on a large, flat rock in front of the images, which seemed to leap and dance in the sunlight. I noticed pottery shards scattered in the sand at the base of the wall and a small basket in which a recent visitor had left feathers, a key, and a miniature basketball. Perhaps this offering was left to thank I'itoi for some good fortune or to ask for help with an illness or need. I looked at the circles and mazes and thought about the creators of these etchings. I imagined that, like my students, they enjoyed a good joke and the company of their friends. I saw them picking up a favorite niece, gathering branches of creosote, creating tightly woven, straw-colored baskets from desert grasses, and carving spirals into rock. I imagined them gazing at Baboquivari, and I looked there, too. I looked back at the petroglyphs and, like Williams, wondered if the images expressed something about an ancient people's relation to open spaces and sacred places.

Williams wanders the open spaces, and when bombs begin blasting the earth around her, she concludes that humans must forge a more reverent, respectful relation to the land. She finds a metaphor for that different relation in silence. "Night in the Cabeza restores silence to the desert, that holy, intuitive silence. No more jets. No more bombs" (124). But there are no people in Williams's silent desert, either. My students, descendants of the people who carved the petroglyphs, were anything but silent, and I could not conclude, after seeing these images and the recent offerings, that the most important lands are those untouched by humans. The petroglyphs provide evidence that, even in the most remote stretches of mesquite and cholla, living beings—both human and nonhuman—have coexisted for centuries. The town of Sells, the hospital, and the basketball in I'itoi's cave are more recent markings on the land than the petroglyphs, but they are evidence nonetheless that the Tohono O'odham still inhabit a living landscape, still respect their sacred places, and—like their ancestors—still work everyday for health and quality of life in the midst of the Sonoran Desert.

Native American Literature and Ecocriticism

In my weekly classes in Sells and San Simon, Tohono O'odham high school students and the American Indian writers we were reading invited me to think more carefully about the insights and challenges that Native American literature offers to the emerging culture of environmental concern and the emerging field of ecological literary criticism. Cheryll Glotfelty, one of the earliest proponents of the study of the relationship between literature and the physical environment, or ecocriticism, notes that, in general, literary scholars have examined the relations between writers, texts, and the world. The "world" is usually synonymous with society—the social sphere. Ecocritics, concerned about the increasingly evident consequences of nuclear testing, overpopulation, acid rain, global warming, and depleted aquifers, ask how literature and literary criticism can be a force for or against environmental change, expanding "the notion of 'the world' to include the entire ecosphere."[10] However, to date, most ecocritics have focused almost exclusively on the nonfiction essays and books of such writers as Henry David Thoreau and Edward Abbey, who, although generally acknowledging the ecological interrelatedness of all things, marginalize or ignore that segment of nature that includes the human or social sphere.

In one of the first and most widely cited essays to argue the value of nature writing and to discuss the theoretical orientation ecocriticism might take, Glen Love decries the limited humanistic vision of most Western literature and the narrowly anthropocentric view of what is consequential in literary study. He notes that the literature in which humans and the workings of human society take center stage is usually considered the most relevant and consequential. "That literature in which nature plays a significant role" is often considered "irrelevant and inconsequential."[11] Even literature written in the pastoral mode, which purports to examine the complex relations of humans to nature, reflects the same sort of anthropocentric assumptions. "Literary pastoral traditionally posits a natural world, a green world, to which sophisticated urbanites withdraw in search of the lessons of simplicity which only nature can teach" (231). But the terms by which "pastoral's contrastive worlds are defined do, from an ecological viewpoint, distort the true essence of each" (231). The "green world" becomes a highly stylized and simplified creation of the humanistic assumptions of the writer and his audience, a place where the main character or characters retreat to sylvan groves in order to attain a critical vision of the good, simple life that will sustain them when they return to the world of human culture, which, despite its complexity, is really the most significant and desirable landscape.

Love argues that many contemporary environmental writers draw on the pastoral tradition but rewrite it. They are creating a "nature-oriented literature" in which there is "a greater understanding of [nature's] complexity, a more radical awareness of its primal energy and stability, and a more acute questioning of the values of the supposedly sophisticated society to which we are bound" (235). They reverse the characteristic pastoral pattern of entry into the green world and return to the more desirable and sophisticated urban world. In their books and essays, contemporary environmental writers assert the greater significance of the green world over the world inhabited by humans.

The pastoral desire to retreat from an increasingly technological, industrialized, urbanized environment into a simpler, cleaner, greener world is perhaps more understandable today than ever. Terry Tempest Williams retreats to the Cabeza Prieta in search of endangered species and a "deep peace" (124). She finds no peace because humans and their technological culture have made saguaro and bighorn sheep expendable targets. Her description of bombs rocking the desert powerfully illustrates why writers and literary critics who are concerned for the environment assert the significance of an increasingly threatened green world over the world of human culture.

As a naturalist, Williams rewrites the traditional pastoral from a perspective informed by a scientific understanding of nature's complexity. The value of her writing rests not only in the ecological information it provides but in its advocacy of nonhuman species and in its indictment of those who destroy the legacy of the land, leaving the human species without the wild places that "elevate and stir our souls" (124).

However, the separation of nature and culture into two contrastive worlds creates blind spots. Williams touches the petroglyphs created by the ancestors of the Desert People but fails to note connections between the absence of modern Tohono O'odham in the Cabeza Prieta and the military assault on bighorn. Cabeza Prieta National Wildlife Refuge, Organ Pipe National Monument, and the United States Air Force Range were established by the federal government in the 1930s and 1940s on lands claimed by the Tohono O'odham. These lands could be represented as "empty" or devoid of human culture only after the Desert People had been expelled from the places they had inhabited for centuries. Once indigenous people were removed, governmental and corporate agencies could represent the region as a blank spot on a map, a sacrifice zone, a target. But the representation of the region as "pristine wilderness" is just as problematic. It assumes that all human culture is exploitative, and it fails to account for the ways in which some human communities have inhabited the land in sustainable ways. It also fails to account for what happens to indigenous peoples after they are removed.

This problem is replicated in ecological literary criticism that focuses solely on writings that assert the greater value of wilderness over lands inhabited by humans because it leaves unexplored the connections between the marginalization and impoverishment of human communities and the exploitation and degradation of the environment. In *Literature, Nature, and Other,* a critical examination of the field of nature writing and ecocriticism, Patrick Murphy observes that several recent anthologies of nature writing acknowledge a "strong sense of the power of nature" in "Native American mythic narratives," but fail to provide any examples of those narratives or any examples of contemporary Native American writing, despite the fact that the Native American Authors Distribution Project catalog lists approximately five hundred titles by American Indian authors, comprising nonfiction, fiction, poetry, and storytelling. The effect of these editors' decisions, according to Murphy, is to "create the impression that Indians have had nothing to say on their own and that they are saying and writing nothing today, literary or otherwise."[12] Also, by defining nature writing as nonfiction books or essays that emphasize the observation of specific, "factual" details about the natural world, the editors of these anthologies privilege a style of writing practiced in the last two centuries predominantly by white male writers such as Henry David Thoreau, John Muir, and Edward Abbey, and by a few white female authors who write in a similar style, such as Annie Dillard and Terry Tempest Williams. Then, based on this narrow definition, they omit the work of American Indian writers from their anthologies because it is infused with stories from the oral tradition, which they describe as "mythic" or "not factual" and therefore not written in the style of the "naturalist."[13]

The problem with the strict codification of what we mean when we say "environmental literature" or "nature writing," Murphy points out, is that it closes the field of ecocriticism to the challenges, voices, and imaginative visions of multicultural peoples and multicultural literatures. Few texts written by contemporary American Indian writers fit the paradigm for a "nature-oriented literature" that exists "outside of human life" (Love 230, 233). In Ofelia Zepeda's *Ocean Power,* for example, there is no "out there" because the desert *is* home, a place where Tohono O'odham cotton farmers and university students—like the "people before them," pull down the clouds and fix the earth, work, go to school, harvest saguaro fruit, and bury the dead with creosote. Whereas the nature writer retreats from human culture to observe the flora and fauna, the American Indian writer maps a landscape replete with meaning and significance for the people who have lived there for long periods of time and often in circumstances in which they have suffered a marginalization and impoverishment connected to the degradation of their environment.

This is not to say, however, that all environmental writers are unaware of the connections between human suffering and the degradation of the environment. For example, as a member of a Mormon community that—out of a sense of patriotism and in the name of religion—blindly trusted the U.S. government when it assured them that nuclear testing would have little effect on their lives, Terry Tempest Williams understands firsthand how environmental destruction can have effects that devastate both human and nonhuman species. In the 1970s, nearly twenty years after nuclear testing in Nevada began, Williams's Utah-based family, most notably her mother and grandmother, suffered and died from breast cancer. Making connections between nuclear fallout and cancer, Williams writes movingly of her family's experience in her most well-known work of nonfiction, *Refuge*. In that book, she notes that when the Atomic Energy Commission, justifying the virulently dangerous nuclear fallout they knew would settle over vast areas of the American West, described the country north of the Nevada test site as virtually uninhabited desert terrain; "my family and the birds at Great Salt Lake were some of the 'virtual uninhabitants.' "[14] Finding common cause with activists around the world, she has traveled to the Nevada test site for such events as the International Mass Demonstration and Non-violent Direct Action to support a comprehensive nuclear test ban. In "Wild Card," a story from *An Unspoken Hunger,* she celebrates the work of activists such as Rachel Carson, whose book *Silent Spring* alerted the world in 1962 to the dangers to human and nonhumans when pesticides enter the food chain; Wangeri Maathai, whose Green Belt Movement in Kenya drew attention to the danger to human communities of de-forestation; and Lois Gibbs, who brought the issue of toxic wastes to mainstream U.S. culture when she began to speak out against twenty-two thousand tons of poisons bubbling up from the underground in the Love Canal neighborhood of Niagara Falls, New York.

But despite her clear understanding of the connections between human suffering and environmental exploitation, when Williams urges her readers, as she does in "Wild Card," to "stand their ground in places they love" (139–40), there is the sense that those places we should defend are wild places—the red-rock country of southern Utah, the Bear River Migratory Refuge, and the Cabeza Prieta National Wildlife Refuge—not Salt Lake City, where her family lives, or the reservations to which the original inhabitants of most places still considered pristine have been moved. Certainly, we need voices calling out for our treasured, still relatively intact natural places. But in the remainder of the chapter, I want to explore what we learn when we listen to the voices of American Indian writers who, for the most part, are not calling on us to defend wild places, but are writing poetry, fiction, and creative nonfiction that is most often set in highly contested areas where people live. *Almanac of the Dead,* for example, is set in several highly contested places on the U.S.–Mexico border and on the border of a Central American rain forest, where Mayan revolutionaries are preparing to "retake" their ancestral homelands. Silko's *Ceremony* and Simon Ortiz's *Fight Back: For the Sake of the People, For the Sake of the Land* explore the effects of corporate nuclear contamination of the Four Corners area on the Pueblo people who have lived there for centuries. Louise Erdrich's *Tracks* is set on the Turtle Mountain Chippewa Reservation, twenty-five years after passage of the Dawes Act allotted Indian land and allowed sections of it to be sold, piecemeal, to logging companies. Sherman Alexie's short stories, collected in *The Lone Ranger and Tonto Fistfight in Heaven,* are set in the urban neighborhoods of Seattle or on the Spokane Indian Reservation.

In the *Environmental Imagination,* Lawrence Buell observes that environmental crisis involves a crisis of the imagination and a need to find better ways of imagining "nature and humanity's relation to it."[15] If this observation is true, then writers and scholars and teachers who are concerned about the increasingly complex environmental crises we face as we move into a new century must be willing to search out the most thoughtfully imaginative works of environmental reflection—not only those that confirm preconceived notions about nature, but also those that challenge perceptions and expand definitions and generic conventions.

Traveling Ajo Way each week, I began to see more clearly why American Indian authors set their imaginative works in noisy, contested landscapes that are alive with myth and history rather than in landscapes that are "silent open spaces." Listening to Tohono O'odham students discuss the writing of Alexie, Silko, Ortiz, or Zepeda and their own compositions, I also began to understand more clearly why American Indian authors are challenging our perceptions about the environment and at the same time helping us to understand the role that the imagination plays in transforming the possibilities for fundamental social and environmental change. All of this gave me insight into why the development and practice of more multicultural ecocriticism matters.

Sherman Alexie and the Power of the Imagination

When Adrienne and I looked out over the landscape on our weekly trips, we saw more than the saguaro, creosote, owl clover, and gold poppies. We did not focus our discussions solely on petroglyphs, I'itoi, or Baboquivari. We passed the Indian Health Service Hospital at Sells, with its large dialysis wing, and discussed how the disruption of traditional diets after the U.S. government restricted hunting and food-gathering activities on tribal lands could be one cause of the high rates of diabetes among American Indian peoples. Adrienne told me about some of the research being done to see how traditional tribal foods such as mesquite-bean flour might be used to prevent and control diabetes. We talked of the white crosses—decorated with mylar balloons, ribbon, and brightly colored plastic flowers—that dot the roadside. A syncretic blend of Indian and Catholic religions, these crosses mark the spots where people have been killed in car accidents. Doctors at the hospital and our Tohono O'odham colleagues at the high schools told us that many accidents on the reservation are alcohol related, and we talked about what happens to a people who, over the course of hundreds of years, are displaced from traditional lands and forcibly educated away from their languages and lifeways. When we passed small houses that would not keep out desert heat or monsoon rain, Adrienne, who had been focusing on federal Indian policy in her graduate work, talked about broken treaty agreements and the low quality of government-built housing. We passed a few houses surrounded by rusted-out vehicles and discussed the ways in which persistent poverty contributes to environmental problems. We could not drive Ajo Way without noticing the patterns of injustice that encompass both people and their environments.

The very presence of Tohono O'odham students in the classroom made me aware that a description of the Sonoran Desert that focused only on animal, plant, and "pristine," unpopulated areas would insufficiently address both the Desert People's long relationship to the land and the connections between social injustices and environmental degradation. Before colonization, the Tohono O'odham were dependent on and shaped by the land they inhabited. They planted corn near the mouths of arroyos to take advantage of summer rains. When necessary, they protected their families from more aggressive tribes making raids on their stores of food. After the coming of Spanish colonial priests and later of U.S. government officials, the threat to their lands and to their quality of life was no longer simply a matter of adverse meteorological conditions or hostile tribes; now the threat was a systematic assault on the entire culture in the form of forced education and imposed reservation borders.

Baboquivari Peak, the cultural center of the Tohono O'odham universe, stands witness to this assault. Because it is visible for one hundred miles in every direction, the mountain is a testament to the history of O'odham-speaking peoples, who once lived far beyond the borders of the present-day reservation.[16] With the 1848 Treaty of Guadalupe Hidalgo and then the Gadsden Purchase six years later, the United States and Mexico split traditional Tohono O'odham homelands without consulting the O'odham. The international border impeded free travel, and many Tohono O'odham families found themselves forcibly separated. In 1916, the United States reduced the Tohono O'odham's land base by three-fourths, when it established a 3.1-million-acre reservation. Later, in the 1920s, the Phelps Dodge Corporation discovered copper on reservation lands, and the United States Congress, by unilateral decree, removed the ore-bearing area from O'odham control: Ajo, located on former Tohono O'odham lands, became a prosperous copper-mining town. But the southern Arizona copper belt, yielding fully two-thirds of all U.S. copper ore, has not economically benefitted the Tohono O'odham tribe, which lost its lands and gained nothing in return.[17]

Because their lands have been split by political boundaries, appropriated for resource exploitation, and cordoned off for national wilderness areas and military bombing ranges, modern Tohono O'odham understand that the roots of poverty, injustice, and environmental degradation lie at the heart of Western culture's favorite story about itself. As William Kitteridge has put it so aptly in *Owning It All*, the "primary mythology of the American West is . . . a mythology of conquest. . . . [O]ur story of law-bringing is a story of takeover and dominance, ruling and controlling, especially by strength."[18] The creation of legal entities such as the Tohono O'odham Reservation or Cabeza Prieta National Wildlife Refuge is the attempt to impose civic law on "Others" of all kinds—desert peoples, animals, and vegetation. The lawmaker presumes a position of power from which to do the lawmaking. Under the terms of this story, the lawmaker can (and does) appropriate Tohono O'odham lands for copper mining or use Cabeza Prieta and the adjoining Barry Goldwater Air Force Range to test the latest military artillery. Tohono O'odham tribal leaders and educators understand that in order to restore health and balance to both human and nonhuman communities in the Sonoran Desert, the Desert People must do more than seek peace in the sonorous silence of wildness. In order to live in dignity and work toward social equality, they must gain access to the power to change the story of conquest and colonization, and create a new story. Consequently, some of the key sites of the Tohono O'odham's struggle for their environment are far from the open-pit mines and the military testing ranges: the battle for the environment is also taking place in schools and universities.

Each time I traveled to Sells and San Simon, it was clear to me that Adrienne and I had been invited into Tohono O'odham high schools not simply because U.S. colleges and universities are seeking to increase minority representation, but because the Tohono O'odham themselves have resisted colonial oppression for hundreds of years and have continually called attention to the interrelated social and environmental injustices committed against their peoples and lands. Many of our students had a strong sense of the role their people's ongoing resistance played in their own educations. When I asked them to read and respond to Louise Erdrich's poem "Indian Boarding School: The Runaways," for example, they wrote essays that included stories about grandparents, aunts, uncles, and parents who had either run away from U.S. government boarding schools because of harsh treatment or who, as a form of protest against being forcibly taken away from their homes and families, had refused to do schoolwork and chores. In these stories, the grandparent or uncle was a hero, a model of courage and independence. But in nearly every case, wrote my students, grandparents or parents ended their stories about their boarding school experiences with an admonishment to the child or grandchild to stay in school and get good grades because education would be one of the keys to the survival of their culture. The implicit message of these stories was that in the last five hundred years, whole tribes had been lost to genocide or disease; treaties had been broken; individuals had been betrayed, murdered, or lost to alcoholism. But like the heroes of the boarding school stories, native people are still here. Tribes such as the Tohono O'odham are increasing not only because grandparents, uncles, aunts, and parents have refused to assimilate, disappear, or give up their vision of the world, but also because they understand that they must—at the same time—learn how dominant culture works. They encourage their children and grandchildren to learn about global politics, U.S. federal policies, corporate law, science, and medicine as well as traditional tribal culture.

If Adrienne and I successfully met the goals of our program, it was in large part because Tohono O'odham high school administrators, teachers, and staff members work day after day, week after week, and year after year to help more students graduate and enter college. We saw examples of their commitment every time we traveled to the reservation. The counselor at Baboquivari High, for instance, knew each student's name and background and updated us weekly on his or her activities and needs. One of the English teachers at Tohono O'odham High worked tirelessly in her own classroom each day and tutored our students on their writing assignments during the week. She also kept in touch with her daughter and other O'odham freshmen who were already at the University of Arizona to make sure they were getting the social and academic support they needed. Our Tohono O'odham colleagues did not use the specialized language of contemporary cultural and literary theory, but clearly they understood that in a world of uneven power relations, where certain groups are routinely silenced and disempowered, gaining access to the power to change the story will require them to search for common ground with people from many differing groups—both Native and non-Native. They saw our course as a tool they could incorporate into their ongoing efforts to imagine a new story and to create a better "environment" on the reservation. Like their ancestors, who called on I'itoi to come out of the cave on the west side of Baboquivari when his help was desperately needed, contemporary O'odham courageously use whatever tools necessary—whether traditional ceremonies or university programs—to ensure the survival of their people and community. They invited Adrienne and me to join them in an alliance to foster their students' imaginations.

Our students came to the class with their own ideas about what relationship an introductory college composition course might have to their futures. Some had strong aspirations to go to college and saw this class as a way to prepare themselves. For others, college seemed remote, maybe even academically or financially impossible, and this class was simply a way to explore the possibilities. Each student imagined a different future for him- or herself. Some of their aspirations were particularly memorable: a young mother returning to high school at the age of twenty wanted to become a nurse because of the injury her toddler had suffered when he accidentally stepped into a cooking fire; a basketball star with a 4.0 grade-point average couldn't decide whether he would study computers, play sports, or practice law; a young man with gang tatoos wanted to write poetry and always had either a Rudolfo Anaya or Tony Hillerman novel on his desk; and a talented writer—who kept getting caught with marijuana because, as she put it, "There is nothing else to do out here"—imagined herself a journalist.

On our last day in San Simon, I collected the students' final essays, and we spent some time discussing them. Most of the students had chosen to write responses to "Imagining the Reservation" from Sherman Alexie's *The Lone Ranger and Tonto Fistfight in Heaven,* which is set not in some pristine old-growth forest somewhere in the Northwest but on contested ground, the Spokane Indian Reservation. My students enjoyed Alexie's writing because it confronts reservation life with the same biting humor that they employ in confronting the challenges they face in their own lives. Alexie addresses alcoholism, suicide, car accidents, poverty, and racism both on and off the rez. His main characters, Victor and Adrian (who have given up beer for Diet Pepsi), face their lives with laughter, resistance, and basketball.[19] Yes, basketball—that was what my students really loved about these stories. Basketball is very important on the Tohono O'odham Reservation and many other American Indian reservations as well. Alexie writes that both male and female basketball players are revered by American Indian communities because "like everybody else, Indians need heros to help them learn how to survive."[20]

In "The Only Traffic Light on the Reservation Doesn't Flash Red Anymore," Victor and Adrian sit on the front porch and speculate that Julius Windmaker—the latest reservation basketball hero, the newest "little warrior"—will be the one to finally "make it all the way": "Julius Windmaker was the latest in a long line of reservation basketball heroes, going all the way back to Aristotle Polatkin, who was shooting jump shots exactly one year before James Naismith supposedly invented basketball" (45). Julius ends up becoming an alcoholic and another legendary figure in the "history of reservation heroes who never finish high school, who never finish basketball seasons" (47). Victor and Adrian observe that "it's hard to be optimistic on the reservation" (49). But they do not give up hope. They sit on the porch and talk "about some kid named Lucy in the third grade who already had a nice move or two" (51). When they see her walking down the street with a basketball under her arm, they tell each other, "that's her," the "little warrior." "God, I hope she makes it all the way" (53).

In "Imagining the Reservation," Victor and Adrian engage in wild speculation: "Imagine Crazy Horse invented the atom bomb in 1876 and detonated it over Washington, D.C. Would the urban Indians still be sprawled around the one-room apartment in the cable television reservation? Imagine a loaf of bread could feed the entire tribe. Didn't you know Jesus Christ was a Spokane Indian? Imagine Columbus landed in

1492 and some tribe or another drowned him in the ocean. Would Lester FallsApart still be shoplifting in the 7-11?" (149). The powerfully direct questions in this passage clearly root Lester FallsApart's problems in historically inequitable social relations between indigenous peoples and the European peoples who colonized the Americas. At the same time, Alexie's queries assert fairly loudly that problems will never be solved until people begin imagining a new story, speculating about how things could be different. Imagination, writes Alexie, can be an "escape. . . . a perfect door . . . a song stronger than penicillin" (152–53). Imagination, the story implies, is the first step toward solution.

The essays students handed in that last day were about a place they had imagined even before they read about Crazy Horse's A-bomb or Columbus's watery demise. In this imagined place, there would be college-prep classes for future nurses and computer programmers, decent basketball courts on which the first Native American Michael Jordans would get their starts, and a youth center so that future poets and journalists would have more to do than join gangs or rely on marijuana for recreation. More students would finish high school and college, return home to help their people, and work to improve their communities and environments. On this future rez, the groundwater would be clean, not contaminated by the open-pit mines and dumps that scar the face of Tohono O'odham lands. Sustainable economic development would provide jobs and end unemployment. Poverty would be eradicated and people would no longer depend on U.S. government welfare checks and commodity foods. The end of poverty and welfare would lead to improved diets, and fewer people would suffer from diabetes. There would be no alcoholism. Using their imaginations to speculate about how things could be different, the young mother, the basketball star, the poet, the future journalist, and their classmates wrote of an environment that means something entirely different from what it typically means to Sierra Club members. For these students, any description of a fight for the environment would have to include the struggle for decent wages, housing, education, and health care.

What is important about my students' writing and about American Indian literature is not only that they raise our consciousness about the ways in which social and natural environments are inextricably connected, but that they imagine the possibilities for fundamental transformative change. As Sherman Alexie's "Imagining the Reservation" and my students' responses to it illustrate, imagination can be the first step to saying "no" to social and environmental injustices. It plays a powerful role in the struggle for survival—for empowerment, recognition, and respect—and in a peoples' emancipation from the oppression of material want, from domination by others, and from environmental degradation.

Only when ecocritics become willing to broaden the scope of their inquiry beyond the generic conventions of nature writing will they be able to account for the kinds of interrelated social and environmental issues that multicultural writers such as Ofelia Zepeda and Sherman Alexie are raising in their nonfiction, fiction, and poetry. Only then will they be able to understand the challenge these writings present to the mainstream environmental community, to the scholarly community, and to ecological literary studies.

My aim in bringing the work of writers such as Terry Tempest Williams, Ofelia Zepeda, and Sherman Alexie together in this chapter has not been to dismiss more conventionally generic nature writing, but to show why writers, environmentalists, scholars, and those interested in developing an ecological literary criticism must expand the field of their vision and the scope of their studies to include other-than-dominant cultures and multicultural literatures. By examining diverse literary representations of how different groups of people understand, live in, and change their environments, we deepen and enrich our understanding of human/nature relationships and gain insight into why the activities that transform nature (planting fields, building cities, establishing reservations, creating wilderness refuges, opening mines) must be understood as fundamentally ecological processes that either contribute to the survival of human and nonhuman species or lead to their destruction. If we are to survive, Williams, Zepeda, and Alexie all seem to be saying, we must imagine new stories about human relation to nature. Our very future depends on it.

Into Contested Terrain

At the end of our final class at Tohono O'odham High School, Adrienne and I returned to our university car and drove east, with the sun hanging low on the horizon behind us. Near Quijotoa, a small O'odham village situated high in the rolling hills between San Simon and Sells, we came to a stop and pulled off the road when a coyote bounded from the brush, running right in front of our car across Ajo Way toward the village cemetery. We stopped in part because coyotes are rarely seen during hot, desert afternoons; they are generally most active during the cooler mornings and at night. We were also curious to know why a coyote would be headed straight into the village in broad daylight. Stepping out of the car into the April heat and the dusty-clean scent of creosote, we shaded our eyes with our hands and watched the coyote pick its way through the O'odham cemetery, with its rows of white, blue, pink, and green crosses decorated with the artificial flowers and shiny mylar balloons that survive the Sonoran sun better than real flowers. Emerging from the cemetery, the coyote—which was unusually large and probably male, with a shiny, thick, golden coat and darker, black striations on its shoulders, back, and tail—headed toward the mission-style chapel in the middle of the village. There are many sub-species of coyote, and many times both Adrienne and I had seen the small, dull-grey version that frequents Tucson's arroyos, but I had seen a coyote like this one only once before.

In the spring of 1990, as I was on my way to the university to teach an 8:00 A.M. class, I was driving down a road where developers were just beginning to cover the hills with identical pink stucco houses. At an intersection, a large golden coyote bounded out of the desert where the bulldozers were already at work clearing ironwood and creosote, and reshaping the hills into flat lots. The coyote glanced at me, then ran across the intersection in the direction of the Tucson Mountains. I felt both elation and sadness: elation because I knew it was an extremely rare thing to see such a healthy, sleek coyote so close to a large urban area and sadness because I knew the bulldozers would erase his tracks, and I would probably never see him again. But six years later, he—or his cousin—emerged from the mesquite and creosote in front of the university car in which Adrienne and I were traveling and trotted across Ajo Way. I have no idea why the coyote felt bold enough to enter the village during the day, but Adrienne and I watched him until he disappeared from view behind the Quijotoa chapel. Adrienne told me that her Diné grandmother taught her that coyote is a messenger and that the direction in which he crosses your path has significance. She was not sure what news our coyote was bringing us, but said she would ask her grandmother the next time she traveled to Dinétah, or Navajoland, for a visit.

Adrienne has never told me what her grandmother said about the coyote we saw, but I have thought about him many times since that day. Scholars believe that both the name *coyote* and the O'odham chapel at Quijotoa cast lines of connection from contemporary American Indian cultures in the American Southwest back to ancient Mesoamerican cultures. The word *coyote* comes from the Aztec word *coyotl* and is associated with the god Heuheucoyotle, the mischief maker. The Quijotoa chapel, one of sixty small churches scattered across traditional O'odham lands in Arizona and Sonora, was not built by Catholic missionaries but by the O'odham themselves for use in what some writers have called "Sonoran Catholicism." Folklorist Jim Griffith notes that the O'odham in Arizona and Sonora seem to have developed this religion over time. It is a kind of "native Christianity" that brings together a complex, yet unified system built from elements of American Indian and European cultures. Griffith observes that the O'odham are not Aztecs, but they are related culturally to Central Mexican people and belong with them to the Uto-Aztecan language family. Also, the architectural features of O'odham chapels and surrounding areas are designed to accommodate ritual processions, music making, feasting, dancing, and games that are reminiscent of the rituals practiced in the great temples and ball courts of pre-Columbian Mesoamerica.[21]

Guiding my vision through the desert, across Ajo Way, and toward the mission chapel, the coyote entered my imagination. I have seen him in Tucson, flicking his ears and glancing askance at the bulldozers clearing the desert. I have imagined him traversing the Tucson Mountains, dancing on the borders of the rez, tracking bighorn, eluding F-16s. He lopes after school buses lumbering down Ajo Way in the direction of Baboquivari High School. I see him sneak into classrooms, where he sits rapt, while teachers and students bring together complex elements of both American Indian and European cultures to forge the tools—and the stories—they will need to create the future. When the school bell rings, he bolts, coming to a stop before the ancient mural at Picture Rock, where he sits down to read some of the first "American literature." His studious demeanor invites me to think about the ways in which American Indian peoples have been creating some of the most searching works of environmental reflection for hundreds, even thousands of years. His path through the desert to the petroglyphs suggests that finding better ways of imagining nature and humanity's relation to it will require going beyond the silent wildlife refuges and nature parks of most American environmental writing; it will require trekking into contested terrain, the same terrain that my students made sure I noticed, the same literary terrain in which contemporary American Indian writers reveal patterns of connection between social and environmental injustices. Emerging from the mesquite near Quijotoa, the coyote crosses Ajo Way, laughing as he transgresses the boundary between nature and culture. He playfully pushes a basketball around the ball court near the chapel, then disappears behind its earthen walls. In my mind, I see him continuing his journey, tracking the same lines of narrative and belief that Leslie Marmon Silko follows in *Almanac of the Dead,* all the way back to the first "American literature"—the hieroglyphic almanacs of the ancient Maya.

In the chapters that follow, my interactions with my students and my encounter with the coyote guide my discussion of the ways in which American Indian writers explore an invisible landscape of myth and history, one that is inextricably bound to the physical geography of the Americas. Infusing their work with ancient creation stories and historical narratives of Mayan resistance to Spanish oppression or the Pueblo Revolt of 1680, these writers reach back more than five hundred years to show us that nature has a history and that some constructs of nature are detrimental to human communities, primarily those of the poor and marginalized. By exposing the historical and ecological effects of certain dominant ideologies on humans and on the nonhuman world, these writers reveal the limitations of such ideologies as theoretical foundations for a just environmentalism and at the same time imagine possibilities for different futures—futures in which it might be possible for humans to live, work, and play *in* nature, but in ways that allow for continued survival of both human and nonhuman species.

With the coyote still trotting through our imaginations, Adrienne and I returned to our car, and I merged back into traffic. When Baboquivari Peak came into view, I was immediately struck, as I always am, by its craggy, granite beauty. I could see the vertical spur on the west face, where I'itoi's cave is located, and I thought of the basketball—left there as an offering to I'itoi by one of my students—in the midst of many other offerings of baskets, feathers, rosary beads, mylar balloons, and ribbons. That basketball stands in my mind as a symbol of how much the American Indian students I have taught over the years are like Victor, one of Sherman Alexie's characters in "Imagining the Reservation."

Victor recognizes the importance of traditional culture, and, at the same time, he lives in a very modern world. He defies stereotypes of the "dying but noble savage" by surviving among the people who created the atom bomb, cable television, and 7-11s. Refusing alcohol and adopting an alternate addiction, Diet Pepsi, he sees that where we need to go is not "back to nature" or a romanticized time before Columbus, but forward to a place we still have need of imagining.

Still thinking of the basketball, I left the Baboquivari Mountain Range and drove through purple clover and gold poppies to Tucson.

CHAPTER 2

Abbey's Country

Desert Solitaire and the Trouble with Wilderness

> In the center of the world, God's navel, Abbey's country, the red
> wasteland.
> —Edward Abbey, *Desert Solitaire*

Into the Canyon

The June sun touched the earth in pillars of light despite the dark clouds
and lightly falling rain. Ankle-deep in the Paria River, with my Camp
Trails pack on my back and my Teva sandals on my feet, I was ten miles
into a thirty-seven-mile hike through a rugged slot canyon in the Paria
Wilderness. Those who have read *Desert Solitaire,* Edward Abbey's
collection of essays celebrating the red, yellow, and orange canyons and
pinnacles of the Four Corners area, often think of this terrain as "Abbey's country," a name that conveys the intense connection Abbey felt
toward "the red wasteland."[1] Abbey's essays and novels have drawn
many a hiker, camper, and tourist to Utah and Arizona, and as I waded
down the shallow stream that is the trail through most of Paria Canyon,
I could hear his words echoing from every sandstone arch and balanced
rock. The light rain falling on my face brought to mind the stories
Abbey relates of people hiking through sun-drenched canyons one min-
ute, then swept away in angry ten-foot-high flash floods the next. So I
was acutely aware of my surroundings: the give of sand, the firmness of
rock, the rise of water, the flash of lightning. I looked at the sheer
vermillion cliffs, so infamous for their inescapability during a flash
flood. This storm looked relatively nonthreatening, the kind of misty,
drizzling rain the Diné call "female rain." However, in the canyonlands,
a storm twelve miles away or some other distant event can have unfore-
seen consequences, so I was paying close attention to every small change
in the river. My reading of the landscape could mean the difference
between life and death.

Abbey has often been described as a voice crying out for the wilderness, but his was not the only voice shaping my reading of Paria Canyon. Four days earlier, curious to see the place about which several of my Diné and Hopi students had written so passionately, I traveled to Kayenta, Arizona, to meet with two of my Diné students and take a drive through Peabody Western Coal's Black Mesa mine. The mine is located on Black Mesa, a magnificent 3,300-square-mile "sky island" so dense with juniper and pinyon that, from a distance, it looks black. To the Diné, Black Mesa is a sacred land of shrines and spirits; it is the Female Mountain whose eternal and natural balance with neighboring Lukachukai, the Male Mountain. Together, these mountains symbolize harmony, which—along with beauty—is the Diné Way.

But during the last twenty years, the mesa has been ravaged by the world's largest coal strip-mining operation. Eleven thousand Diné and one hundred Hopi people, living on jointly occupied land on Black Mesa, are facing eviction and forcible relocation because of the passage of the Relocation Act, a federal law ostensibly mediating a land dispute between the Diné and Hopi but which the people themselves argue simply facilitated the opening and expansion of the mine.[2] The beleaguered people who refuse to leave their homelands and the sacred shrines located there now drink from wells that have been contaminated by toxic levels of copper, lead, and arsenic from the mining operations. Residents also suffer from respiratory illnesses they blame on the excessive coal dust that results from blasting at the mine.[3]

In *Desert Solitaire,* Abbey laments the mineral speculation and mining that has pocked the Four Corners area generally and discusses Black Mesa specifically, but the focus of his book is still "Abbey's country," a place located somewhere outside the contaminating reach of human culture. The Diné, on the other hand, have responded in more concrete ways to the social and ecological threat posed by the world's largest open-pit coal mine. Some of the people living closest to the mine have formed the Dinéh Alliance, a group of Diné people who have pledged to fight for social and environmental justice for the people and for the land.

In this chapter, by bringing *Desert Solitaire* into dialogue with some of the observations of my Diné students and with a still emerging U.S. environmental justice movement, I examine how conceptions of "wilderness" create blind spots in the mainstream environmental movement that excuse us from thinking seriously about how our everyday activities in culture have consequences that flow out into "nature." I also examine how these blind spots prevent us from understanding broad socioecological processes that lead to environmental degradation in the first place and explore the reasons why an ecocriticism that focuses solely on works such as *Desert Solitaire* holds little promise for activating concrete social and environmental change.

The Construction of Wilderness

From Kayenta, I traveled to the Lees Ferry Campground on the Colorado River, near Utah's Vermillion Cliffs, where I began my trek into Paria Canyon. As a young man, Abbey was drawn to these same brilliantly red cliffs, first visiting the Four Corners region as a seventeen year old, then later—after service in the military during World War II—returning to explore its canyons, mesas, mountains, and rivers. In 1947, he moved to Albuquerque to pursue a degree in philosophy from the University of New Mexico and spent most of the rest of his life in the West. During the summers of 1956 and 1957, he worked as a seasonal park ranger in Arches National Monument, near Moab, Utah, accumulating four volumes of notes and sketches that became the basis of *Desert Solitaire*. In 1959, he was among the last to travel by boat through Glen Canyon before construction of a dam submerged the canyon under the waters of Lake Powell. The elegiac narrative of his farewell journey through Glen Canyon, which became the longest chapter of *Desert Solitaire*, remains one of the most evocative descriptions of red-rock country ever written. *Desert Solitaire*, considered his best work, launched Abbey's career as an essayist and novelist and defender of the desert Southwest.

Hiking through the two-hundred-million-year-old Navajo sandstone of Paria Canyon, which in a few places is so narrow that I could stretch out my arms and touch both dark-orange, slick-rock walls, I could easily imagine why Abbey described this dramatic country as refuge, bedrock, "a different world, older and greater and deeper by far than ours."[4] On his ten-day trip through Glen Canyon, Abbey spent two days exploring a side canyon much like the one in which I was walking. His subtle description of Escalante Canyon captures the power of the twin forces of water and time that combine to create the spectacular carved-rock canyons of the Southwest. He writes: "The canyon floor averages about fifty feet in width but the curving walls are at least five times that high, without benches or ledges, sheer, monolithic and smooth as if carved in butter, paralleling each other in a sort of loosely jointed ball-and-socket fashion, each concavity matched by a corresponding convexity on the opposite wall. And all this inspired by the little stream that swings through the rock and the centuries" (201). Abbey knew that to spend any time at all in such a place is to experience a world very different from the world of New York City, Salt Lake City, or Tucson. The sheer scale of the walls produces a sense of the most profound wonder, shifting our vision, revealing the smallness of humans and their endeavors, inviting us to acknowledge that the plants and animals and physical landscapes are not of our making; they have their own reason for being quite apart from any meanings that we might attach to them. To his own question "What does the desert mean?" Abbey answers, "It means nothing. It is as it is and has no need for meaning. The desert lies beneath and soars beyond any possible human qualifications" (219). This response illustrates Abbey's greatest strength as an environmental writer: he celebrates, honors, and respects the autonomy of the natural world.

In the tradition of John Wesley Powell, John C. Van Dyke, Mary Austin, and Joseph Wood Krutch, who wrote lyrically of the West's arid lands, Abbey revels in the rugged beauty of the desert. But as Don Scheese notes in his assessment of *Desert Solitaire,* Abbey wrote with a difference of temperament from most other nature writers. Distinguished by his harsh, iconoclastic, extravagant narrative voice, Abbey advocated not just love for wild lands but political activism. Because he openly participated in monkey-wrenching acts to preserve wilderness (such as pulling up a government road surveyor's stakes), Abbey became a kind of green prophet, drawing many a backpacker and prospective monkey-wrencher into the "back to nature" cult of the 1960s and the "back to the wilderness" movement of the 1970s. However, Abbey's most lasting contribution, notes Scheese, is to the field of nature writing: "he articulated new arguments, distinguished by a rhetoric of rage, for wilderness preservation; and he advocated political activism in order to defend wild nature. . . . Abbey's life and work have become a counterfriction against those forces that would destroy wilderness."[5]

Yet it is precisely because his writing has been so widely influential—

drawing thousands to America's desert wilderness areas and inspiring such movements as Earth First!—that we must raise questions about some of the more troubling contradictions in Abbey's assumptions about wilderness. At various points in *Desert Solitaire,* he constructs nature as "escape," but at others as "home." As escape, wilderness becomes a paradise, an Eden, a place that existed before the corruption inherent in the civilized world. In this paradise, we are born again; we leave our former selves and learn to know our true selves. In the "Author's Introduction," Abbey clearly states that he is not writing a book primarily about the desert and his purpose is not to understand the intricate workings of nature (x); rather, he has come to the wilderness to experience the freedom of the natural world, to recover the true self he has lost to the corrupting influences of his artificial life in the city. During the two years he worked at Arches, Abbey spent six months of the year as a park ranger and the other six months as a welfare caseworker in Brooklyn. He heartily preferred the canyonlands to what he termed "that miscegenated misalliance of human and rodent called the rat race" (298). His months in the desert afforded him the opportunity to "evade for a while the clamor and filth and confusion of the cultural apparatus," to "confront, immediately and directly if it's possible, the bare bones of existence, the elemental and fundamental, the bedrock that sustains us" (6).

Abbey's vision of the desert as a wilderness escape taps into a thoroughly historical shift in perception about the natural world. As environmental historian William Cronon details in his essay "The Trouble with Wilderness," only 250 years ago in American and European history *wilderness* meant "deserted," "savage," "desolate," "barren"—connotations that were anything but positive. But by the end of the nineteenth century, this view had changed. Henry David Thoreau's 1862 declaration that in wildness was the preservation of the world suggests the shift in values occurring in the United States. As great expanses of wild country fell under the plow and the ax, many people, under the influence of romantics such as William Wordsworth and John Muir, came increasingly to value those ever-shrinking rugged terrains in which one might go to perceive the divine or the sublime in nature. No less important, adds Cronon, "was the powerful romantic attraction of primitivism, dating back at least to Rousseau—the belief that the best antidote to the ills of an overly refined and civilized modern world was a return to simpler, more primitive living."⁶ Frederick Jackson Turner's 1893 "Frontier Thesis," the classic academic statement of the closing of the frontier and of the myth of primitivism, so powerfully entered the American imagination that it has been a part of American cultural traditions for more than a century. According to Cronon, Turner's thesis argued that easterners and immigrants, "in moving to the wild unsettled lands of the frontier, shed the trappings of civilization, rediscovered their primitive racial energies, reinvented direct democratic institutions, and thereby reinfused themselves with a vigor, and independence, and a creativity that were the source of American democracy and national character" (76). Seen in this way, wild country becomes not only a place of religious redemption and national renewal, but the last bastion of rugged individualism.

In the tradition of Owen Wister's *The Virginian* and Zane Grey's *Riders of the Purple Sage,* Abbey's *Desert Solitaire* laments not just the taming of wild country but the passing of the rugged individuals who lived in that landscape of endless freedom. Leaving the "foul, diseased, hideous cities" and all the "useless crap" of modern society behind, Abbey, with his friend Ralph Newcomb, puts out into the Colorado, delivered—for a time, at least—into an older, better, more pristine world, a world that is quickly passing, perhaps already gone. Describing his experience as one of the last men to float through Glen Canyon before it was dammed, he writes: "Cutting the bloody cord, that's what we feel, the delirious exhilaration of independence, a rebirth backward in time and into primeval liberty, into freedom in the most simple, literal, primitive meaning of the word, the only meaning that really counts. The freedom, for example, to commit murder and get away with it scot-free, with no other burden than the jaunty halo of conscience" (177). On the river he is free to be himself, a man with no past, no responsibilities, no job, no entanglements. In a very telling passage that refers to the wife he has left in Albuquerque, he jauntily asks his friend Newcomb, "Do you think it's fitting that you and I should be here in the wilds, risking our lives amidst untold hardships, while our wives and loved ones lounge at their ease back in Albuquerque?" (182). "Yes," answers Newcomb.

Like the rugged individualist, who is almost always masculine in gender, Abbey goes to the wilderness. There, a man can be a real man. Abbey writes: "there are no women here (a blessing in disguise?)" (83). William Cronon points out that since Theodore Roosevelt's day, frontier individualists have feared the emasculating tendencies of civilization's comforts and seductions. The irony is that men who felt this way more often than not came from elite-class backgrounds. "[T]he very men who most benefitted from urban-industrial capitalism were among those who believed they must escape its debilitating effects. If the frontier was passing, then men who had the means to do so should preserve for themselves some remnant of its wild landscape so that they might enjoy the regeneration and renewal that came from sleeping under the stars, participating in blood sports, and living off the land" (78). From the end of the nineteenth century, as the frontier was perceived to be closing, wild land became less and less the site of permanent homes or productive labor and increasingly associated with recreation for the affluent. People who already lived and worked in rural areas or on the frontier were generally familiar with the rigors of life in "uncivilized" places, so they did not fantasize about life in the "wild." Thus, celebrating wilderness became a culturally constructed activity mainly for city dwellers who could afford to pay for train tickets to the West, where big-game guides and backcountry residents served as romantic surrogates of a more rustic age.

Of course, Abbey was no captain of industry or big-game hunter. He proudly claimed to be a redneck born and bred on a submarginal farm in Appalachia, cultivating a rough-around-the-edges, beans-and-bacon, working-class persona. But by the time he published *Desert Solitaire* in 1968, he had worked himself into the middle class—at least educationally—by way of the GI Bill. He steadfastly refused to submit to the "creeping strangulation of the clean white *collar* and the rich but *modest* four-in-hand garrote" (178, emphasis in original), *choosing* instead, to work for fifteen summers as a park ranger and fire lookout. I emphasize the word *choosing* for two reasons. First, Abbey strictly separated nature from culture and chose nature. He did not go back to nature for recreation, an activity he associated with cars and trailers and motorboats and water skiing. Rather, he held himself above all that; he was *participating with* the wilderness, spiritually re-creating himself in the tradition of Henry David Thoreau, confronting immediately and directly the bare bones of existence. Second, Abbey was free to make the choice to re-create himself in nature because both his place in a graduate school (Abbey spent ten years earning bachelor's and master's degrees in philosophy at the University of New Mexico) and his job with the Park Service, while not exactly lucrative, afforded him the privilege of having large amounts of time to read and write and explore wilderness areas.

Abbey's wilderness experience is predicated not solely on his educational and professional resources, but on his *choice* to participate in and to perpetuate—through his writing—what has become, since the end of the nineteenth century, a uniquely white, middle-class fantasy that side-steps race and class relations. This fantasy creates a place outside history where it is possible to have the comforts of civilization *and* a pure, pristine wilderness in which to escape the "corruption" of civilization. In his assessment and critique of Abbey's writings, Peter Wild notes that Abbey, the "middle-class maverick," offers his readers a "marvelous dualism," the Edenic paradise that the middle class "never had but thinks it has lost, or thinks it should have."[7] Wild is careful to point out that the middle-class cannot be stereotyped as to financial or educational or political position, but by far most of those "mole-skinning their blisters" in the backcountry are well-heeled doctors, lawyers, nurses, and English professors (18). (Wild cites a recent Forest Service study noting that only 0.8 percent of backpackers are farmers and 6.3 percent blue-collar workers. My Paria Canyon *Hiker's Guide* seems to confirm this conclusion by noting that "peak use periods at Paria Canyon usually coincide with spring breaks at colleges and universities.") Speculating about the reasons for Abbey's appeal to the middle class, Wild concludes that Abbey taps into the romanticism that has lain at the center of the middle class since the birth of the republic: the notion that it is possible to "have it all," a comfortable wood-framed house in the suburbs *and* a beautiful, old-growth forest. The problem, Wild argues, is that Abbey's writing ends up having the same effect as Novocaine in a dentist's office: it is comforting, but not the cure for decay. The heroes of Abbey's novels confirm this point: according to Wild, they are "agog on John Denver visions of Rocky Mountain highs but thwarted by unpleasant realities of abuse and overuse, of crowded peaks and Winnebago-choked high-ways" (22).

In *Desert Solitaire,* Abbey touts the wilderness as a place of primeval "liberty," "freedom," and "independence" (177), implying that it is a place in which we are all equal, all on the same footing. But my visit with Diné students in Kayenta, who struggle each semester to find the grants and scholarships to allow them to continue attending college and whose summer jobs allow them little free time for hiking, made me very conscious that none of the people I met on the Paria Canyon trail were Diné—despite the fact that the Diné *live* and *work* all over the region. This is not to say, however, that American Indian people do not ever visit national parks or wilderness areas, or that economic factors alone keep them away. Rather, as Simon Ortiz implies in his poem "Grand Canyon Christmas Eve 1969," when American Indians visit national parks, it is with a different set of perceptions than those of hikers who enter a culturally invented wilderness to "get back to nature." Ortiz writes of his visit with his young son Raho to the Kaibab National Forest on the South Rim of the Grand Canyon. He and Raho go to the forest not to escape entanglement with family or to slip the corrupting influence of civilization, but to spend time in a place their grandfathers "talked with bears and wolves."[8] At the canyon's rim, Ortiz "breathes the earth" and pays respect to "my mother earth," praying that his family will be given the strength "and subtle timelessness of stones and mist and beauty" (185–86).

By evoking his grandfathers, Ortiz makes apparent the problematic assumptions at the core of a socially constructed conception of wilderness. The movement at the end of the nineteenth century to set aside national parks and wilderness areas could begin only at the conclusion of the Indian wars, *after* the prior human inhabitants who once called these areas home were taken captive and moved onto reservations. Once the former inhabitants had been ejected from national parks and their earlier uses of the land redefined as inappropriate or even illegal, notes Cronon, "tourists could safely enjoy the illusion that they were seeing their nation in its pristine, original state" (79). Ortiz's "Grand Canyon Christmas Eve 1969" works to expose just how culturally invented notions of uninhabited wilderness are. Camping with his son in the Kaibab Forest, Ortiz needs wood to prepare a meal. A nearby U.S. Forest Service sign instructs campers that they may not collect wood around their campsites. Instead, they must pay for the wood that the Forest Service sells in neat packages for eighty-five cents. Thinking, "This is ridiculous. / You gotta be kidding. / Dammit, my grandfathers / ran this place," Ortiz deliberately ignores the sign and gathers firewood, mumbling, "Sue me" (188).

Ecocriticism and a Literature of Hope

The notion that we can somehow escape the history of American race and class relations and our own connection to the problems inherent in urban-industrial civilization by lighting out for the wilderness produces

an odd sort of selective blindness, one that often ends up being replicated in the work of ecocritics who focus solely on writers who separate
nature from culture. Abbey sees clearly that the root of our ecological
crisis is cultural, but seems blind to his own connections to that culture.
He shrewdly critiques the culture of what he terms "Industrial Tourism," a form of national park sightseeing in which people remain sealed
in their air-conditioned cars and never walk in the sun and sand, never
sweat, and never touch a tarantula or scrape their knee on a rock. He
sharply criticizes the government for domesticating the wilderness by
building more and more roads to accommodate the Industrial Tourist
and calls into question the "big business" of Industrial Tourism—the
motel and restaurant owners, gasoline retailers, and corporate oil executives who profit from the dollars of tourists who refuse to sleep in a tent
or leave the paved loop drives through national parks that begin and
end at a gas station. He also admits that his own books will—although
drawing attention to the need for wilderness preservation—adversely
affect wilderness by attracting more people to the national park system
and its proliferating loop drives. Knowing well that his warning will be
ineffective, he writes: "Do not jump into your automobile next June and
rush out to the Canyon country hoping to see some of that which I have
attempted to evoke in these pages. . . . [M]ost of what I write about in
this book is already gone or going under fast. This is not a travel guide
but an elegy" (xii).

   At the same time that he criticizes the Industrial Tourist and clearly
sees his own complicity in the disappearance of "true wilderness," he
also propagates the illusion that by getting out of your motor home,
your car, or your speedboat, by entering the wilderness on foot or non-
motorized boat, you can somehow slip your own entanglement in civilization and escape into prehistory, a place that existed before humans
began to leave their imprint on the world. Thousands of the most banal
and unadventurous types of tourist, he observes, have a "real" wilderness experience each year by climbing Mt. Whitney or hiking to the
bottom of the Grand Canyon on foot or by riding on the back of a mule.
The one thing these hordes of "self-propelled tourists" have in common
is that they are "hungry for a taste of the difficult, the original, the real"
and that they refuse "to live like sardines in a can" (56).

   By separating the "real," "original" wilderness from "false" civilization, Abbey creates a blind spot, releasing himself—and all of us—from

responsibility for those institutions and those industrial and agricultural landscapes that shelter and benefit us. He holds himself aloof from these benefits, as if he could essentially separate himself from urban-industrial civilization simply because he rejects its values. But the U.S. government—builder of dams—was footing the bill for his education and providing him with a summer job, both of which gave him the opportunity and resources to spend time in the wilderness. Also, like most wilderness adventurers who do not make their own outdoor gear or forage for their food, Abbey packed a rubber boat, hiking boots, beans and bacon, and canned fruit for his trip through Glen Canyon, none of which he produced himself.

Abbey's response to places that are not "pure, original nature" is to retreat ever farther into the wilderness. Floating down the Colorado, he takes a big drink of river water with his lunch, acknowledging that the water, although far from a source of human biological contaminants, is probably polluted with radium, uranium, and vanadium from the many corporate and private mines in southern Utah. He thinks: "when a man must be afraid to drink freely from his country's rivers and streams that country is no longer fit to live in. Time then to move on, to find another country" (184–85).

In *Seeking Awareness in American Nature Writing,* ecocritic Scott Slovic argues that nature writers are epistemologists, students of the human mind rather than activists in any concrete sense of the term. Certainly, Abbey himself supports this conclusion when he writes that he goes to the wilderness not to study nature, per se, but to recover his true self, to confront the "bare bones of existence" (x, 6). Slovic observes that nature writers, although usually not advocating direct political action, do in a sense advocate an awareness that might possibly lead to political action. Nature writing "is a 'literature of hope' in its assumption that the elevation of consciousness may lead to wholesome political change."[9] Illustrating his point, Slovic quotes from Judy Lensink's interview with Abbey in Steven Trimble's *Words from the Land:* "I think that poets and writers, essayists and novelists, have a moral obligation to be the conscience of their society," Abbey told Lensink, adding that "I think it's the duty of a writer . . . to try to make the world better, however futile that effort might be" (99). It could be argued that Abbey, employing his particular brand of cantankerous rhetoric, seeks to make the world a better place by alerting readers to the fact that a national treasure, our precious wilderness, is fast disappearing, and we better do something to save it. The assumption here—one made by many environmental writers and critics—is that, as Slovic states, "a problem of some kind that receives public attention is likely to be corrected" (171).

However, the trouble with this assumption is clearly illustrated by Abbey's passage about contaminated river water. Although literature in which the author reflects on nature may lend itself well to epistemological speculation, and although writers and critics may freely choose to address or not address certain genres of writing or political issues on the basis of their individual talents and preferences, writing that separates nature from culture holds little promise of activating concrete change because it fails to reveal the social, political, and economic forces that lead to and justify exploitative, unsustainable uses of the natural world. If the only original and real wilderness must be completely untouched by human culture, and if wilderness adventurers must retreat farther and farther from civilization to find it, then humanity and nature are at widely opposite poles; humans, then, are excused from thinking seriously about how their everyday activities in culture have consequences that flow out through the river channels or float through the air into nature. This conceptual split relieves them of the responsibility of learning what an ethical, sustainable relation to nature might look like because they are endlessly searching for a last, best, untouched, uninhabited paradise.

As we move into a new century with increasingly complex, interrelated social and environmental crises, an environmental "literature of hope" may reawaken our sense of beauty and fuel a deeply spiritual concern for the preservation of unique wild places and biological diversity. But the journey of one nature writer into a wilderness preserve can tell us only about the small-scale ecological processes occurring in one particular place. Although thought-provoking and inspirational, such accounts are insufficient for understanding the broader socioecological processes that lead to environmental degradation in the first place.

Wilderness as Home

There are no springs the last twelve miles of the Paria Canyon trail. The river picks up speed and grows larger from the run-off of several small tributaries. The trail moves out of the water and up onto the boulder-

strewn sides of the canyon, which widens and becomes more dusty and
hot because the canyon walls are no longer monolithically high and so do
not cast long, cooling shadows. There is an abundance of water, but it is
unsafe to drink. At the last spring, I carefully refilled all my water bottles
with enough water to take me to the end of the trail because, as my
Hiker's Guide warned, the Paria River is polluted not only with micro-
organisms such as giardia (which can be removed by means of a backpacking water filter), but also with herbicides and toxic substances that
water filters cannot always remove. Each time I crossed the chemical-
laden river, I thought about the uranium-laced Colorado River water
from which Abbey drank in 1959. Then and now, the water illustrates
something professional ecologists and environmental historians have
been saying for more than twenty-five years. There are few, if any, places
on the earth untouched in some way by humans and their cultures;
therefore, it is an illusion that there is a natural paradise outside of
culture to which we may retreat.

The natural world is and has always been, according to William
Cronon, "far more dynamic, far more changeable, and far more en-
tangled with human history than popular beliefs about 'the balance of
nature' have typically acknowledged" (24). Humans have indeed polluted and degraded the environment with agriculture and industry. But
they also have played a role in shaping many of the landscapes that we
think of as "natural." From the Amazon rain forest in South America to
the old-growth forests and river valleys of the U.S. Pacific Northwest to
the desert grasslands of the U.S. Southwest, the diversity and patterns of
plant species cannot be explained without accounting for the deliberate,
long-term use of fire by indigenous peoples.[10] In short, notes Cronon,
the work of environmental historians "has demonstrated that human
beings have been manipulating ecosystems for as long as we have rec-
ords" (25). And though a knowledge of long-term human intervention
in the environment does not excuse the wide-spread abuses of the natural world by urban-industrial civilizations, it does call into question,
Cronon points out, "the familiar modern habit of appealing to nonhuman nature as the objective measure against which human uses of
nature should be judged" (25).

Abbey's construction of wilderness as home does exactly this: it sets
up an opposition between nature and culture by which to measure the
failings of the human world. Seeking to articulate the importance of

wilderness and the reasons why we should preserve it, Abbey writes: "[T]he love of wilderness is more than a hunger for what is always beyond reach: it is also an expression of loyalty to the earth, the earth which bore us and sustains us, the only home we shall ever know, the only paradise we ever need if only we had the eyes to see. Original sin, the true original sin, is the blind destruction for the sake of greed of this natural paradise which lies all around us—if only we were worthy of it" (190). The construction of wilderness as natural and unfallen and as a *home* we must fight to protect is comforting and seductive, but such a construction necessarily represents civilization as fallen, unnatural, less important. Abbey draws an analogy between "the blind destruction for the sake of greed of this natural paradise" and "original sin"—an allusion to Eve's first bite from the apple, an act that gave her knowledge of the present, everyday world, but that also meant she and Adam would forever be barred from Eden. The problem with Abbey's analogy (besides the fact that it lays the fall of the natural world at the feet of women) is that it makes humans unworthy of pristine nature. To be "natural," wilderness must be remote from civilization and untouched by humans, who are, according to Abbey, unworthy because they destroy nature for greed and because their common, everyday living in industrialized civilization increasingly encroaches into the purity of nature. By this definition, the only human activities permissible in the wilderness would be contemplating the beauties of nature and trying out new, high-tech camping gear.

My point is not that environmental destruction should be accepted as inevitable or natural; it is that wilderness, couched in terms of an epic battle to save our Edenic home, makes all other social, political, and moral concerns seem trivial. Problems (whose victims are mainly people) occurring in places no longer considered "wild" seem less important. Backpackers, rock climbers, and river runners—who carefully follow the "leave no trace" backcountry ethic, packing out every Zip-lock bag and Ramen Noodle package—often live less carefully when they return to the city, forgetting that their houses were built from wood from the forest and that their electricity is produced by dams or coal-burning generating stations. They feel somehow less responsible for the forest that has already been clear-cut, for the land at the edge of an urban minority neighborhood that is being used to dispose of toxic industrial waste, and for the reservation in the corner of the state where a multinational coal-mining corporation is contaminating an aquifer with toxic levels of arsenic and copper. In short, our conceptions of wilderness often give us permission not to care about problems that occur in "unnatural" or—and this is very often a key issue for mainstream environmentalists—"overpopulated" places.

In *Desert Solitaire,* for example, when Abbey turns his head from the Glen Canyon Dam to Dinétah, or Navajoland, in order to critique what he considers the overpopulated Navajo Reservation, he goes back into a romanticized prehistory, to the time of the Anasazi, who left "seven hundred years ago and won't be back for a long time" (114). After a cursory discussion of the rock art of the "primitive savages" and superficial speculation about why the Anasazi might have disappeared (116), he skips the history of Anglo-European colonization of American Indian lands, the history of language loss, and the institution of the reservation system. Instead, he plunges directly into an analysis of the "Navajo's troubles," which, he emphasizes *repeatedly,* can be traced to their "extravagant population growth" (119). In his chapter titled "Cowboys and Indians Part II," he writes that the introduction of white medicine has reduced the Navajo infant mortality rate—though it is still higher than the white infant mortality rate. "Are the Navajos grateful? They are not. To be poor is bad enough; to be poor and multiplying is worse" (118). Having assumed the right to speak for wilderness, Abbey assumes the right to speak for the people who live there, even to know their innermost feelings about the imposition of government health services. Some Abbey readers might argue that Abbey is employing his infamous rhetoric to call attention to one of the most pressing social problems in the United States. In the chapter from which I am quoting, they might add, Abbey calls for social justice and for a more equitable sharing of the nation's wealth as a way to end the poverty of the Navajo. To that argument, I would concede that Abbey does indeed call for a "social justice" that would entail "carving some of the fat off the wide bottom of the American middle class" (124), but I strongly question any formula for social justice that requires making "birth control compulsory" for the Navajo people (124).

In Kayenta, musing further about the poverty in evidence among the Navajo, Abbey admires an "old Longhair" standing in front of the Holiday Inn who refuses to allow his picture to be taken by a white woman, but Abbey fears that the younger generation will soon be turning "tricks for the tourist trade" and supporting themselves with a few "coal mines here and there" (123–24). This construction of a younger generation of Navajo as fallen and of "traditional" Navajo as somehow more genuine, real, or authentic (like the construction of civilization as fallen and wilderness as genuine, pristine, and uninhabited) is, simply put, a flight from history. It fails to acknowledge that the same people that Anglo-European Americans constructed as closer to nature and part of the wilderness landscape (and therefore classified as savages and compared to animals) are the people who have been colonized, exploited, and relegated to the poverty inherent in the reservation system. Abbey's separation of nature from culture, his single-minded focus on wilderness preservation, and his self-appointed position as solitary voice crying out for "Abbey's country" allow him to dismiss the legitimate efforts of the Navajo to overcome their poverty and marginalization—whether through the tourist industry, college scholarships, or leased mineral rights—as their desire to be "dark-brown white men" (120, 124). Constructing their actions as unnatural, untraditional, and inauthentic, he trivializes their poverty and suffering, and flippantly stereotypes them as "sheep and goat raising families still hanging on in the backlands" (120).

In his discussion of the "cult of the wild," Abbey anticipates my critique somewhat, but his—I would argue willful—flight from history blinds him to the contradictions inherent in his own construction of wilderness as home and to the rich possibilities embedded in his reference to Pueblo Indian constructions of home. He writes that many believe that the "cult of the wild" is simply the fantasy of those who have never had to work the land to make a living, grow their own food, or build their own house. These "hard-headed realists" tell "us that the cult of the wild is possible only in an atmosphere of comfort and safety and was therefore unknown to the pioneers who subdued half a continent with their guns and plows and barbed wire" (191). As proof that the "hard-headed realists" do not know what they are talking about, he offers the examples of Henry David Thoreau, John Muir, John James Audubon, and George Caitlin, "who endured hardships and privations no less severe than those of the frontiersmen" and who "wandered on foot over much of our country and found in it something more than merely raw material for pecuniary exploitation" (191).

As exemplars of the wilderness ethic he is advocating, Abbey selects other white men of privilege who *chose* to move through landscapes in

which the previous inhabitants have been removed or were being removed. There, they are free to re-create themselves transcendentally
and to describe or paint the natural world and the indigenous inhabitants from the standpoint of Euro-American science and art. These men
have no need to exploit the land for material gain because, like Abbey,
they have come to revel in nature—to study, write, map, or paint the
landscape. Abbey concludes that if urban-industrial society rejects the
example of men like Muir and Caitlin and continues to exploit the land
for its greedy pecuniary purposes, then all of us "will understand what
the captive Zia Pueblo Indians meant when they made a song out of
their sickness for home: My home over there, / Now I remember it; /
And when I see that mountain far away, / Why then I weep, / Why then
I weep, / Remembering my home" (192).

Unfortunately, Abbey himself does not understand the import of the
song he quotes. In fact, the song refers to the ten-year captivity of
seventy Zia Indians. In 1689, nine years after their involvement in the
successful Pueblo Revolt, which expelled the Spanish, the Zia were at-
tacked by Domingo Jironza Petriz de Cruzate, who crushed the pueblo,
reestablished Spanish rule, and carried off the seventy captives to El
Paso del Norte. The remaining Zia, while waiting for the captives to
return, rebuilt their pueblo and, as they had for centuries, began once
again to cultivate floodwater gardens of corn, beans, and squash in side
canyons above and below the Pueblo.[11] The home that the Zia captives
lament, then, is not a place outside of history, a *wilderness* as Abbey uses
that term; rather, it is a place in which the Zia built structures, lived, and
cultivated gardens, a place targeted by the Spanish for a bloody sacrifice
to colonial objectives. Most importantly, it is a place to which the Zia
captives returned, a place where people, despite hardship and suffering,
rebuilt their lives and replanted their gardens.

Home as Middle Place

To understand the Zia captives' fierce historical attachment to place and
the continuing attachment felt by contemporary Pueblo and Diné peoples, one must understand something about the creation/emergence and
migration stories of Southwestern American Indian tribes. For centuries, explains Leslie Marmon Silko, Pueblo and Diné peoples have
told stories of their ancestors' emergence from the earth into the present,

everyday world. After their emergence and during the course of their long migrations, their ancestors marked their route by remembering, telling, and retelling incidents that occurred near a certain boulder, mesa, spring, or river crossing—an act of the imagination that forever bound them culturally to specific geographical features in the landscape and to the region's flora and fauna.[12] Eventually, each tribal group came to a "middle place" or place that had been prepared for them by their gods.[13] There, they built their pueblos and cultivated their gardens.

Today, despite five centuries of oppression, repression, and dispossession, the Diné and Pueblo peoples still feel a deep connection to lands that resonate with cultural and personal meaning and significance, lands that are alive with story. They still identify a place of emergence somewhere within their traditional homelands—usually a small spring edged with mossy sandstone and full of cattails and watercress. They still tell the emergence and migration stories from their oral traditions, still recognize the places where the events of the stories took place, still cultivate gardens of corn and beans and squash, and still see the places where they live as a middle place in which nature and culture are not separate, but inextricably bound.

In the ancient stories from the oral tradition, in historical stories that speak of colonial tyranny, revolt, and resistance, in songs of home created by those taken captive, and, today, in contemporary poetry and fiction, members of southwestern American tribal groups recognize a profound irony. The "Place from Which All Life Emerges" (as it is called by the Acoma) has been designated a National Sacrifice Area, and the people who emerged from the earth have been targeted as a Sacrifice People. Colonizing governments and multinational corporations have sunk mines deep into the earth to extract not life, but the radioactive substances used to power technologies that could abruptly end all life. Removing valuable natural resources from large open-pit mines, mining companies unleash a myriad of other nonradioactive but toxic substances that poison the earth and its people more slowly. At Black Mesa, for example, natural springs have gone dry, the mosses and cattails have disappeared, and water table levels have dropped dramatically as Peabody Coal pumps more than 1.4 billion gallons of groundwater a year, mixes it with crushed coal, then sends the mixture through a slurry pipeline to the Mohave Generating Station in Nevada. Peabody also ships coal by rail to the Four Corners and Navajo Generating Stations in

New Mexico and Arizona, where it is burned to produce electricity for Los Angeles, Las Vegas, Phoenix, and Tucson. The filthy plumes of smoke spewed into the atmosphere by these stations often extend across the polychrome desert for more than 150 miles, and astronauts have reported the smoke from these plants as one of the few human-made objects visible from space.[14]

In their freshman composition classes, several of my Diné and Hopi students have written movingly about the effects both the mine and the generating stations have had on their homes and relatives. They write of the federal government's interference with Indian cultures, of the pressure to convert from a subsistence economy to the U.S. wage economy, of high unemployment since the 1940s, and of the lack of economic development and jobs on their reservations. They write of the almost unopposed move, during the 1950s, of multinational mining corporations into economically depressed reservation lands, where local populations were easily converted into economic hostages and their environments turned into a toxic sacrifice zones. At Black Mesa, Peabody promised the Diné people who signed the first mineral lease in the 1960s that residents would always have clean water and air, and that the company would provide homes in the area with electricity. Thirty years later, few homes have electricity, the air is continually laden with coal dust, and the mining operation has contaminated the Moenkopi wash system on which Black Mesa residents depend for water. For weeks at a time, Benally Spring, a tributary of the wash system, flows with thick black water caused by leaks in Peabody's coal-slurry pipeline.[15]

One Diné student, writing about the toxic environment in which she lives, contextualized her essay with an account of her family's complex relationship to the Black Mesa mine. She speculated that mainstream environmentalists might call for an immediate end to the mining operations and a cleanup of the sacred but now-scarred mesa. However, such a call would fail to recognize that not all the people working for Peabody at Black Mesa are distant multinational corporation executives intent on depleting the earth's resources. Financially, her family depends almost completely on employment with Peabody. If the corporation slowed down or ceased operations at the mine, both her family and the community would be economically devastated. She was in college and studying to become an engineer in part because of a scholarship from Peabody. Putting both human and nonhuman residents of Black

Mesa at the center of her concerns for the environment, she wrote about her plan to return to the reservation after she graduated and work for Peabody. Enthusiastic, optimistic, and determined, she planned to work for changes in the company's mining operations that would lead to more responsible and balanced uses of the earth's resources. She would bring to the task both a knowledge of traditional Diné beliefs about human relation to the land and a knowledge of engineering.

Like the Zia captives, contemporary Pueblo and Diné students, environmental justice activists, storytellers, and poets necessarily conceptualize the fight to protect their home in more complex ways than many mainstream American environmental activists and nature writers. Locating nature in cultural histories that often include painful memories of colonial oppression and the daily environmental consequences of racial marginalization, they do not lament the loss of an imagined paradise. They recognize that for centuries their ancestors have been manipulating their environments—burning the grasses, cultivating the floodplains, and building pueblos of red rock. They claim the right of human beings to derive a living from the land, but in ways that are, to use words from Simon Ortiz's poem "Mid-America Prayer," "responsible / and proper."[16] They call us to imagine the sacred not only in wild places, but right where we live. What would it mean to discover our home or a middle place wherever we are, whether in a national forest, in the city, on the farm, in the garden, or even in a mine? In the next chapter, by bringing Ortiz's *Fight Back: For the Sake of the People, For the Sake of the Land* into dialogue with *Desert Solitaire,* I explore this question. By examining the issues raised by Ortiz and environmental justice activists, my aim is to illustrate how the study of multicultural literatures offers us rich ground in which to root a better, more culturally inclusive, politically effective environmentalism and a more satisfying, theoretically coherent ecocriticism.

CHAPTER 3

Simon Ortiz's Fight Back

Environmental Justice, Transformative
Ecocriticism, and the Middle Place

The voice of the people must be heard for justice on Black Mesa to ensure the protection and survival of the people. The struggle is to protect sacred land, religion, and the survival of a traditional way of life from corporate interests.
—"Dinéh Alliance Press Statement,"
Black Mesa, Arizona, Friday, 21 March 1997

We acknowledge ourselves
to be in a relationship that is responsible
and proper, that is loving and compassionate,
for the sake of the land and all people.
—Simon Ortiz, "Mid-America Prayer," *Fight Back: For the Sake of the People, For the Sake of the Land*

A National Sacrifice

Today, many Diné and Hopi—dry-crop farming and sheep herding on Black Mesa—struggle to continue living a traditional way of life, despite state and corporate encroachment on their lands and exploitation of their water and mineral resources. Unlike Edward Abbey, who occasionally drank contaminated water on trips down the Colorado, the people of Black Mesa have no choice but to drink from contaminated water sources and breathe dust-laden air because their *homes* are located near the world's largest coal strip-mining operation. But they are not retreating to the wilderness to find a better, more pristine locale. They are staying put and fighting for their homes in decidedly modern and nontraditional ways. Using the Internet and the federal courts, they have moved outward their concern for a specific place, making connections to a broader social and environmental justice agenda.

Citing both a 1992 Environmental Protection Agency report that conceded that minority and low-income populations are subject to environmental risks more often than nonminorities and middle and upper classes, and a 1994 Clinton administration Executive Order, which redefined environmental hazards in low-income and minority communities as a civil rights issue, one group of these people, the Dinéh Alliance, filed suit in July 1995 against the U.S. Office of Surface Mining, Reclamation, and Enforcement and Peabody Western Coal. They demanded that the federal courts refuse to renew Peabody's mineral lease with the Navajo and Hopi tribes until the corporation obtains the consent of local residents, identifies sacred shrines and burial sites scheduled to be destroyed by mining operations, takes responsibility for blasting damage to local homes, stops harassing local residents to relocate, and ceases polluting the groundwater and the air. On 11 March 1996, Judge Ramon Child ruled for the Dinéh Alliance, vacating Peabody's Kayenta mine permit.[1] A subsequent ruling overturned Judge Child's decision. Years later, area residents still complain of respiratory illnesses, rashes, and cancers they blame on the excessive coal dust from the blasting and the contamination that leaks into the groundwater from the mine. Undeterred, the Dinéh Alliance is appealing the appellate court's decision.[2]

The open-pit mine on Black Mesa is just one example of the state and corporate exploitation of both American Indian people and their lands that can be found throughout the Four Corners, a region about which Simon Ortiz writes movingly in *Fight Back: For the Sake of the People, For the Sake of the Land.* Ortiz does not refer to the lands that are the focus of his book as "Abbey's country"; rather, he points out that by 1972, the region had become so toxically contaminated by the military testing of nuclear bombs and the mining of uranium and coal that the Nixon administration sought to have it designated a National Sacrifice Area.

Based on Ortiz's experience growing up in the Acoma Pueblo and working in the early 1960s in the uranium-mining and processing industry near Grants, New Mexico, *Fight Back*, a mixed collection of poetry and prose, draws connections between the twentieth-century sacrifice of American Indian people, their fight to protect their communities and resources, and the Pueblo Revolt of 1680. That year, Pueblo people rose against the civil, religious, and military rule of the Spanish, who, for more than one hundred years, had been stealing the Pueblo people's lands and resources, using indigenous peoples as slave labor, and forbidding them to practice their religions. In a well-planned and armed revolt, a loose coalition of oppressed, dispossessed, and poor Diné, Apache, Pueblo, detribalized Indians, and poor Hispanic people forcibly expelled the Spanish. For the next twelve years, writes Ortiz, "our homeland was free of the dire social conditions that had caused the people to revolt."[3]

In this chapter, through a discussion of *Fight Back,* I explore the other-than-dominant concepts about *nature, place,* and *justice* that undergird the emerging movement for social and environmental justice by examining how the Acoma people come to understand the natural world through working in their gardens. In a discussion of the pueblo garden, I explore why notions of wilderness can do little to help us answer questions about how to live ethically in a world where whole regions and groups of people are sacrificed to state and corporate objectives, or to teach us how to confront and transform the large-scale economic and political processes that give rise to most social and environmental problems. I also examine the aspirations of writers, scholars, and ecocritics to help transform the world, and argue that if we want to find answers to our most difficult social and environmental questions, we must come home from the wilderness, take a hard look at the middle place where culture emerges from nature, then help to build alliances of people intent on fighting the forces that exploit both humans and their environments.

The Myth of the First White Man

According to their oral traditions, Simon Ortiz's ancestors (the Acoma Pueblo people, or *Aacqumeh hanoh* as they are called in their own language) emerged from the earth, living first in Chaco Canyon in present-day New Mexico, then migrating northward to Mesa Verde in present-day Colorado. Sometime later, say the elders, the Aacqumeh hanoh migrated southeast, coming, after many trials, to their high orange-and-red mesa, which rose up from a sea of lush, waist-high grass. They built a new pueblo at the top of the mesa, calling it *Aacqu,* or "Which Is Prepared," because they had been told by their gods in prophecy about a defensible mesa already prepared for them, on which they would establish their city, and the fertile flood-plain fields surrounding it, where they would plant corn, beans, pumpkins, melons, and squash. In all his work, including *Going for the Rain, A Good Journey,* and *Fight Back: For the Sake of the People, For the Sake of the Land* (all reprinted in *Woven Stone*), Ortiz writes of the ways in which his perspectives on both nature and culture were shaped by the Aacqumeh hanoh. Some of the experiences that inform his writing begin with his work as a boy in the centuries-old fields of his ancestors. In the shade of sandstone cliffs, remembers Ortiz, he loved to run barefoot through the sandy soil as his father plowed the family's fields. Following his father behind the family plow and work horses, he dropped corn seeds spaced one footstep apart, then scattered pumpkin and melon seeds and covered them all with a thin layer of the soft soil. In the evenings, after the planting was done, he played games, hunted, ran foot races with other boys, and explored the nearby boulders and cliffs until his mother called him to supper.

The Acoma people like the Laguna, Zia, Zuni, and Diné peoples— have been planting corn for centuries, and there is perhaps no better symbol than corn to represent the ways in which nature and culture cannot be separated in the middle place. According to Ortiz, corn emerges from the earth and is recognized as the food on which most southwestern tribes depend for their survival. There is, therefore, a sacred relationship between the earth and the people: the people respectfully care for and till the earth, and the earth regenerates the human body when people eat corn. Corn, writes Ortiz, cannot "be regarded as anything less than a sacred and holy and respected product of the creative forces of life, land, and the people's responsibilities and relationships to each other and to the land" (346). When corn in all its forms—seed, plant, food—is spoken of, Ortiz adds, it is given a sacred nature because of the all-important place it holds in the life and culture of Native American people. It is a symbol of the very essence of humankind's tending and nurturing of the land—a product of physical, mental, and emotional work.

Like millions of people from pole to pole who gain a more intimate knowledge of nature by hunting animals, gathering fruits, furrowing fields, planting seeds, eliminating pests, and harvesting plants, Ortiz learned some of his first lessons about the land by manipulating nature to produce food. In *Going for the Rain,* he vividly recalls an incident that took place in a field his father was plowing. This event taught him something about the processes of life in nature but also about his father's and his people's relationship to the nonhuman world. During a spring planting at Aacqu, writes Ortiz in the poem "My Father's Song," he is following his father's plow, as he had many times before. But on this day, his father stops, stoops to the earth, and calls his son over to see a mouse's burrow unearthed by the plowshare. Very gently he scoops "tiny pink animals / into the palm of his hand" and tells his son to touch the small, newly born creatures (58). Later, father and son move the mice to the edge of the field, where they place them in a shady spot in the soft moist sand. In Ortiz's memory of this incident, nature and culture, earth and language mingle. "I remember the very softness / of cool and warm sand and tiny alive / mice and my father saying things" (58).

When most European Americans have wanted to think about their relation to nature, they, unlike the Acoma people, have not gone to the garden, that middle place between nature and culture, but to the wilderness, that place they imagine as untouched by human culture. Many American naturalists and nature writers, making a case for an original relation with nature, imagine what the country must have looked like when mythical "first white men" entered newly "discovered" lands for the first time and surveyed a world with no marks of human culture on the landscape. The most popular first white men are often Meriwether Lewis, William Clark, and Daniel Boone. In the Southwest, Francisco Coronado, traveling up through the river valleys of Arizona and Utah, is put forward as that most honored of first white men. But in fact, Ortiz emphatically notes, when the Spanish arrived in the sixteenth century, they found Aacqu surrounded by small, well-ordered farming communities (341). In much the same manner as Ortiz and his father, who would plant their corn several centuries later, these people cultivated and harvested a variety of plants, generously sharing the fruits of their labors with the first Spanish soldiers they encountered. The Spanish admiringly noted the irrigation system that the Aacqumeh hanoh had built from the river to their fields, comparative in design and technology to those in Mexico. They were duly impressed by the city's defensible location high atop a magnificent mesa, commenting in their journals on the cleanliness and orderliness of the streets and on the richness of a people clothed in cotton fabrics and handsomely dressed animal skins.

First white men, observes environmental historian Richard White, are fascinatingly sympathetic figures, but they are culturally constructed viewers of the natural world who exist somewhere outside human history. In the nature writer's narrative, they enter the landscape as bearers of environmental original sin and mark the beginning of change and history. Indigenous peoples are granted certain timeless "spiritual" or "traditional" knowledges, but they are not credited with the capacity to make changes.[4] The problem, argues White, is that the research of environmental historians and closer readings of the journals of men such as Lewis and Clark do not bear out this narrative. Lewis and Clark, like the conquistadores who first entered Aaqu, were quite aware they were moving through landscapes where human work had altered nature. In their journals, White points out, they describe "Indians farming, hunting, fishing, and grazing their animals. Their journey west was punctuated by fires set by Indians to shape the landscape, influence the movement of animals, or signal each other" (176).

Narratives grounded in the myth of the first white men not only fail to acknowledge the history of the landscapes through which the first European explorers of North America moved, but also romanticize nature. Since the mid–nineteenth century, writes Michael Pollan in *Second Nature,* a meditation on gardens and gardening, Americans have prized the notion of a natural refuge far from the messiness of the human estate. Fixing on what Henry David Thoreau—the last important American writer to have anything to say about gardening—called the "higher laws" of nature, they ascribe to wilderness a certain immutable order to which the human world can only aspire. This notion of an orderly, balanced ecosystem can be wonderful and powerful and useful, argues Pollan, when it acts as a kind of taboo in our culture, a check on our inclination to dominate and spoil nature.[5] However, ecologists now freely admit that even the concept of an ecosystem is only a theory, a metaphor of our making, a human construct imposed on a much more variable and precarious reality. Nature has no grand designs. Rather, an incomprehensibly various and complex set of circumstances—some of human origin, but many not—determines the future of any given environment. Nature may possess certain inherent tendencies that theories about order and balance can help to describe, but chance events can divert the course of natural processes into an almost infinite number of different channels. Scientists now tell us, Pollan concludes, that contingency plays nearly as big a role in natural history as it does in human history (216–17).

Working yearly in their gardens, the Acoma accepted contingency, both their own and nature's. In the oral tradition, writes Ortiz, the

people do not romanticize nature, but speak of its danger, its capricious-
ness, its mystery. They tell of war, crisis, and famine, of "eras when
catastrophe came suddenly, inevitably, and perhaps necessarily when the
people had not paid careful heed to their responsibilities. . . . The oral
tradition does not ignore bad times and mistakes that people have made
throughout their history" (345). They understood there would be times
when torrential floodwaters would sweep through fields, obliterating
their labors; occasions when lightning, striking a tree or a meadow,
might ignite the landscape; years of drought when crops would fail; periods of starvation; occasions when an animal might steal a child, when a
tree might fall and break a human limb. Accepting nature as neither all
good nor all bad, they learned to live with ambiguities, to see patterns,
and to mimic natural processes in the cultivation of their gardens.

They did not see their own farming practices, though passed down
from generation to generation, as providing some sort of mystical protection to the land or to themselves. They understood that people make
mistakes that sometimes lead to environmental crisis. The Acoma oral
tradition implies that human environmental overuse, and perhaps warfare, may have combined with natural events such as drought to neces-
sitate the people's migration from the magnificent Pueblo Bonita in
Chaco Canyon to subsequent locations at Mesa Verde and Acoma. Cata-
strophic events and human miscalculation required people at times to
confront, alter, or change tradition. Lessons learned from the past were
woven into story and song, and passed down by word of mouth to be
remembered and heeded. These stories, about times of bounty and
times of crisis, were always told in "mythic proportion," Ortiz explains,
"in order to impress upon those hearing that there are important lessons, values, and principles to be learned" (345).

The Acoma oral tradition encourages the people to remember and
learn from the past. Their uses of this tradition illustrate that human
culture, though blamed by some environmentalists and nature writers
for the "death of nature," can play a role in teaching humans to observe
and remember, to share their experiences, and, most importantly, to
restrain themselves. Nature, writes Pollan, "does not teach its creatures
to control their appetites except by the harshest of lessons—epidemics,
mass death, extinctions" (232). For these fates to be avoided, culture—
human laws, metaphors, technology, and narratives about human relation to the natural world—must point us in the right direction. Nature

did not call Ortiz to the furrow to see the tiny mice; his father did. By moving the mice out of the way of the plow, the elder Ortiz, guided by his culture, teaches his son that because humans are dependent on many other forms of life, they must humbly, respectfully, and thoughtfully take into account the interests of nonhuman nature whenever possible. However, he also clearly recognizes that humans must alter their environments to survive. Unlike Thoreau, who, according to Pollan, romanticized wild nature to the point that he felt "guilty about discriminating against weeds . . . and . . . couldn't see why he was any more entitled to the harvest of his garden than the resident woodchucks and birds" (4), the elder Ortiz moves the mice and continues to plow.

Pollan observes that when Thoreau declared in *Walden* "that he would prefer the most dismal swamp to any garden," he essentially banished the garden from American writing on nature (5). Leaving behind domesticated terrain, Thoreau writes off culture as irredeemable and the middle place as fallen, a move that anticipates Edward Abbey's declaration that when river water becomes too contaminated to drink, we must search for a river, somewhere else, that still runs sparkling clean and clear. But what happens to the "nature" left behind? What happens to the bean field when the weeds and the woodchucks invade or when developers decide to build a subdivision there? What happens to the swamp after someone drains it or to the sparkling river after corporations dump chemicals into it? How do the humans who remain behind in these fallen places—those unable to move to cleaner, clearer environments—live? Our notions of wilderness as a place far from humans and their messy history, of nature as a pure expression of natural law, Pollan rightly argues, will not help us with these questions. In *Fight Back,* Ortiz implies that we must start looking for the answers to these questions not "out there" but in the trailer parks where the poor and marginalized live, in the mines where multinational corporations exploit human and mineral resources, and in the middle place where humans, guided by their culture might learn to "change things in a good way."

Understanding Human Relation to the Natural World Through Work

Fight Back is shaped and honed by work: Ortiz's own early work in Acoma fields, his later work for low wages at the Kerr-Magee uranium millsite, and his lifelong work as a writer. The book is set near Deet-seyamah, or "The North Door," the Acoma farming village where Ortiz grew up in the 1940s and 1950s. Located sixty-five miles west of Albuquerque, Deetseyamah is called "McCarty's" on U.S. and New Mexico maps in recognition of the Irishman who operated the water pumps that kept Sante Fe Railway steam engines running. Ortiz re-members Acoma elders anxiously watching the nearby Río de San José dwindle to a trickle. They talked about the days when the river ran sparkling clear, abundant, and fast, when it rained often enough that the grass surrounding the mesa grew waist high. In those days, there were a number of springs, and the Río de San José was fed by Kaweshtima, or "Snowed Peak," and by Ambrosia Lake. During the late summer rains, the people could see silvery ribbons of water running from the uplift of mesas west of Aacqu, then threading through canyons and spilling into their corn fields. But in the 1880s, the region began experiencing long periods of drought; with the construction of the railroad, a logging town, and the Bluewater Dam in the 1930s, there was only enough water for a very few people to continue farming. Those who were no longer able to practice the subsistence agriculture of their ancestors were driven by poverty into the U.S. wage economy. They took jobs with the railroad and later, in the 1950s, in the uranium and coal mines pro-liferating throughout the region.

The two decades in which Ortiz attended school were years of devas-tating change for the Acoma people. This was the era of Indian Termi-nation and Relocation, the names of two post–World War II U.S. fed-eral programs that sought to terminate all federal services, ties, and recognition of Indian reservations and to relocate tribal people to Dallas, Chicago, San Jose, Los Angeles, and Cleveland. Though the federal government's termination policy did not directly affect Acoma Pueblo, many Acoma people were lost to relocation or to jobs on the railways, which took them away from their communities for long periods of time. Forced by economic need to take a job laying track for low wages, Ortiz's father spent weeks, months, and even years away from his fam-ily, feeling lost, lonely, and powerless. In "Final Solution: Jobs, Leav-ing," Ortiz writes poignantly about his father's departures from the train depot on Sunday afternoons. The children would cry, "Goodbye. Goodbye Daddy, / please come back. Please don't go" (318). But "Sur-rounded by the United States, / we had come to need money" (318).

There were groceries, clothes, and roofs to buy. Because the river and springs could no longer provide enough water for the fields, his father could not provide for his family solely through farming. The only solution was change in the form of the railway job that took the elder Ortiz to Arizona, California, Colorado, Kansas, and Texas. At home, Ortiz's mother waited in anger: anger at having her husband taken away; anger for the abuse of alcohol she understood as her husband's attempt to cope with the separations from his family; and anger for the Acoma blood, bone, muscle, skin, sweat, and heart lost to keep U.S. railways in good repair.

Despite the alcoholism and anger, Ortiz's father never quit encouraging his children to fight for their homelands and people, and in his heart he never left Deetseyamah. Like the Zia Pueblo captives, he returned to his fields when he could and found strength and wisdom in work. In "Mama's and Daddy's Words," Ortiz's father chants words that are reminiscent of the Zia captives' song for their home, words that express love for the land and hope that his children will have a life free from oppression: "This is the land / It is our life, your life, / my life, life" (329). He encourages his children to learn all they can about the rapidly changing world in which they find themselves, telling them, "You young people / you have a chance" (329). Describing his work in the fields, on the railroad, in a sawmill, and with a road gang, he explains that it was never easy, adding that his hands were often torn, his back strained, and his skin burned by the sun (329). But in plowing earth, cutting lumber, and laying railway tracks, he learned about the world in the same way his ancestors learned: through work. Most importantly, his work took him out into the world of the "Mericano," or American, where he gained insight into a culture unlike his own, a culture "that was bent upon a kind of destruction that was total and undeterred and over which [the Acoma] seemed to have no control" (346).

At one time, the Acoma people dealt capably with nature's indifference, its contingencies. In their oral traditions, Ortiz points out, they had a system of knowledge that made it possible for them to cope with changes and to develop "further knowledge to deal with new realities" (349). But after the Spanish and later the Mericano entered their homelands, depleting the natural resources on which they had depended for centuries, the people became dependent on the wage economy and experienced change, alienation, and loss on a scale unprecedented in their cultural memory. However, just as they always had before, the people went out into the changing world and incorporated into their oral traditions the understanding they were gaining of both social and environmental changes. They linked stories of the tall grass, abundant harvests, and clear, fast-running water with stories of oppression and loss—not out of a sense of nostalgia, but because they were making connections. The disappearance of the grass, the barrenness in their fields, and the poverty of their families were undeniably linked to the Mericano appropriation of their best lands, to the poisoning of coyotes and prairie dogs, and to the pumping of groundwater. In the stories they tell about the time after the coming of the Mericano, writes Ortiz, the people are very definite about the responsibility of the "rico," or rich, for their difficulties. The Acoma are "very sure who the rich are; they are the ones who have money, possession, power, and the U.S. law on their side. The rico are those who . . . took the land; they are those who cause the people to become indebted and dependent" (351). So, when Ortiz's father, singing a song for his home, encourages his children "to fight / by working" (329), he is not simply lamenting a bygone era; he is urging them to follow in the tradition of their people, to learn about the inextricably interrelated natural and cultural histories of their region through work, and to "fight back" by remembering and making connections that will enable them to resist unjust oppression.

Toward a Garden Ethic

Never forgetting his father's words and songs or the lessons embedded in the oral tradition, Ortiz writes from a perspective that accounts for one of the most striking differences between the literary texts of many American Indian writers and those of Edward Abbey and many American nature writers. Abbey equates human labor in nature with destruction while celebrating the virtues of recreation in nature: backpacking, climbing, rafting, setting up camp. However, Ortiz gained his understanding of the human relation to nature in his family's fields and in a Kerr-McGee uranium mine, the places where he began not only observing the oppression of his people and the destruction of their lands, but seeking to understand and write about the underlying reasons for that destruction.

His father had hoped Ortiz might carry on his people's fight through a type of work less physically debilitating than railroad work, so he encouraged his son to go to school. But in the 1950s, Native Americans were hardly encouraged by their predominantly white teachers to go to college or into the professions. Ortiz—a prize-winning high school student who read voraciously, wrote poetry, earned good grades, and knew that he wanted to become a writer—never even considered college an option. When he was nineteen years old, having never met a writer and having no idea of how to become one, he took a job as a laborer with the Kerr-McGee uranium-milling operation at Ambrosia Lake. "I had a job," he recalls, "and for poor people with low education and no skills and high unemployment, that is the important thing" (357). During the year he spent in a mill crushing and leaching yellowcake, before a labor strike idled Kerr-McGee workers and gave him a reason to find his way into college, he put his back, muscles, and heart into the work and his creative and scholarly insights into his writing.

Twenty years later, having refined his insights and forged his political consciousness in the illuminating fires of the Civil Rights era and the emerging third-world national liberation struggles of the 1960s, Ortiz looked back to the Pueblo Revolt of 1680 and wrote *Fight Back,* which builds on and further analyzes the connections between Mericano colonization and the environmental degradation already embedded in the oral traditions of the Pueblo peoples. In poems and prose, he argues that the corporate colonization of the Four Corners region is nothing less than history repeating itself, this time in relation to who suffers the consequences of modern-day environmental pollution. The Pueblo rebellion was against theft of land and resources, slave labor, religious persecution, and unjust tribute demands. Three hundred years later, many of the same conditions existed, a result of the activities of multinational corporations. In "To Change in a Good Way," one of the poems based on his experiences working in the uranium industry, Ortiz powerfully illustrates that what is at stake is not only the survival of the Aacqumeh hanoh or the Diné or other southwestern American Indian peoples, but the survival of "all people of this nation" (360). Through the friendship of a Laguna Pueblo couple, Pete and Mary, and an "Okie" couple, Bill and Ida, he shows that if the quality of life of poor and marginalized peoples is not taken into account in our fight for the environment, then no one's quality of life will be assured, and it will make no difference whether or not we preserve and protect "natural wilderness and cultural parks" (360).

At the Ambrosia Lake mining area, Ortiz saw clearly that Kerr-McGee was set up to benefit the "rico," and its managers operated according to an ethic that did not have "people and the land and their continuance as their foremost concern" (360). Just as poverty and oppression drove seventeenth-century Pueblo people to form an alliance with the mestizo and the Diné in order to overthrow the Spanish, low wages and unsafe working conditions in the twentieth century led to friendships at Kerr-McGee that might not have occurred outside the workplace in the racially tense climate of the United States in the 1950s. Because of his own background and experience, Ortiz was sensitive to the condition of all workers, no matter what their race. He observed many similarities and differences between Indian and Anglo miners, noting that many of the working-class whites, who had recently immigrated to the area from West Virginia and Oklahoma, were "not far removed from land-based backgrounds" (22). Like the Acoma, they were farmers, dispossessed of their lands by drought and poverty, and drawn by economic need to New Mexico, where they took jobs in the mines. Ortiz did experience racism at the hands of some of these men, one of whom turned out to be the first "hard-core bigot" the young Ortiz had ever met. But for the most part, he found working-class whites to be "hardworking, earnest, loyal to their group, even clannish, opinionated and blunt in their speech" (22). Bill, an "Okie" electrician's helper who works with Pete in the mine, is modeled on these men.

In the poem, Bill and his wife Ida leave Oklahoma in the late 1950s for a job at Kerr-McGee's Ambrosia Lake uranium mine and a small trailer home in the company town of Milan. Carpooling to Section 17, Bill becomes friends with Pete, who spends his after-work hours raising sheep and cultivating the same small plot of land where his Laguna ancestors had raised chili, sweet corn, squash, and beans. Even after twenty years of working in the New Mexico mine, Bill's roots are still in Oklahoma soil, and he dreams of making enough money to return home and buy a piece of land. "You're lucky you got some land, Pete, / Bill would say. / It's not much but it's some land, / Pete would agree" (309). Later, the two wives meet in the town grocery store and go over to Ida's trailer to drink Pepsis. Ida, taking Mary out to her garden, confesses to being unfamiliar with New Mexican soil, which is different from Oklahoma's. She shows Mary her wilted lettuce and radishes and the corn that has failed to thrive in the hard red clay of the trailer court. Mary tells Ida that her soil needs "something in it," that she needs to break up the heavy, packed clay. She promises to come back the next weekend with some sheep dung to knead into the soil. The next spring, Ida proudly produces chili, corn, lettuce, carrots, and tomatoes in her garden.

Ida's garden suggests one of the most recurrent themes of *Fight Back*: to survive, humans must recognize a reciprocal relationship with the land. Humans necessarily change the environments in which they live, building shelters, cultivating gardens, raising livestock, and deriving the other materials that sustain them from the land. As William Cronon observes, "Calling a place home inevitably means that we will *use* the nature we find in it, for there can be no escape from manipulating and working and even killing some parts of nature to make our home."[6] Because each act of use unavoidably changes nature, continued human survival means that people, like gardeners, must think carefully and responsibly about the uses to which they put the land. As Ortiz observes in a discussion of the relation of people to nature, the land will be productive and serve humanity only when people find ways to "serve the land so that it is not wasted and destroyed" (360). Mary, having served her fields all her life, recognizes exactly what Ida's soil lacks and shares that information with her, thus helping her to become more responsive to a specific place, to the unique New Mexican soil of her garden, to the kinds of plants that will do well there, and to the arid climate. Enriching and lightening the hard red clay with sheep dung, Ida establishes a reciprocal relationship with the land, putting her time and care into the ground so that it will become more sustainably productive. She demonstrates that not all uses of the land need to be destructive, that some acts can change the land "in a good way."

When Bill's beloved younger brother, Slick, on a second tour of duty in Vietnam, is killed by stepping on a U.S. landmine, Pete and Mary come to Bill's trailer, bringing feathered prayer sticks and some Indian corn they have grown in their garden. Pete's gifts and his instructions on how to use them give Bill insight into the economic, social, and political connections between his work for low wages in dangerous mine shafts and Slick's death in a jungle made dangerous by the U.S. army. Pete tells Bill to plant the corn, a symbol of the sacred relationship between humans and the earth, as a reminder that Slick will now be given back to the earth, to grow like a seed. Pete further instructs Bill to put the prayer sticks, which symbolize Slick's travel from this life to another place of being, somewhere he thinks Slick might be able to help "change life in a good way" (314). A week later, after returning from the funeral in Oklahoma, Bill places the prayer sticks deep in the mine shaft where he works, humbly asking Slick to "help us with our life here," to watch over the men in the mine so that no one will be injured or killed as a result of the corporation's refusal to properly reinforce the dank mine shafts with enough timbers and bolts. The next spring, Bill and Ida plant the corn in their garden, smiling to think that Slick is helping them "hold up / the roof of Section 17" and break up "that clay dirt too" (317).

By juxtaposing Bill and Ida's garden with a dangerous minefield in Vietnam and the dangerous Kerr-McGee mine shafts, Ortiz confronts the abstract ethics that serve to explain and justify state and corporate oppression of nature and "Others" (read: people of non-European races, people of the underclasses, and nonhuman species). At Slick's funeral, Bill's relatives claim that Slick "done his duty for America," that he sacrificed his life to keep the world safe for democracy (315). But Bill's work with Pete in a uranium mine operated by those whose objective is both profit and global nuclear domination gives him insight into the connections between the linked oppression of nature and Others in both the United States and Vietnam. Though he grew up in a state desig-nated "Indian Country" by a government that forcibly removed entire tribes to the region at the end of the Indian Wars, he had never met a Cherokee in the Ozark Hills or a Creek in Muskogee. Pete and Mary are "the first Indians he'd ever known" (315). He had grown up with the notion that his "past folks" had lived a hard life, fighting off Indians in order to "build homes / on new land so we could live the way / we are right now, advanced and safe / from peril" (315). Knowing Pete and Mary, however, makes Bill realize that the Indians who were relocated in Oklahoma were humans like his own "past folks" and that the myth of a "new land" was created by those who stood to benefit in some way from the sale or enclosure of lands formerly inhabited by indigenous peoples.

Though it is painful to admit, after twenty years of working for sub-sistence wages in a dangerous place, Bill realizes that Slick did not die for democracy. He died because he was poor, and he needed a job to pay for his motorcycle, and his economic need led him to a dangerous place where he accidently stepped on a U.S. landmine. The only Americans living "advanced and safe," Bill bitterly tries to explain to working-class relatives with little education and no understanding of the larger forces that drew Slick to Vietnam, are those with the power to remove people from their homelands, create armies of the poor to "fight for democracy," legislate the protection or sacrifice of "new lands," or operate highly profitable mines in the midst of economically depressed Indian communities. With Slick's death and Bill's insight, Ortiz illustrates that the same economic, social, and political forces that destroy Indian communities "will surely destroy others" if the poor and the working class and the "white middle class, who are probably the most ignorant of all U.S. citizens" do not come to a concrete understanding of "what Aacqu and her sister Pueblos in the Southwest are fighting for when they seek time and time again to bring attention to their struggle for land, water, and human rights" (360–61).

Ortiz reveals that the forces that draw lines of protection around sacred, wild, "new lands" are the same forces that write off other landscapes as "fallen" and hand them—along with the people who live in them—over to the jurisdiction of laissez-faire economics. Consequently, the wilderness ethic and the corporate ethic, antithetical as they might at first appear, are really mirror images of each other. Both, argues Michael Pollan, propose "a quasi-divine force—Nature, the Market—that left to its own devices, somehow knows what's best for a place" (223). The real power of both of these ideas and the reason why they draw so many adherents is their very abstraction. In a country as large and geographically various as the United States, observes Pollan, it is probably inevitable that we will favor abstract ideas that have the power to simplify and unite—grids, monocultures, wildernesses, supply-side economics—because they "can be applied across the board, even legislated nationally" (226).

Given the choice between nature and those landscapes that have "fallen" to the market, Americans have chosen nature. But when faced with difficult questions such as what to do about the acid rain killing some of their most cherished old-growth forests or what to do about the poisoned groundwater killing the people who live in marginalized communities, they have no answers. Their oversimplified concepts of the world as "wilderness" or "sacrifice zone" give them permission to behave as if they have no relation to nature and allow them to ignore the ways in which their own existence in the middle place is connected to acid rain and unsafe industrial workplaces. Pollan argues that if we want to solve our most pressing environmental problems, we must acknowledge our relation to nature and construct an environmental ethic that tells us as much about using nature as about not using it. He suggests that a "garden ethic," although it will never speak as clearly or univocally as the wilderness ethic, makes sense precisely because it proposes "different solutions in different places and times" and seeks local answers to local questions (226).

In "Returning It Back, You Will Go On," Ortiz illustrates exactly why we need an environmental ethic or "garden ethic" that accounts for local differences. Again, he contrasts a Pueblo garden with a corporate landscape in which oil and mining companies set up operations on Indian land and, without regard to the health of local environments or local people, begin extracting mineral resources to sell to distant power companies in distant places. In a sense, nature, like the corporation, is indifferent to the rightness or wrongness of these activities and indifferent to human survival. Humans may, if they choose, destroy the land for profit, exploit economically and politically disempowered people, even burden the environment to the extent that it is rendered unfit for human life. "The land," writes Ortiz, will "let you" (331). But such irreversibly destructive practices are unthinkable to the Pueblo farmer, who gently sings to her plants while watching them grow, who harvests the plants to feed her children, and who, with great care and planning and "compassion and love," serves her soil so that it may serve her again the next year. Operating in accordance to a garden ethic, she recognizes that the health of specific places suffers under the imposition of abstract practices that are better suited to other places or best not practiced at all. She understands that one soil may be rich and loamy, whereas a hard, red clay may need to be broken up with sand, compost, or sheep dung; each place is different, and the gardener pays close attention to those differences and responds accordingly because she knows that her success is not ordained. Because nature is indifferent to the fate of the garden and to the fate of humans, the gardener is obliged to pay close attention to specific places, to observe and remember, to learn from mistakes, to share experiences, and to use restraint. Only by tending to the ground with this kind of attention and care—only by returning something back—will the land be regenerated and "life go on," Ortiz suggests (331).

Ortiz sees that the dualism separating nature from culture cloaks the "wildness" that can be found in the Pueblo farmer's fields, in trailer court gardens, and in urban areas where the majority of Americans live. Moreover, by honoring the Exotic Other who lives far way, perhaps in a rain forest, perhaps doing some kind of "authentic" or archaic work in nature, the wilderness ethic gives us permission to ignore the Other who lives next door, working in a field or a factory or a mine. But a garden ethic teaches us to live more responsibly in the specific places we inhabit, to acknowledge our embodiment in the natural world, to honor the wildness we find all around us. Just as Ortiz's father stooped to honor and respect the tiny mice but moved them because he understood that we must change things "in a good way" to survive, humans can honor the wildness they find in the middle place by thinking carefully about their relationships to nature and to Others of all kinds, both human and nonhuman. William Cronon writes, "Learning to honor the wild— learning to remember and acknowledge the autonomy of the other— means striving for critical self-consciousness in all of our actions. It means that deep reflection and respect must accompany each act of use, and means too that we must always consider the possibility of nonuse. It means looking at the part of nature we intend to turn toward our own ends and asking whether we can use it again and again and again— sustainably—without its being diminished in the process" (89–90). Most importantly, it means not excusing ourselves for the ways we live *in* nature by romantically imagining that nature is "out there."

As a result of his interactions with Pete and Mary, Bill acknowledges that "us Okies . . . maybe / have been wrong sometimes" (317). He takes responsibility for his own and his people's intentional and unintentional acts of oppression toward nature and Others, rejecting his former narrow, socially constructed attitudes about people of other races, species that are not human, and lands that are considered fallen. For the first time, he begins to understand the broader social, economic, and political forces that connect him more closely to people like Pete than to those who profit by destroying natural resources and exploiting economically disadvantaged people in unjust wars or unsafe mines. The prayer sticks he leaves in the mine shaft symbolize the ways in which humans, by virtue of being alive, unavoidably leave indelible marks on the world, but who, when guided by an ethic that makes people and the land and their *continuance* the foremost concern, can make responsible choices about the kinds of marks they wish to leave.

Like the Zia Pueblo song for home and the elder Ortiz's song for his children and his land, Simon Ortiz writes poems that are songs of hope, songs that imagine how people might "change things in a good way." However, this is not a nature writing that turns its back on the middle place, drawing attention to environmental problems in the simple hope that raising individual consciousness might lead to wholesome political change. Rather, it is a nature writing that recognizes that the people of Deetseyamah are still drinking water contaminated by the uranium-processing mills that closed in the 1980s when the market for uranium bottomed out, but that remain a toxic presence in the community. It is a literature, as I show in the next section, that rests its hope in organized community resistance to social and environmental injustices.

Justice and a Sense of Place

Most of us would accept that the conditions under which the poor and marginalized live and work in toxically contaminated regions are both socially and environmentally *unjust,* according to the commonsense meaning of the word. However, by persuasively showing that too many colonized peoples have suffered at the hands of Western imperialism's particular brand of justice, the postmodern critique of universalism has effectively rendered any one definition or application of the term *justice* problematic. In "That's the Place the Indians Talk About," Ortiz illustrates why specific places are the preferred terrain of environmental justice movements and why questions of justice fall squarely into a middle place between universalism and particularity, where they move back and forth dialectically, whirring and grinding, like the forces of the earth itself. In a short paragraph introducing the poem and the narrator of the poem, Ortiz recalls a gathering at a naval station in California, where he met an old Paiute man wearing thick glasses and a cowboy hat. A lifelong range rider and migrant laborer, the Paiute elder explained to Ortiz why he and his people returned yearly to Coso Hot Springs, a place considered sacred by Shoshonean people. Ortiz transforms the elder's words into a chantlike poem that recalls the old Paiute's memories of years before the U.S. government appropriated and fenced the lands surrounding the hot springs, transforming a place of healing into China Lake Naval Station, a center for the development, experimentation, and testing of military weapons.

Before its enclosure, Shoshonean families from Nevada, Utah, Arizona, and California would return annually on foot or by horse-drawn wagon to Coso Hot Springs to pray, sing, talk, bathe, and drink the healing waters. Putting the water on their hands and faces and bodies, the elder chants, the people would "get well, all well" (321). They listened to "the stones in the earth rattling together," felt the ground, hot and shaking, whirring and grinding, and heard the "moving power" of the earth (322). But during World War II, the U.S. Navy locked out the people and forced them to "talk with the Navy people / so they can let us inside the fence" (323). Resentful and angry about having to ask permission to listen to the earth, to use its power to "keep ourselves well," the Paiute people resist what they consider to be the unjust appropriation of traditional lands by returning each year by car, by wagon, and on foot to "the place the Indians talk about."

The Shoshone people's concern for Coso Hot Springs powerfully illustrates why the concept of *place* plays such a key role not only in the fight to protect and preserve the environment, but in most American nature writing as well. Some of the fiercest battles for the environment—Hetch Hetchy Valley in Yosemite and Glen Canyon in the Four Corners area, to name just two—have been waged over the issue of the destruction or preservation of valued environmental qualities in particular places. In much American nature writing, there is an inherent hope, an abiding faith, that writers may be able to aid in this battle by reawakening a sense of the beauty of local places and, as a result, reactivate a sense of care for the environment. *Place,* as it is most often used in this literature, means much more than a point on a map, a geographical location. It is the sights, sounds, and experiences that humans associate with a location; it is space humanized.[7] A sense of place, writes Kent Ryden, takes in more than the physical features of the landscape; it takes in the deep and subtle meanings that people assign to those landscapes. It "results gradually and unconsciously from inhabiting a landscape over time, becoming familiar with its physical properties, accruing a history within its confines."[8] Some of the most persuasive environmental writing, explains Lawrence Buell, rests on the belief that a true sense of place cannot be built on superficial contact with one place or another, but that it requires a deep, contemplative familiarity with the flora and fauna, geologies, and histories of human occupancy in specific places. Writers who "speak a word for nature," to use Thoreau's phrase, attempt to increase our feel for "places previously unknown and places known but never so deeply felt" by defamiliarizing the familiar, teaching us to see things new, and inviting us to "contemplate the individual fact in relation to whatever truth [seems] to flower from it."[9]

However, as humanistic geographer David Harvey points out, the connection between ecological sentiments and place deserves some critical probing. The intimacy of many place-based accounts—Thoreau's *Walden* being an exemplary case—yields "only limited natural knowledge embedded in ecological processes operating at a small scale."[10] He argues that the "penchant for regarding place as a privileged if not exclusive locus of ecological sensitivity rests on the human body as 'the measure of all things' in an unmediated and very direct way" and often "ends up fetishizing the human body, the Self, and the realms of human sensation as the locus of all being in the world" (303–4). Although such knowledge may fuel a deeply spiritual concern for the preservation of the ecological diversity and uniqueness of specific places, it is insufficient to understand broader social and ecological processes occurring at scales that cannot be directly experienced and that are therefore outside of phenomenological reach.

For the Shoshonean and other American Indian peoples, the fight for sacred places and traditional homelands is not simply about preserving valued environmental qualities in specific locations or gaining deep experiential knowledge of nature. For them, unique geologic features within their homelands are often alive with the mythic, historic, and sacred meanings of their cultures; these places are expressive of a particular way of life, and when threatened, they become symbols of the threat to distinctive cultural identities. The fence surrounding Coso Hot Springs stands as a stark reminder that contemplative reflection on nature's wonders cannot, of itself, lead to a clear understanding of the processes at work when one culture disturbs or destroys the basis of another culture's identity and violates a people's human rights by making the continued practice of their traditional lifeways difficult or impossible. Indian people must necessarily come to an understanding of broad processes operating on a large scale, Ortiz argues, because their lands and lifeways are continually threatened by those "who have money

[and] possession" and who use "Mericano power and the law to control affairs that had been formerly the people's to control" (351).

When the Shoshonean people speak through the fence that separates them from the hot springs, in essence they demand an end to five hundred years of injustices in the Americas. However, the fence raises a fundamental question: Which conception of justice is more just? By separating two peoples, the fence symbolizes two differing conceptions of justice, each with its own distinctive qualities, integrities, and meanings. Appealing to the political and economic theories of Thomas Jefferson and Alexander Hamilton, the Mericanos or ricos, writes Ortiz, justified appropriation of Indian lands because it was needed to raise the capital required by an emerging world power (349). Later, political leaders and government scientists justified the appropriation and radioactive contamination of Indian lands because it was necessary to develop and test the weapons of mass destruction that would keep the world democratic and free. Relying on concepts of justice that had no foundation save the arbitrary effects of power in arbitrary places and times, the rico needed no conspiracy to steal Indian lands; they "simply took it" (343). But American Indian people have not given up their lands without a fight. Taking up positions of resistance all along the fence of Mericano justice, they appeal to different concepts of justice, concepts embedded in other cultures, languages, and relationships to the land. They demand their right to "talk to the hot springs power," thereby claiming their right to social, cultural, spiritual, political, and ecological self-determination. The fence thus reveals that concepts of justice, like concepts of nature, are, as Harvey points out, socially constituted "beliefs, discourses, and institutionalizations expressive of social relations and contested configurations of power that have everything to do with regulating and ordering material social practices within places for a time" (330).

At the China Lake Naval Station, "justice" is used as a weapon, a monolithic absolute, an abstract notion of order resting on transcendent "higher laws" that have no grounding in local experiences, geographical conditions, or social relations. Wielding this "universal" concept like a sword, the navy people impose "justice" on the "the moving power of the earth, / the moving power of the People," attempting to sever the Shoshone from a place that speaks to them of their cultural identity (324). Inside the fence, the navy people carry on their activities without regard for the Shoshonean people's cultural and spiritual health or for their relation to Coso Hot Springs. But the processes of the earth are dynamic, unpredictable, contingent; the stones moving under the earth cannot be fenced. The people, like the forces of the earth, continue to sing, to talk, to return. They understand that "for a while" they must talk through the fence, but soon they will "talk to the hot springs power again" (323–24). Because of their long experience dealing with colonial oppression, they recognize that justice is dependent on the individuals, groups, and places involved. They also recognize that conceptions of justice can change. They have felt the earth, a seemingly immovable entity, moving. If they keep returning to Coso Hot Springs year after year, seemingly immovable Western concepts of justice could shift as well.

If we admit, to use the terminology of postmodern literature, that the *situatedness* or *positionality* of whoever is making the argument is relevant, if not determinant, to understanding the particular meaning put upon a concept, can there ever be a universal notion of justice to which we can appeal? History is littered with past attempts to create just societies, which have crumbled into tyranny or dissolved into violence. To argue for a particular definition of social justice, Harvey writes, has always implied "appeal to some higher order criteria to define which theory of social justice is more just than another. . . . An infinite regress of argument then looms as does, in the other direction, the relative ease of deconstruction of any notion of social justice as meaning whatever individuals or groups, given their multiple identities and functions, at some particular moment find it pragmatically, instrumentally, emotionally, politically, or ideologically useful to mean" (330). From this perspective, justice has no universal meaning. This does not mean, however, that we must discard the notion of justice. In the same way that conceptions of wilderness have been a powerful mobilizing force in the American environmental movement, acting as a check on human inclination to despoil the environment, the acceptance of justice as a foundational concept can be useful in the regulation of human affairs. For example, the United Nations charter on human rights is enshrined in a declaration of universal human rights that is firmly entrenched in notions of rightness, fairness, and justice. These notions are so powerful, Harvey observes, that "we seem powerless to make any political decisions without appealing to them" (332).

In recognizing that attaining and maintaining justice will be an ongoing, daily, yearly effort, the Shoshonean people in Ortiz's poem and growing numbers of environmentally focused, place-based groups such as the Dinéh Alliance recognize justice not as a monolithic order but as a process that must move and shift continually between universal concepts and particular places. Moving from universality to particularity, these groups might employ certain notions of "justice," "saving Mother Earth," "changing things in a good way," or "protecting the sanctity of nature" as useful foundational concepts to help them talk about the need to regulate human relationships to other humans and to nonhuman others, but at the same time, their goal will be to work collectively toward a particular set of social and ecological goals in a specific place. Moving in the other direction, from particularity to universality, they may find that gaining political power will require them to expand out from the confines of their particular issues of origin and embrace a more universal social change agenda.

The Search for Common Ground

In Bill's friendship with Pete, Ortiz hints at the reasons why fighting the large-scale forces that undergird the exploitation of people and places will require the formation of alliances of like and unlike people. Just as Bill's interactions with Pete give him a greater appreciation of cultural differences and a better understanding of the ways in which both men are caught up in large-scale forces that have local and global consequences, small place-based groups often recognize that their movements of opposition may take on greater historical significance if they make connections to a more general movement. Members of different groups must search for ways to cross the problematic divide between action that is deeply embedded in *place*—in local experience, power conditions, and social relations—and action that seeks to confront and transform the large-scale economic and political processes that give rise to environmental problems. However, what counts as nature among people of color, ethnic and minority groups, and working-class people of all races is historically dynamic and culturally specific, so there are often wide differences in perception about "the environment" between these groups that may either be productive of or militate against the formation of alliances.

In order to form effective alliances, racially and culturally diverse groups must find common ground by framing their experiences in ways that mobilize them to work unitedly. These groups often find that common ground, writes Giovanna Di Chiro in "Nature as Community," not by seeking deep experiential knowledge of nature, but in the experience of alienation from nature, from their environments, and from their sense of place (312–13). The historical experience of being forced off one's land, shipped to America on slave ships, prevented from maintaining long-standing relationships to sacred sites, obligated to move long distances to pursue an economic livelihood, or detached from one's place and sense of place in some other way has resulted in very different relationships to the environment for American Indians, African Americans, Mexicans Americans, and those who, because of class and racial oppression, must live in forsaken, highly polluted inner cities or industrial areas. The process of coalition building can begin only when members of these diverse groups proceed with the hard work of recognizing the other groups' specific experiences with social and environmental inequalities. They may begin at widely differing points, but in the process of dialogue they may be inspired to form alliances when they discover they share some of the same experiences with racism, economic hardship, toxic poisoning, and feelings of alienation from their surroundings and sense of place.

Many naturalists and nature writers hold that the only hope of environmental salvation is one based on a deep understanding of, commitment to, and resacralization of place. However, members of the Acoma community, the Black Mesa community, and other communities fighting for social and environmental equality confront and complicate this notion by demonstrating that not all experiences people associate with place are connected to the beauty of flora and fauna. Some of the deep and subtle meanings that people assign to beloved places may be associated with forced removal, environmental degradation, urban sprawl, or toxic poisoning. Although the city and other supposedly fallen landscapes are often represented by nature writers as menacing, noxious, and threatening to the survival of the natural world, the overwhelming majority of Native Americans, African Americans, Mexican Americans, Asian Americans, and Latinos in the United States live in urbanized or industrialized areas. For members of these communities, the predicament of the "sustainable" city or the rural areas where they live is just as crucial as the predicament of threatened wilderness. By exploring

their various experiences with and understandings of their environments, members of these diverse groups can deepen and enrich their
own understandings of human/nature relationships and gain insight
into how they might work together for a more just and inclusive environmentalism that refuses to separate ecological issues from social
justice considerations.

Environmental Justice and Transformative Ecocriticism

Although countless groups of people in the Americas have struggled for
freedom, justice, home, and place both before and since the Pueblo
Revolt of 1680, small environmental justice groups such as the Dinéh
Alliance have only recently become a significant political force in the
United States. These groups owe their emergence onto the world stage
to three well-publicized and representative events. The first, the celebrated case of Love Canal, came to the attention of the nation in 1977
when residents of a working-class neighborhood in New York found
their basements full of noxious liquids that were adversely affecting the
health of their children. The second incident took place in Warren
County, North Carolina, in 1982 and brought together hundreds of
predominantly African American women and children, as well as local
white residents, who used their bodies to block trucks from dumping
toxic PCB-laced dirt into a landfill near their community. A third event
occurred in the mid-1980s, when the city of Los Angeles proposed
locating a 1,600-ton-per-day solid waste incinerator known as LANCER
(Los Angeles City Energy Recovery Project) in the center of a low-
income, predominantly African American neighborhood. Members of
the community organized Concerned Citizens of South Central Los
Angeles and after mobilizing a citywide network of community organizations and local political and business leaders, they successfully blocked
construction of LANCER. The vigor of these environmental justice protests and the involvement of a wide range of civil rights organizations
and community leaders focused the nation's attention on what has since
become known as *environmental racism*—a term that has come to mean
the deliberate targeting of minority communities for toxic waste facilities, the official sanctioning of life-threatening poisons and pollutants in

those communities, and the exclusion of people of color from leadership in the environmental movement.[11]

From the start, writes Giovanna Di Chiro, the gender, race, and class composition of the environmental justice movement has distinguished it from that of the mainstream environmental movement, "whose constituents have historically been white and middle class and whose leadership has been predominantly male" (300). Because many environmental justice activists associate mainstream environmentalism with the preservation and protection of "wild" areas defined as places where people are not and *should not* be in large numbers, they are often reluctant to call themselves "environmentalists" at all. Di Chiro writes that when Concerned Citizens of South Los Angeles first approached organizations such as the Sierra Club and the Environmental Defense Fund, they were informed that "the poisoning of an urban community by an incinerator facility was a community health issue, not an environmental one" (299). A few environmental organizations, most prominently Greenpeace, later joined Concerned Citizens, swayed by the argument that a broadly based environmental movement must reconceive of "nature" and the "environment" as those places and sets of relationships that sustain a local community's way of life. However, the most heated battles fought by environmental justice groups still almost inevitably begin with the struggle to redefine social justice, local economic sustainability, health, and community governance as "environmental issues."

As I have attempted to show with this dialogue between Edward Abbey, Simon Ortiz, and a still emerging U.S. environmental justice movement, different cultural groups rest their notions of wilderness, justice, and place on widely differing foundational beliefs about nature and the environment. But in the academic world, to evoke the notion of "foundational beliefs" is to invite icy stares, callous sneers, and nervous hand rubbing, thanks in large part to the inroads that hypercritical currents of thought such as poststructuralism, postmodernism, and deconstruction have made throughout the world. Although I agree that postmodernist critique has decisively shown us why foundational beliefs must be carefully scrutinized and questioned—and I hope this chapter supports that argument—it is often the case that groups armed with strong and unambiguous foundational beliefs are more passionately committed, vigorously enthusiastic, and successful in achieving their goals than groups whose only foundational belief is a skepticism that meanders aimlessly through ethereal space, detached from specific places, cultural identities, or particular issues. The contrast between groups such as the Dinéh Alliance, which are working for and often effecting concrete social, political, and environmental change, and large academic organizations, which often seem as if they champion only skepticism and ambiguity, has led many in the creative and critical arts to reflect on their roles and the role of their profession in the struggle to preserve the environment.

In the introduction to *The Ecocriticism Reader,* Cheryll Glotfelty observes that many working in the field of contemporary literary studies find themselves facing a dilemma. In the postmodern age, literary studies seems mired in a state of change so rapid that the critical contours of the profession are redrawn every few years in response to the latest, "hottest" theory (xvi). Noting some of the positive effects of postmodern thought in the academy, Glotfelty writes that social movements such as the Civil Rights and women's movements of the 1960s and 1970s—both of which were powered by postmodern critique of dominant power relations—transformed literary studies by demanding that the profession take account of the issues of race, class, and gender, and that it expand the canon to include the work of women and multiethnic writers. Despite this focused attention on pressing contemporary issues, literary scholarship remains curiously ignorant of the "most pressing contemporary issue of all, namely, the global environmental crisis" (xv). In response to this lack of attention, a small group of people came together in the late 1980s and early 1990s to form the Association for the Study of Literature and the Environment (ASLE). As an interdisciplinary group of environmentally concerned writers and scholars, Glotfelty writes, ASLE recognizes as a fundamental premise "that human culture is connected to the physical world, affecting it and affected by it" (xix).

However, those involved in the ecological study of literature often work from foundational concepts about nature and the environment that obscure the connections between environmental degradation and environmental racism. As a result, ecocriticism has been "predominantly a white movement," writes Glotfelty, calling on her fellow writers, scholars, and environmentalists to make stronger connections between the environment and issues of social justice (xxv). Glotfelty's challenge is provocative because an implicit separation between social and environmental issues is evident in many essays written by literary critics who study literature and the environment. For example, in "Revaluing Nature," one of the first essays to address the emerging field of ecocriticism, Glenn Love celebrates a "nature-oriented literature" in which there is an implicit or stated regard "for the nonhuman" (230). This literature offers a needed corrective, he notes, to a profession in which a heavy emphasis is placed on deconstructionist, Marxist, psychoanalytical, feminist, and multicultural theories. Love observes that "[r]ace, class, and gender are the words which we see and hear everywhere at our professional meetings and in our current publications," but there has been little regard exhibited for the environment (226). He argues that it does not seem unreasonable to suggest that an ecocritical reinterpretation and reformation of the literary canon to include works such as *Desert Solitaire* could have "far greater" influence "than any critical movement which we have seen thus far" (236). The words *far greater* imply that ecocritics would emphasize the importance of environmental issues over social issues and that the movements to open up literary studies to discussions of race, class, and gender have nothing to do with opening up literary studies to discussions of environmental issues.

I do not believe that Love is adverse to literary approaches that take race, class, and gender into consideration. Clearly, his criticism is directed at what he and many other critics see as the increasing emphasis in literary studies on postmodern theories that seem to have no practical relevance outside the ivory towers of academia and that are characterized, to use his words, by their "obscurity and inaccessibility to all but other English professors" (236). This distinction is important. Even if we accept that the emphasis on theory in the profession has led to a certain debilitating descent into ambiguity and skepticism, we need to be careful not to dismiss the important issues associated with postmodernism—race, class, and gender—or to ignore the ways in which social issues are connected to environmental issues.

We ignore these connections at our own critical peril. For example, in his assessment of *Desert Solitaire,* Don Scheese describes Edward Abbey as a "secular prophet of the modern religion of environmentalism," noting that Abbey "believed that he stood for time-honored American values produced in response to the frontier: independence, self-reliance, self-sufficiency."[12] Given that most early ecological literary criticism focuses on the work of solitary white, male writers who enter the wilderness to "confront the bare bones of existence," it is not surprising that Scheese—in an otherwise thoughtful and valuable discussion of *Desert Solitaire*—fails to critique the inherent racism, classism, and sexism in America's "time-honored" frontier values. Scheese's lack of consideration of the issues of race, class, and gender produces gaps in his criticism: like Abbey, he does not acknowledge the frontier as a place of genocide and removal, a place unwelcoming to women and dangerous for Others. Had he brought these issues to his analysis, it would have been difficult to ignore how time-honored frontier values shape Abbey's construction of wilderness in *Desert Solitaire* as a place that should be limited to "men on foot" (55). Wives and other females are best left lounging in the cities (182); indigenous sheep-raising people and their untraditional offspring need not apply (116, 120); and, unfortunately, people too elderly or too young to move through rugged terrain under their own power are best left safely at home (61). In short, for Abbey, the timeless wilderness is not a specific place, but an abstract notion of refuge for solitary white men in good physical condition.

Ecocritics consistently claim to have aspirations to make a difference in the profession and in the world. "We have witnessed the feminist and multi-ethnic critical movements radically transform the profession, the job market, and the canon," writes Cheryll Glotfelty, urging colleagues to work for similarly transformative effects by raising consciousness about environmental crisis (xxiv). But as long as ecocritics base their work on abstract notions of wilderness, where individuals seek a solace that excludes everyone except those like themselves, their critical work will remain theoretically incoherent and politically ineffective in its aim to protect threatened environments. Again, Glen Love's essay, though well-intentioned, serves to illustrate this point. Love argues that through either some massive ecological crisis or a genuinely new enlightened sense of environmental awareness, those in literary studies must soon recognize "the integration of human with natural cycles of life" (235). It must happen, he concludes, "that our critical and aesthetic faculties will come to reassess those texts—literary and critical—which ignore any values save for an earth-denying and ultimately destructive anthropocentrism" (235). The phrases "earth-denying" and "ultimately destructive anthropocentrism" render his critical objective of working to understand human integration into natural cycles theoretically incoherent because they imply that we would not be working for a place in which humans live and work ethically *in* the natural world, but for a place outside of human culture where solitary individuals occasionally go to hike and climb and seek a heightened awareness of nature's wonders.

An ecocriticism based on such abstract and ultimately ahistorical notions of wilderness would lack the power to transform the profession or the world, and for some of the same reasons that Love decries the emphasis on theory. Love is not specific about which characteristics of postmodern critical theory he is referring to when he argues that literary criticism is retreating "ever further from public life" (236), but if he is referring to theories of identity that posit an endless play of "difference" or "otherness," then I would agree that he is right to call for a "needed corrective." Postmodernism posits that all knowledges are "situated" in a heterogeneous world of difference and that all sorts of problems arise when privileged individuals or groups purport to speak for Others. However, critics such as David Harvey and Nancy Hartsock, whose work Harvey cites, argue that conceptions of infinite fluidity of multiple and shifting identities become, as Harvey expresses it, "vulgar" when they block the "capacity for directed action" by "the sheer confusion of identities" (357). In other words, "vulgar" notions of situatedness assume that none of us can ever throw off the shackles of our personal histories or consider what the condition of being Other is all about. The argument goes something like this: because she is Acoma and female, she could not possibly have anything to say about the condition of being a white male in New York City; or more commonly, because he is white, male, and middle class, his vision will be bounded by his position in the world, and he will never be able to understand the condition of or speak against the oppression of anyone whose identity is construed as Other.

Postmodernist theorists have shown, I think persuasively, that biographies *do* matter, that they *do* shape our visions of the world. But "somewhere between the vulgar essentialist view [of identity] and the potentially infinite fluidity of multiple and shifting identifications," as Harvey has put it, "there has to be sufficient common ground established (however contingent) to give direction (for a time and in a place) for political action" (357). Because meaningful social and political change almost always involves groups of people coming together in specific places to work for agreed-upon objectives, a first step in the process must be to seek to understand the Other's historical experiences and foundational cultural concepts. The critic's task in this process, observes Nancy Hart-sock, is to pay close attention to and theorize not only the differences between diverse individuals and groups of people but the "similarities that can provide the basis for differing groups to understand each other and form alliances."[13] With different degrees of theoretical sophistica-tion but with equal degrees of concern for their profession and the world, Harvey and Hartsock—and Love—are all calling for a "needed corrective" to the disorienting aspects of postmodern theory, one that encourages scholars to bring their theoretical work down to earth, to ground it in specific places, to collaborate with particular groups of people for effective transformative change. As Love puts it, we must recover the lost "social role of literary criticism" (238).

Edward Abbey has been something of an icon among ecocritics, and few have undertaken a critique of his work from the perspective of race, class, or gender. But he himself understood—albeit, in his quirky way— that one white man, working alone, even one who loved wilderness as passionately as he did, could not bring about transformative change or stop the large-scale social and political processes encroaching on the places he loved. This is evident in an incident he recalls in *Desert Soli-taire* in which he meets and engages in a bit of small talk with govern-ment engineers working to build and pave the road that will attract an increasing number of tourists to Arches National Monument. After the engineers leave, Abbey drives behind their government-issued jeep, pulling up carefully placed survey stakes. But the road is built anyway: "As I type these words," Abbey laments, "all that was foretold has come to pass. Arches National Monument has been developed. The Master Plan has been fulfilled" (51).

Abbey's response is not to call like and unlike people together to work for the preservation of a valued place. Rather, without saying exactly why or how, he writes that we must preserve wilderness because "We may need it someday not only as a refuge from excessive industrialism but also as a refuge from authoritarian government" (149). This kind of rhetoric, however inspirational or consciousness raising for a generation of middle-class environmentalists and nature lovers, cannot be the basis for meaningful or directed political action because it does exactly the thing that many ecocritics find so disturbing in postmodern theories that posit an endless play of individual differences: it gives us permission to give up on the difficult, time-consuming, often confusing work of making connections with other people, with understanding their experiences and differences, and with finding common ground on which to stand and fight the forces that exploit both people and their environments.

Transforming the world, then, will take much more than bringing people to an awareness of their differences or to a consciousness of environmental crisis. To use the counsel of Simon Ortiz's father to his children, it will take work, and it will not be easy. As Ortiz's characters Bill and Pete and Ida and Mary discover, it is not difference alone that matters, it is working to understand our differences and similarities (not sameness) sufficiently well so that we can come together in the middle place—the place where social and environmental problems originate—to work for transformative change. The work that ecocritics can do—their task, as I see it—will be to employ their training in literary, environmental, and cultural studies not to prove the impossibility of foundational beliefs about difference, nature, wilderness, justice, or place, but to work for more plausible and adequate foundational concepts that make critical interpretation and political action meaningful, creative—and possible. Seeking to understand and change the local, national, and global processes that give rise to social and ecological problems, they would help us understand how power relations are produced through social action and how these relations acquire the particular significance they do in certain places and situations. In this way, ecocritics would facilitate the formation of alliances by framing human experiences in ways that encourage us to be responsible to each other and to the places we inhabit.

Building on Simon Ortiz's notion of the Pueblo farmer as one who seeks to understand the reciprocal relationship of humans to the natural world and on Michael Pollan's notion of the gardener as one who works to understand how humans might use—or not use—nature responsibly, we might see the writer's, critic's, and teacher's task as the development of an aesthetic and ethic that embraces both the human and the natural. Both Pollan and Ortiz point out that concrete results in the garden depend on an understanding of how nature's large-scale patterns work on a small scale in specific places. This might mean that, like gardeners or environmental justice activists, literary critics might move at times from a large-scale pattern or theory to a specific place—asking, for example, how differences in ecological, cultural, economic, political, and social conditions get produced and how those differences manifest themselves differently in specific places. At other times, they might move from a specific issue outward to a more universal foundational concept or theory—asking, for example, how radically different socio-ecological circumstances imply quite different approaches to the question of what is or is not just. But theory and place must always be inextricably linked because the insertion of actual physical, geographical place considerations into abstract theoretical considerations offers profound insights—or disruptions—into how a theory or foundational concept might actually work in the world.

No More Sacrifices

On the last ten miles of the Paria Canyon trail, my knees ached under the weight of my pack as I hiked up hills of ancient blue volcanic ash and crossed sparsely vegetated fields of prickly pear cactus and yucca. Sunburned and grubby, I no longer changed to my sandals to ford the river, but sloshed through the water in my hiking boots, appreciating the cool sponginess of my insoles against my hot, aching feet. I had been in the canyon for five days, and now, looking forward to getting back home, where a hot shower, fresh clothes, and my bed awaited me, I began pushing myself a little harder. Nevertheless, when I looked up into the cobalt sky and saw a red-tailed hawk circling, I had to sit down, breathe, and watch, marveling at the way it sailed on the updraft, tipping its wings one way and then the other. At that moment, I thought I understood perfectly what Abbey meant when he wrote that "wilderness is not a luxury but a necessity of the human spirit, and as vital to our lives as water and good bread" (192). Wild rivers, slot canyons, hawks, and blue volcanic hills are vital to our sense of who we are as humans, and we should celebrate their existence and work to ensure their preservation.

But if I walked through the Paria River without feeling both the natural and cultural forces swirling around my feet, if I imagined that by packing out all my garbage, I was actually "leaving no trace" of my presence in the natural world, then my reading of the landscape could do nothing to help me confront and transform the processes that draw lines of protection around some areas but write off others as sacrifice zones. As I observed at the beginning of chapter two, our readings of the landscape can mean the difference between life and death. I was referring to the literal necessity of keeping a close eye on the weather and the water while hiking Paria Canyon, but I meant more than simply that. Euro-American readings of the landscape have assigned "nature" to those mythical places untouched by human culture. At the same time, the human and nonhuman populations considered closest to nature and part of the "wilderness" landscape are deemed Others who are in need of control and domination. The places where they live are defined and interpreted as either valuable national treasures or expendable sacrifice zones. Thus, Euro-American readings of the landscape have literally meant the difference between life and death for entire species and communities.

In *Fight Back,* Simon Ortiz illustrates that until we find common ground on which to form alliances of like and unlike people who stand and fight the oppression of all those—both human and nonhuman— whose identities have been construed as Other, expendable populations will continue to be expended, and sacrifice areas will continue to be sacrificed. In "We Have Been Told Many Things But We Know This to Be True," he offers us a place to come together and begin our search for that common ground: work. Because all the elements of human survival are extracted from the natural world, and because most of us must work to live, work is the link that binds humans to other humans and to nature. By recognizing our relation to the natural world and to work, we acknowledge ourselves to be in "vital relation / with each other" (365). This recognition behooves us to accept responsibility for the consequences of our own lives and work together for transformative social and environmental change.

Ortiz emphasizes that working together, forming effective alliances, will require a recognition of kinds and degrees of human intervention in the natural world. In Kerr-McGee's Ambrosia Lake uranium-processing mill, Ortiz learned that there is a kind of work that is exploitative, that gives nothing back. This work is carried out by "liars, thieves, and killers" who refuse to take responsibility for their actions (365). These people are not necessarily the loggers, ranchers, farmers, or miners that mainstream environmentalists often vilify; rather, they are the individuals or groups who do not have the people and the land and their continuance as their foremost concern, and who are willing to sacrifice everything to their colonial, political, and economic objectives.

In contrast, in his father's fields, Ortiz learned there is a kind of work that "is creative" and encourages "reliance" among all living things (325). This work does not romanticize nature as separate from culture but recognizes the complexity of a world in which we must alter, manipulate, even destroy elements of nature as a condition of our survival. It acknowledges that humans are "reliant" on other life forms and so must take the interests of nonhuman nature into account—humbly, respectfully, and *thoughtfully* making choices about their use or nonuse (325). It does not demonize Others or make distinctions based on race, class, or gender, or on whether or not people do hard physical labor as opposed to white-collar work. Rather, it encourages diverse groups of people to see their "vital relation" to each other, to move toward an understanding of their differences and similarities, and to come together for common causes in specific places. Only by working together, by recognizing that we "are in a family with each other," will we "have life" and continuance (324, 325). Only then, Ortiz emphasizes in the concluding essay of *Fight Back,* "will there be no more unnecessary sacrifices of our people and our land" (361).

As *Desert Solitaire* and many of the critical works assessing it clearly illustrate, environmentalists, writers, and scholars who identify nature with leisure open themselves to charges of elitism and racism, and close themselves off from the possibility of finding common cause with those who redefine the environment as the places where we live, work, and play. By taking the position of the rugged individualist, a solitary voice crying out for the red wasteland, Abbey relegated himself to the politically ineffective—and lonely—effort of standing guard at the borders of wilderness. On the other hand, Simon Ortiz's effort to come to terms with work brings people of diverse races and classes together in the pages of his writing and unites issues as diverse as workplace safety and sustainable agriculture, toxic sites and sacred shrines, depleted aquifers and community health, economic development and wilderness protection. In *Fight Back,* we hear not one voice crying out in the wilderness, but "the moving power of the voice, / the moving power of the earth, / the moving power of the People" (324).

Part of our task as community members, environmentalists, writers, scholars, and critics, then, must be to call attention to the social and environmental links between our own work, the work of others, and the natural world. By failing to account for the necessity of work, we give ourselves permission to ignore how our own actions in the middle place lead to environmental degradation in places that have been written off as fallen. If we are white collar and middle class, working in some air-conditioned office, buying our groceries in a supermarket, we often have no sense of where our food, homes, heat, and power come from. "What have we to do with Black Mesa or the Mohave Generating Station or the Glen Canyon Dam?" we ask. We are not extracting and crushing coal, mixing it with groundwater, or sending it through a pipeline to a distant generating station. We are not multinational corporation executives or coal miners or dam builders. Our work, we tell ourselves, destroys nothing, poisons no living thing, so we absolve ourselves of responsibility. But in my own case, every page of this book was written on a computer powered with electricity produced, in part, at a generating station that burns coal extracted from Black Mesa. My work, though seemingly clean, is no less innocent than the blast detonated by a Diné worker or the order to blast signed by a Peabody executive. I cannot blame Peabody entirely for the respiratory illnesses suffered by the Diné and Hopi who live near Kayenta and by the surrounding communities. I cannot separate myself from responsibility for poisoned groundwater simply because I live far enough away from the consequences of my work that I do not breathe air laden with particulates or feel my house shudder every time an explosion cuts deeper into seams of coal on a sacred mesa.

By examining the writing of Edward Abbey, I admit to focusing on an environmental writer whose books and essays take a radical (or conservative, depending on one's viewpoint) position on the separation of nature and culture and on the refusal to accept responsibility for the consequences of our lives, our histories, and our work. Not all American nature writers and critics, however, construct wilderness in such extremely dichotomous terms as Abbey, and many have thoughtfully approached the subject of work and examined the lives of humans who respectfully learn about the natural world through work. Both Gary Synder and Barry Lopez have written with great sensitivity to the fact that in traditional American Indian communities there was no conception of wilderness, but rather a perception of the natural world as home, a place where humans manipulate the elements of nature in order to survive. John McPhee and Gretel Ehrlich have written with great sensitivity about traditional human cultures guided and circumscribed by the rhythms and capacities of nature in the Pine Barrens of New Jersey and in the grasslands of Wyoming. McPhee's "pineys" and Ehrlich's ranch workers, notes critic Kent Ryden, are portrayed not as despoilers of the earth but as "folk manipulators of the landscape," people who are subtly and intrinsically part of the environments they inhabit. McPhee and Ehrlich typify those nature writers who listen "carefully to people in order to understand their traditional uses and interpretations of the landscape, examining the landscape itself as providing clues to human culture. In so doing, they bridge the gap between the human and nonhuman that looms so large in American nature writing and ecocriticism."[14]

McPhee's and Ehrlich's literary works and Ryden's criticism suggest the fruitful new angles on environmentalism and ecocriticism that open up when we attempt to come to terms with the implications of human labor in the natural world. This chapter suggests the further possibilities that open up for environmentalists and scholars when they incorporate multicultural perspectives and literatures into their study and critical practice and when they refuse to ignore the issues of race, class, and gender. Literary works such as *Fight Back* appeal to other-than-dominant concepts of nature, justice, and place, concepts embedded in other cultures, other languages, and other relationships to the land. These works show us a relation to nature other than domination and exploitation, one that acknowledges the wildness not only "out there," but all around us—in the middle place that encompasses both nature and culture.

Cultural Critique and Local Pedagogy

A Reading of Louise Erdrich's *Tracks*

[P]eople of color have always theorized—but in forms quite different from the Western form of abstract logic. And . . . our theorizing . . . is often in narrative forms, in the stories we create, in riddles and proverbs, in the play with language, since dynamic rather than fixed ideas seem more to our liking. How else have we managed to survive with such spiritedness the assault on our bodies, social institutions, countries, our very humanity?
—Barbara Christian, "The Race for Theory"

The Official and Vernacular Landscapes

Every summer for six weeks, the University of Arizona campus becomes home to a new group of high school students who hail from the reservations, barrios, urban neighborhoods, and rural areas of Arizona. Having been accepted into the Med-Start Program, which introduces ethnically underrepresented and economically disadvantaged students to the medical professions, seventy-five sixteen- and seventeen-year-old boys and girls flood noisily, excitedly, nervously into the lobby of their dorm on the first morning of the program. For many, it is the first time they have been so far away from home, the first time they have been to a city as large as Tucson, or the first time they have been on a university campus. If they live in some of Arizona's higher elevations, it might also be the first time they have experienced the unrelenting heat and humidity of a rainy season in the Sonoran Desert.

In those first hours, while greeting their peers, they put on a confident, "yeah, I do this all the time" face. But most wave good-bye to their parents with some apprehension and uncertainty, emotions they endeavor to keep hidden from the others. Working to allay their concerns, experienced counselors gather them into small groups, pair them with a roommate, and help them get settled into their rooms. Later, each counselor leads his or her group on a tour of what, for most of the students, is an intimidating landscape of towering buildings, asphalt streets, concrete bike paths, and an expansive, grassy mall, lined on either side with palm trees. One of the first stops on this tour is the University Medical Center, an imposing complex of buildings where the students will spend their mornings studying anatomy, attending surgeries, and "shadowing" doctors, physical therapists, and nurses on their daily rounds. Subsequent stops include the Chemistry Building and the Humanities Building, where the students will spend their afternoons taking courses in science and composition, and attending weekly readings given by such poets and novelists as Sherman Alexie, Patricia Preciado Martin, and Alberto Rios, who spend time with the students discussing the reasons why poetry and fiction are important—especially for those who want to be healers.[1]

As a program coordinator and composition instructor, I had the privilege to work with participants in the Med-Start Program for seven summers. Each year I helped greet the students as they arrived at the Tucson campus, then walked with them as they left their dorm to enter what might be thought of as the "official landscape" of Euro-American culture—a phrase loosely based on the distinctions John Brinckerhoff Jackson makes between the "vernacular" and the "official" in his analysis of landscape.[2] The vernacular landscape is a folk landscape in which people are attuned to the contours of home and place; it is a living, breathing landscape where geological features such as Baboquivari Peak on the Tohono O'odham Nation or a cherished Catholic cathedral in a South Tucson neighborhood are alive with meaning and significance, where people, whether they live in rural or urban areas, can tell you the names of their neighbors and the names of the trees, where they have a sense of the rhythms of local culture. This landscape is the familiar, intimate landscape that most Med-Start students leave when they depart for their summer adventure on the Tucson campus.

The official landscape, as Brinckerhoff defines it, is an extraction-oriented landscape, imposed by government and corporation on local geographies without regard for local peoples, cultures, or environments. I say the students were entering the official landscape as they walked out onto the palm-lined university mall because the campus sits on land close to the Santa Cruz River, where the Tohono O'odham once cultivated floodplain gardens and where, later, Mexican American peoples grew flowers and vegetables in *milpas* sheltered from the searing Sonoran sun by the towering cottonwoods growing along the riverbanks. Today, the city of Tucson extracts so much groundwater to keep swimming pools filled and golf courses and university malls green that the water table has dropped dramatically, and the river and the cottonwoods have disappeared. The Tohono O'odham no longer plant corn in the mouths of arroyos, and the Mexican American barrios and milpas have been removed to make way for the Tucson Convention Center and an interstate freeway. Because Euro-American educational systems, dating back at least to Descartes, have supported the imposition of the official landscape, in part, by promoting the notion that the powerful and educated must separate local concerns from universal truths, the University of Arizona campus (indeed, all university campuses in the United States) might be read as a metonomy for the social and institutional power that grants state and corporate entities the authority to remove, extract, develop, and pave over the vernacular landscape.

For centuries, students entering the official landscape of Euro-American higher learning have been taught to become citizens of a world city of ideas and books; to renounce, minimize, or ignore their citizenship in their own families, cultures, and vernacular landscapes; to value the universal; and to embrace an aesthetic that supposedly transcends time and place.[3] This age-old tradition has had all sorts of historical consequences for poor and marginalized and for people of color, who view family, culture, and place as primary—not the least of which has been their exclusion (until relatively recently) from U.S. institutions of higher learning and a discrediting of their traditional knowledges, literatures, and arts. This historical exclusion and the stories told about it by those who have been excluded are often at the root of the apprehension and uncertainty some Med-Start students feel as their parents drive away from the dorm. For example, if a student is American Indian and the first in her family to be college bound, stories about grandmothers, fathers, or uncles who were marginalized socially and educationally by being forcibly sent away from an intimate, familiar landscape to government boarding schools where they were stripped of their names, cultures, and languages will almost certainly play a role in how she experiences her educational journey into the official landscape. If a student is African American, his perceptions will be shaped, in part, by stories about laws passed to prevent his forebears from learning to read and write, about their struggle to gain admittance to U.S. educational institutions, and about the institutionalized racism they faced once they got there.

However, the resistance, persistence, and triumph embedded in these stories often provides strong motivation for students to enter the official landscape, despite their doubts and concerns regarding what the experience may hold for them. When asked to write about what compels them to seek a college education, Med-Start students often mention historical figures such as Harriet Tubman, W. E. B. Du Bois, Chief Joseph, Martin Luther King Jr., César Chávez, or some member of the family or community who contested the official landscape through activism or resistance—sometimes by participating in the Civil Rights movement, sometimes by obtaining an education despite the obstacles, or often by quietly persevering in a heroic effort to provide their children with more educational and economic opportunities than they themselves were afforded. Many American Indian students, for example, tell stories about sitting as children on the laps of grandmothers or fathers or aunts who told them stories about running away from their boarding school, sneaking off into corners to speak forbidden tribal languages with friends, or passively resisting injustice by failing to perform schoolwork or chores in expected ways. These stories distinctly embody an attitude of resistance to the federal government's efforts to control Indian people by depicting the storytellers as courageous for their resistance. At the same time, the stories often end with grandmother or father or uncle admonishing the child to stay in school, and they thus show acceptance of education as a positive goal. These kinds of family and community stories help hundreds of students step out into the official landscape armed with a courage and strength gained in the vernacular landscape.

Programs such as Med-Start (as well as Women's Studies, American Indian Studies, African American Studies, etc.), which aim to alter the contours of the official landscape of the United States by welcoming the children and grandchildren of ethnic and minority groups into colleges and universities, are unique in many ways because they owe their very existence in academia to the struggles of national figures such as Martin Luther King Jr. or of activists working at the community level or of other less-visible, but no less extraordinary people (grandmothers telling stories to children sitting on their laps). None of these people necessarily had as their goal the creation of new scholarly fields or programs. But the individuals working in literary and cultural studies—especially those whose scholarly and pedagogical work focuses on the literatures of marginalized groups—recognize, remember, and honor the struggle of these people by remaining committed to the goals of the Civil Rights movement. They see themselves as working for specific peoples living in specific places and are intent on doing academic work in ways that move us toward a future that looks nothing like the landscape of Euro-American domination and control.

A Valorizing Academicism versus Local Pedagogy

In his 1992 presidential address to the Modern Languages Association, Houston Baker observed that the Civil Rights movement challenged the academic community to acknowledge that immersing college students in the ideas and theories of Western Europe and New England did not necessarily move us toward the creation of a more just and equal society. As a result, many academic professionals came to regard the classroom not as a place for the transfer of placeless universals from professor to student, but as a locale "for critically reading one's self and the world with the goal of changing both."[4] Speaking specifically to those working in literary and cultural studies, Baker suggested that working for transformative social change will take more than the incorporation of multicultural literatures and perspectives into the curriculum; it will take the committed practice of a *local pedagogy*, one informed by a better understanding of local peoples, cultures, histories, and geographies. Teaching multicultural literatures and perspectives almost certainly broadens a student's knowledge of diverse cultures, but if everyone across the United States is teaching the same multicultural literary works, the same Native American novel, or the same Chicana poetry in the same ways, there is the danger, Baker argued, that "our resolute inclusiveness amounts to no more than a thoughtless pandering to high-flown, abstract ideals" (404). To avoid the dangers of standardizing or of normalizing our discussions of race, class, and gender, we must invite our students into a discussion of the ways in which literary works are rooted in the particulars of place and time, and make connections between the works they are reading and the ways in which they themselves are rooted, to go back to the terms I have been using in this chapter, in a vernacular landscape.

Most teachers and literary critics would agree that literature has something to teach us about being human, something universal that transcends the limits of historical and geographical origin in its meaning and beauty. But literature cannot teach us about the literal places our students might take us unless, in our classroom discussions, we grant them pedagogical license to bring their own knowledges and cultures into the classroom. Yet, how can we invite local and regional cultures into the room or make connections between those cultures and what our students are reading or even recognize who the students in our classes are if we know nothing about local cultures or are so blinded by our own academic specializations that we cannot see what our students have to offer? The first step of a local pedagogy, then, would take us outside our classrooms to walk across our campus malls or the local convention center parking lot (both of which represent a general cartography of white, man-centered legitimacy and control), toward the banks of a once free-flowing but now dry, unshaded riverbed, where we would stand for a time and contemplate past and present histories of the indigenous, local, and regional cultures that still survive just outside the campus gates.

Back in our classrooms, we would look around the room and notice who is sitting there, then teach in ways that would provide our students with educational experiences that accommodate in some manner the irresolvable tension between the local and universal, the vernacular and official. Recognizing that our students and their communities are often in touch with knowledges and forces beyond our own lives and academic specialties, we would practice a local pedagogy that might look something like the Med-Start Program. The instructors who teach in this program employ many conventionally accepted pedagogical methods to teach students anatomy, chemistry, and composition, but they also invite students to bring their own local knowledges into the academy. After shadowing doctors at the Medical Center and reading Leslie Silko's *Ceremony* or Rudolfo Anaya's *Bless Me, Ultima* for their composition classes, students of American Indian or Mexican American descent might write personal essays about how the traditional healing practices of a Diné medicine man or a Mexican American *curandera* present additional or complementary alternatives and further possibilities to accepted Western medical practices. If an ecological perspective teaches us to see everything as connected to everything else, then the practice of this kind of local pedagogy might be thought of as "ecological" in that it encourages students to see connections, to envision a middle place between the local and the universal, and to contest campus landscapes where Western philosophies that separate science from story, history from health, and economics from ecology are literally reflected in the built environment.

Describing his presidential address as a "summons" to a renewed life in teaching, Baker recalled an incident that occurred during a course he was teaching on African American women's literature. One evening, a young black female student attempted to make connections between her reading of Phyllis Wheatley's poetry and her own contemporary experiences, but Bake reprimanded her, telling her that in his classroom, students will root their discussions in theory and forms of literature, not descend into the realm of the personal experience or the local landscape. Later, a walk across his own university landscape made him more cognizant of the virulent racism still institutionalized in a row of fraternity houses prominently located on a prestigious and heavily used corridor of the University of Pennsylvania—called Locust Walk. Baker began to wonder how the experience of his young black student—who had to negotiate her way past the white fraternity houses each week on her way to class and who therefore endured the racial slurs inevitably hurled at her by fraternity members—shaped her reading and discussion of Phyllis Wheatley's poetry. But having denied her the opportunity to bring her personal experience into his classroom, he saw that he had denied himself and his other students the benefit of her mapping of the connections between the local landscape and his official, literary one. He concluded that if our students' classroom experiences are to provide them with the tools to build landscapes different from the Locust Walks of this country, then we will need to allow our students to chart the contours of their local landscapes and experiences and to bring their "maps" into the classroom. This kind of "local mapping" must be considered integral to the development of useful and practical reading skills for the twenty-first century (405).

Yet too often, as Baker's own story illustrates, teachers, scholars, and students of literature are encouraged to be more concerned with other critics' texts and with the development of theory-informed reading skills than with learning to map the shared connections between literature and local people and landscapes. In this official literary landscape, theory is commodified and becomes the basis on which scholars are hired and promoted in academic institutions, a curious critical environment, observed Baker, that often leads to a "valorizing academicism" or an inverse correlation between the intellectual achievements of the scholar-teacher and the amount of time, energy, and patience he or she devotes to the classroom and to students (405).

Baker's concerns echo those of many women-of-color critics who question the privileging of certain postmodern modes of theorizing in university courses, especially those focused on the study of literature. In *Making Face, Making Soul,* a collection of the creative and critical writings of women of color, critics such as Gloria Anzaldúa and Barbara Christian do not dismiss theory *tout court.* We need to theorize our most pressing social problems, they point out, in order to understand how we might work collectively for change. But in academia, the definitions of what counts as theory are often very narrow. Theory is thought of as those inaccessible texts addressed to a privileged, predominantly Anglo-European social group and characterized by words such as *profound, serious, substantial,* and *consequential.* Theory is constructed as the antithesis of story or fiction, which is often described with words such as *playful, imaginative,* and *nonserious.* Christian and Anzaldúa observe that it seems highly suspicious that just at the moment when writers of color are producing literature that emerges from the vernacular landscapes they inhabit—literature that reclaims or reinvents identities and unmasks the power relations of the world—theory is invested with more status than literature. They challenge literary and cultural critics to pay renewed attention to fiction, poetry, and creative nonfiction, not just as literature, but as a way of "doing theory in another mode."[5]

In the spirit of speculating about the kinds of readings that might work to move us away from a valorizing academicism and toward pedagogies that aim to develop a shared sense of responsibility for local situations, I move now into a brief discussion of theory and argue for the practice of a transformative cultural critique that would help us build a more just and equitable world. I then offer a reading of Louise Erdrich's *Tracks* that I hope is suggestive of why cultural and literary critics should treat multicultural literatures not only as literary work but as theoretical work that gives us insight into how marginalized groups have always challenged the official landscape of Euro-American domination and control. I end the chapter by coming back to my Med-Start students and briefly discussing how this kind of reading might be employed in the practice of a transformative local pedagogy.

Transformative Cultural Critique

In chapter three, I explained why conceptions of the natural world as wilderness end up being theoretically incoherent and politically ineffective, and I drew some connections to the ways in which conceptions of identity that posit an endless play of difference and "otherness" block the capacity for effective alliance and directed action. I challenged literary and cultural critics to bring their theoretical work down to earth, to make it relevant by continually moving back and forth between the universal and the local, and by working for transformative change with particular groups of people in specific places. Feminist critics Gloria Anzaldúa, Barbara Christian, and Teresa Ebert argue for something very similar. Contemporary academic theory, they observe, is often considered irrelevant by community leaders and grassroots activists working among the poor and working classes because it seems to hold little promise for moving us toward collective social and environmental change.

In an essay arguing for a cultural studies that eschews academicism and works toward concrete social change, Teresa Ebert articulates the differences she sees between postmodern theory and "transformative cultural critique." Dominant forms of postmodern theory, Ebert explains, seek open access to the free play of signification (through parody, irony, and experimentation). These theories advocate cultural equality through semiotic activism and rearticulate the notion of politics solely as a language effect, substituting "valuation for critique and affirmation for opposition."[6] In other words, this kind of theory affirms already existing social differences, and sees this affirmation as, in itself, an effective mode of social resistance to dominant culture. No attempt is made by those who engage in this kind of theory to explain why and how social, racial, or economic differences came into being or how existing social institutions might be collectively changed so that (economic) resources and cultural power might be distributed without regard to gender, race, class, or sexuality.

In effect, postmodernist theories intimate the end of transformative politics, making emancipation or the collective social struggle to end exploitation simply a metaphysical project: a metanarrative. Instead of explaining how we might work toward transformative social change, Ebert observes, these theories place emphasis on "pleasure—pleasure in/of textuality, the local, the popular, and above all, the body *(jouissance)*" (7–8). Scholars who engage in postmodern critique often share a commitment to overturning the dualism that associates women and "Others" with the body in ways that negatively and systematically represent them as ruled by their bodies instead of by their minds. In opposition to this alienating abstraction, they posit the body as a concrete, anticonceptual, material knowledge that is both disalienating and creative. They argue that the *experience* of the female body—its pleasures, desires, and needs—locates women in a specific, particular, material knowledge of daily life and involves them in creative, nondominating relations of nurturing and connection with others.

The problem, writes Ebert, is that pleasure and desire "can be the overriding concern only for classes of people (middle and upper) who are already 'free' from economic want. . . . This fetishization of pleasure validates the priorities and privileges of the middle class—in spite of its attention to the 'pleasures' of others—for it produces a cultural studies that largely erases the needs, conditions, and exploitation of the working poor and the impoverished underclass, an underclass that is often denied basic economic and human rights, an underclass that is overwhelmingly not 'white'" (8). Furthermore, by taking refuge in a seemingly anticonceptual biological, biographical, textual body free from economic want or racial marginalization, postmodern critics often remove the "body" from history, affirming social differences but failing to explicate how systematic practices of exploitation based on socially constructed gender, race, sexual, and class differences operate.

Some significant parallels might be drawn between writing that conceptualizes nature as wilderness—and heralds the "death of nature"— and writing that, though claiming to be anticonceptual, essentializes the body as a concept and intimates the end of transformative politics. Both, for the most part, are produced by writers and scholars who are, regardless of race or nationality, predominantly middle-class professionals largely from North America, Britain, and Australia, and who are thus part of the minority of the world appropriating the majority of the world's resources. Both types of writing obscure the effects on each of us of socioeconomic and ecological forces that require us to work in the biophysical world for our own survival and place us within a class system that does not give us all equal access to education, money, privilege, or power. Both posit that there can be no middle place or common ground on which we might come together to develop a sense of our shared situation.

As I stated in the previous chapter, writers and scholars are free to address any subject or issue they choose on the basis of their individual talents and preferences. However, writing—whether creative or theoretical—that erases the needs, conditions, and exploitation of the underclasses and simply validates social differences cannot provide like and unlike people with enough common ground on which to come together and find answers to urgent questions about the exploitation and suffering of the poor and marginalized in economically depressed and ecologically degraded areas of the world. Theories that indulge in the pleasure of the text or invite us to "play" can be insightful, even necessary when they problematize or denaturalize dominant meanings and open up space in which to create new meanings. But if we want to transform society, we need theories that do more than valorize academicism, theories that emerge from a middle place between the universal and the local, theories that do cultural work in the world, theories that provide us with explanatory critique and alternatives for change, theories that give us the tools to build a more socially and environmentally just society.

If we want to create landscapes different from Euro-American landscapes of domination and control, we will need to articulate our different positions, analyze and explicate the underlying bases of social and ecological injustices, and find common ground by exploring our shared situations and responsibilities. But how can we come together or find that common ground if we are speaking a language to which only the elite few are privy? This is not to dismiss out of hand the language in which most postmodernist theoretical texts are written; all professional fields have specialized languages only a few individuals are trained to read, and specialized language is often necessary for articulating complex concepts. But if at the outset we determine that we are working not to reach the few, but the many, then that determination will guide the orientation we (writers, critics, teachers) take in our work, the language we use, and the purposes for which our work is intended. The problem with most postmodern theory is not that the language is often difficult to read, but that dense metaphysical language, as Gloria Anzaldúa has observed, "does not translate well when one's intention is to communicate to masses of people made up of different audiences" (xxv).

Women-of-color critics note that only relatively recently have women, people of color, and the poor and working classes been given access to those cultural and institutional practices—education and literacy— through which individuals are enabled to produce new concepts and legitimate them. Historically, they have been restricted in their ability to produce academically accepted theories and concepts, silenced by a privileged few, who excluded their knowledges from what might be termed the "official landscape of academia." But if theory, to use Ebert's useful definition, is a way of knowing that reveals that "what 'is' is not necessarily the real/true but rather only the existing actuality which is transformable," and if the role of cultural critique is "the production of historical knowledges that mark the transformability of existing social arrangements and the possibility of a different social organization" (9), then it becomes entirely possible to see how traditional folktales, proverbs, trickster stories, and animal tales might be considered "theory." If the aim of cultural critique is not the free play of signification or cognitive delight—the joys of knowing—but explication that makes connections and clarifies why certain complex concepts matter in people's lives and how they operate in society, then it also becomes entirely possible to see how stories might be just as effective as academic prose at conveying complex concepts. As Barbara Christian assures us, "people of color have always theorized—but in forms quite different from the Western form of abstract logic. And . . . our theorizing . . . is often in narrative forms, in the stories we create, in riddles and proverbs, in the play with language, since dynamic rather than fixed ideas seem more to our liking."[7]

Moreover, if the aim of cultural critique is to reach people outside the academic community—people of all races and classes, people such as my Med-Start students and their families, people who still have ties to a vernacular landscape—then it becomes possible to understand why writers, storytellers, and even critics might prefer fiction, narrative, and poetry to the often stilted prose associated with academia. For those who have struggled for decades to make their various voices heard, Christian argues, the poetry and fiction emerging from traditional stories and folktales and from specific places and particular communities are not simply "an occasion for discourse among critics but . . . necessary nourishment for their people and one way by which they come to understand their lives better" (336). Consequently, if we want to understand what multicultural communities and literatures have to teach us about theory and how they are offering tools honed in the vernacular landscape to people stepping out into the official landscape, we will need to read literature *as* cultural critique. The reading of *Tracks* that follows is intended to illustrate this point.

The Oral Tradition as Cultural Critique

Chippewa writer Louise Erdrich has never claimed to be writing literary criticism or cultural critique or to be writing for an audience of literary critics. She has said that she sees her primary audience as American Indians, who she hopes will "read, laugh, cry, really take in the work."[8] A member of the Turtle Mountain Band of Chippewa,[9] she adds that her novels are shaped by the constantly "changing, ongoing, vital, oral and literary traditions" of her tribe.[10] Chippewa oral tradition can be described as "ongoing" and "vital" because variant versions of the myths and stories have always shifted and changed depending on the storyteller, his or her personality, the occasion, the location, and the audience.[11] A storyteller often revises and retells a story, and the audience, already familiar with the stories as traditionally told, understands that the storyteller's version is an interpretation of the traditional text. Although new versions of a story might not be called literary criticism by community members, they can be seen as a criticism and commentary on the tale as previously told.

In the sense that every new telling of a traditional story is a critique of earlier versions of the story, *Tracks* enters into a kind of critical conversation with past and present tellers of traditional Chippewa myths. The novel assumes an implicitly theoretical stance by taking up traditional stories about bears, wolves, bearwalkers, lion-monsters, manitou, and *windigo,* and transforming them into a narrative that constantly transgresses boundaries between oral narrative and written narrative, past and present, questioning and reinterpreting each in order to create new stories from old elements.

Erdrich also invokes the sense of an oral performance by offering the perspectives of two narrators—Pauline and Nanapush—who tell the story of Fleur, the last female survivor of the Pillager clan. Both narrators tell their versions of Fleur's story in the first person, as if their audiences were present and engaged in the act of judging which narrator's version is the more credible. In alternating chapters, Pauline speaks directly to the reader, and Nanapush speaks to Fleur's grown child, Lulu. Analyzing Fleur as if she were literally a text, each narrator finds evidence to formulate a general theory to explain events that occurred on the reservation from 1912 to 1924.

Because Fleur is a member of the respected Pillager family, leaders in the tribe and members of the powerful bear clan, it is not surprising that both narrators associate her not only with stories about bears, but also with stories about several traditional Chippewa totemic animals. At times, Fleur, with her "teeth, strong and sharp and very white,"[12] embodies the traits of the mythic Wolf. On other occasions, with her "skin of lakeweed" (22), thin green dress, and damp, tail-like braids (18), she is associated with Misshepesshu, the lake monster. Like a totemic animal, Fleur combines the elements of many texts—Wolf, Misshepesshu, and Bear—in complicated and mysterious ways. As a text, she opens the oral tradition to the possibility of new interpretations, revealing—to revisit Teresa Ebert's explanation of the role of cultural critique—that "what 'is' is not necessarily the real/true but rather only the existing actuality which is transformable" (9).

Throughout the novel, however, Erdrich is careful to point out that Fleur's ambiguity, which becomes a metaphor for the openness of transformational myths to resignification, is not an invitation to endless interpretive play for the sake of play. Her concerns parallel those of critics such as Barbara Christian and Gloria Anzaldúa, who decry the uses of theory when it becomes mere metaphysical abstraction rather than explanatory critique grounded in the history and politics of community and place. In traditional Chippewa society, individual members of the tribe did not seek knowledge for the sake of knowledge or fast for a vision or seek contact with one of the gods merely to satisfy their own curiosity. Although the gods, or manitou, were thought of as personal beings who were generous and given to sharing their power with humans, they were sought with great caution and usually only if help was urgently needed to answer a question of grave social concern.[13] When Nanapush urges Fleur to seek contact with her helper, Misshepesshu, Fleur is distraught over her inability to pay the taxes on her land. "Go down to the shore," Nanapush urges her. "Make your face black and cry out until your helpers listen" (177). This scene implies that stories about transformational beings—and the novel *Tracks* itself—open the oral tradition to the possibility of resignification and recontextualization, but only for the purpose of answering urgent questions that face the community.

In transforming the oral tradition to create Fleur, Erdrich creates a kind of middle place between the oral tradition and contemporary literature. Her text—Fleur—has many faces, no fixed identity, and cannot be brought into any kind of order because she is being "told" by two narrators whose interpretations of the "text" often contradict each other. Like the oral tradition itself, Fleur becomes the object of continual telling and retelling, a narrative strategy that draws readers themselves into the middle place to participate, along with Erdrich, in the theorizing process. As if they were at an actual storytelling session, readers must "listen" to both Pauline's and Nanapush's stories, carefully weighing each interpretation against what they know about each narrator and then engage in some cultural critique of their own.

Imposing an Official Landscape

Most literary critics agree that readings are situated within a system of social, political, economic, cultural, and personal circumstances that direct readers to *particular* readings and, further, to *particular* constructions of reality. Through her narrators, Erdrich explores how different conceptions of reality are situated, theorized, and constructed. Like literary theorist Mikhail Bakhtin, she is interested in how a monologic Voice of Authority can impose an official landscape without regard to local people or places, whereas multiple voices and points of view can reveal the possibilities inherent in the invisible, vernacular landscape. She illustrates this concept by showing how each narrators' interpretation of Fleur is shaped by his or her relation to authority and tradition. In the novel, authority is represented by the Catholic Church and by the grid—or official landscape—imposed by the U.S. Congress after passage of the Dawes Act. Tradition is represented by Chippewa culture and by an invisible, vernacular landscape alive with the spirits of the recent dead and noisy with the voices of Wolf, Bear, Misshepesshu, and other manitou.

The narration of *Tracks* begins in 1912, twenty-five years after the Dawes Act divided Indian lands into individual holdings, purportedly for the purpose of promoting self-supporting farming and ranching among American Indian peoples. In actuality, the bill provided no provisions for seeds or for farming and ranching equipment, but did provide detailed provisions for the reduction of Indian lands and the sale to whites of unalloted lands. Passage of the bill led to massive dispossession and starvation, which weakened indigenous communities and made members of these communities more susceptible to disease. The staggering number of deaths disrupted tribal social relations forever and led to the sale of unclaimed allotments to whites, who became the owners of great tracts of land within reservation boundaries.

In the wake of the federal government's imposition of the reservation system on Chippewa communities and of the passage of the Dawes Act, both Pauline and Nanapush lose their entire families to disease and are unsure about how to move forward in a rapidly changing world. Both search the intimate, vernacular landscape that once provided the Chippewa with a theoretical understanding of their world for answers to the urgent social questions that face them. But they end up on opposite sides of the question of allotment. Pauline and her adopted family, the Morrisseys, argue that lands lost to death with no heir and lands foreclosed because starving people cannot earn enough money to pay their taxes should be put on the auction block (173–74). Nanapush and his adopted families, the Pillagers and Kashpaws, are "holdouts," believing that tribal lands should continue to be held communally.

A mixed-blood descendant of both whites and Puyats (members of a little respected Chippewa clan traditionally assigned the role of butchers and skinners), Pauline turns her back on the disease and death she attributes to the inferiority and backwardness of Chippewa culture and embraces the world of white culture: "I wanted to be like my mother, who showed her half-white. I wanted to be like my grandfather, pure Canadian. That was because even as a child I saw that to hang back was to perish" (14). Pauline is described by Nanapush as tall, skinny, invisible, and greedy, characteristics that the Chippewa associate with the windigo. In traditional Chippewa tales, windigo is a giant skeleton of ice that represents the fear of winter starvation and cannibalism. It is said that people "go windigo" when a dangerous spirit takes possession of their soul, causing them to become greedy, gluttonous, and have an insatiable desire for human flesh. As A. Irvin Hallowell explains, the fear of the windigo is really a fear of excessiveness of any kind. In Chippewa culture, a balance, a sense of proportion must be maintained in all interpersonal relations and activities. Hoarding or any manifestation of greed is discountenanced. Even overfasting for spiritual knowledge is judged to be "as greedy as hoarding."[14] Pauline, who acts "afflicted, touched in the mind" (39), is judged by Nanapush to be windigo not because she rejects her Chippewa heritage but because her need for status leads her to excessive behaviors that exhibit no feeling for other humans.

While living in the off-reservation town of Argus, for example, Pauline watches coldly as Fleur is raped by her employer and two other men. Then she cooly closes the door to the meat locker where the men who raped Fleur are waiting out a tornado, an act that results in the immediate death of two men and the slow demise of another. Six years later, she kills in cold blood again: this time, she strangles her lover, Napoleon Morrissey, the father of the child she abandons. Later, she absolves herself of any responsibility for the murder, observing, "I felt a growing horror and trembled all through my limbs until it suddenly was revealed to me that I had committed no sin. There was no guilt in this matter, no fault" (203).

Despite the murder, which goes unsolved, Pauline enters a Catholic convent, greedy for spiritual knowledge and determined to take the vows of a nun. She has come to believe that her people, like the buffalo, are dying out (140). Turning away from a culture she judges to be doomed, she gives herself a "mission" to "name and baptize" and lead her people to the "new road" of Christ—away from the traditional Chippewa four-day road to the afterworld (140). Aligning herself with the authority of the church, she begins to speak as if she herself were greater than Christ—a disembodied Voice of Authority. She molds her interpretation of Fleur's story to fit this single-minded vision of theological certainty, linking Fleur—and her bear power—to traditional Chippewa ceremonies, cures, dances, and love medicines. Fleur, she believes, is the "hinge" on a door that can swing open or closed, keeping people from entering on "Christ's Road" (139). So Pauline appoints herself door monitor and gives herself the responsibility of preventing Fleur from swinging the door open.

Speaking to anyone who will listen to a Puyat, Pauline, who claims to want to close the door on the invisible landscape, nevertheless opens it occasionally when she sees an opportunity to increase her own status as an "authority" on Chippewa culture. Making Fleur the target of her vicious rumors, Pauline reminds people that when Fleur returned from Argus, she lived alone at Matchimanito Lake. A "young girl had never done such a thing before" (8). Citing Fleur's anomalous actions and her inherited bear power, Pauline accuses Fleur of wielding the malign powers of a bearwalking sorcerer, or one who transforms herself into a bear in order to use her power for self-aggrandizement. According to Chippewa oral traditions, bearwalkers manifest their evil power by appearing as bright lights at night, stealing the fingers and tongues of the dead, and causing the dreaded affliction most associated with bear-walkers, "twisted mouth."[15] Fleur, Pauline lets it be known, has gotten herself into some half-forgotten medicine that causes her to mess with evil, place the heart of an owl on her tongue, carry the finger of a child in her pocket, and afflict a Morrissey with twisted mouth (122).

Pauline's mission to "close the door" on her people and her community is clearly linked to the abstract forms of logic on which the hierarchies of Western culture have been based, hierarchies that place God above humans, humans above nonhumans, and "civilized" cultures above those considered primitive. To support and maintain this official, hierarchical landscape, Pauline must close the door on a vernacular landscape in which gods walk among humans, the boundaries between humans and nature are permeable, and everything in the natural world is connected to everything else. She must turn a blind eye to whatever does not fit into the official landscape being imposed on the Chippewa and on their lands by church and state. She must not notice, for example, the connections between malnutrition and U.S. government policies. When she visits Fleur and her family, she ignores the starvation they are obviously suffering. Although Fleur is malnourished and struggling to carry a pregnancy to term, Pauline, who eats meals daily at the convent, shows up at Fleur's door and asks, "You wouldn't have a little scrap to eat . . . ?" (142), knowing that Fleur will not refuse to feed a guest. When, during the course of this visit, Fleur goes into labor, delivers a premature child, and nearly dies, Pauline does nothing to help. Watching Fleur's face drain of color, she remembers, "I knew this look and I was fascinated, rapt, as at other death- and sickbeds" (156). Pauline's "reading" of Fleur's circumstances and of the circumstances of the community erases the needs, conditions, and oppression of the Chippewa people and makes no connections between the U.S. government's allotment of small portions of land to individual tribal members and the simultaneous imposition of restrictions limiting traditional food-gathering activities. She situates herself above this reality, coldly abstracting herself from the social, material, and environmental struggles of her people.

Because she has so closely aligned herself with the voices of the official landscape, Pauline's words are suspect among her own people, which is perhaps the reason why she is narrating her story to no one in particular. The suspicion with which she is regarded calls attention to the fact that her abstract vision of the world is not rooted in local history and takes no account of the community. She is fully aware of her complicity in the attempted silencing of the vernacular landscape. After murdering her lover, she justifies the act by claiming that she has not murdered a man but tamed the lake monster, who is not a lake monster at all, but Satan: "I believed that the monster was tamed that night, sent to the bottom of the lake and chained there by my deed" (204). She links the silencing of the lake monster with the imposition of the official landscape. The morning after the murder, she recalls with malicious satisfaction, "a surveyor's crew arrived at the turnoff to Matchimanito in a rattling truck, and set to measuring. Surely that was the work of Christ's hand" (204). Trivializing the inevitable displacement and suffering that will follow the division and sale of tribal lands, she adds: "The place will be haunted I suppose, but no one will have ears sharp enough to hear the Pillagers' low voices, or the vision clear enough to see their still shadows" (204–5).

By removing her people from history and attempting to cut them off from an oral tradition and culture that once provided them with tools to interpret and understand the world around them, Pauline gives her people no alternatives, no avenues of resistance, and no hope of opposing the official landscape being imposed on the vernacular landscape. Obfuscating rather than explicating, obscuring rather than revealing, Pauline's reading of Fleur illustrates how cold, theoretical abstractions that are rooted in greed or in a need for personal aggrandizement and that take no account of local voices in the landscape can literally silence those voices forever.

Contesting the Official Landscape

Unlike the morbid Pauline, Nanapush is associated with life, community, laughter, and healing, and he is constantly challenging authority and established order. Although he is only "fifty winters old" when he begins his narration of Fleur's story, his life has spanned the end of the nineteenth century and the beginning of the twentieth. Somehow, he has survived fever, pox, spotted sickness, broken treaties, and dispossession. Clearly making connections between disease and the land losses associated with broken treaties and the Dawes Act, he understands that his entire family died from diseases contracted after they were forced onto reservations. Where "[people] were forced close together," he states, "the clans dwindled. Our tribe unraveled like a coarse rope, frayed at either end as the old and new among us were taken" (2). At one point, he is so overcome by sorrow he decides to die, but like the Chippewa trickster Nanabozho, he recovers somehow, saving himself "by starting a story. . . . I got well by talking. Death could not get a word in edgewise, grew discouraged, and traveled on" (46). He uses his meager strength to help others, taking the seventeen-year-old Fleur to his cabin after discovering her, half frozen, among the bodies of family members who have succumbed to starvation and consumption.

Nanapush implies that his narration of Fleur's story is a kind of ceremony he is performing for Lulu, Fleur's only living child, who, as a teenager, returns to the reservation filled with bitterness toward Fleur for sending her away from an intimate, familiar landscape to an official one—the government boarding school. At the school, Lulu attempts to run away, but is caught and severely punished, made to wear orange-colored clothes, scrub long sidewalks, and kneel for hours on broomstick handles. Calling on the manitou to help him, Nanapush uses story, song, and rattle to create a ceremony that will heal Lulu. His story of Fleur is like a chant: "She sent you to the government school, it is true, but you must understand there were reasons: there would be no place for you, no safety on this reservation, no hiding from government papers, or from Morrisseys . . . or the Turcot Company, leveler of a whole forest" (217).

The position of Erdrich's two narrators in relation to Chippewa culture and to Euro-American governmental and religious authority gives readers some intimation of how the once happy, confident Lulu became a hurt, resentful child. Pauline, a Catholic nun who eventually becomes "Sister Leopolda," a convent schoolteacher in Erdrich's *Love Medicine,* represents the voices Lulu would have encountered in the official landscape. Supporting and maintaining the landscape of officialdom, Pauline—and Lulu's teachers—see education as the transfer of placeless "universal" knowledge to the children in their charge. They close the door on the significance of the children's own cultures by insisting that they are only the superstitions of a primitive people. Thus, the voices of officialdom rob the children of their first confidence in being able to understand and interpret the world around them and in knowing how to move within it.

But where voices of officialdom rely on institutionally sanctioned ideologies and theories to constrict, transfix, objectify, and dehumanize, Nanapush insists on employing the transformative, emancipatory aspects of cultural critique to confront the violence of controlling systems—be they governmental, religious, economic, or textual. He teaches Lulu that her heritage and traditions are not meaningless superstitions. Through Fleur's powerful bear-clan bloodline, the old ways course into the modern world. Through Fleur, Nanapush tells Lulu, the manitou speak: "Turtle's quavering scratch, the Eagle's high shriek, Loon's crazy bitterness, Otter, the howl of Wolf, Bear's low rasp" (59).

Nanapush is not romanticizing the vernacular landscape; rather, he is illustrating for Lulu how Fleur's ties to the living, breathing landscape of the manitou provide her with an alternate vision, one that assures her that the official landscape is not necessarily the real/true, but only the existing reality, which is transformable. By telling and retelling Fleur's story to Lulu, Nanapush is engaging in an age-old interpretive process: opening the ancient traditions and stories of his people to the possibility of reinterpretation and resignification. Though the invisible landscape is being destroyed by those who seek to replace it with an official landscape, he encourages Lulu to find answers to the urgent social and ecological questions facing the community by leaving the door open to a continuing dialogue between the old world and the new.

Nanapush's interpretation of Fleur's story makes strong connections between the marginalization of people and the degradation of the environment, showing Lulu how the imposition of an official landscape leads directly to Fleur's dispossession from Matchimanito Lake and results in Lulu's being sent away to boarding school. Once, Nanapush recalls, the Pillagers met all their needs by trading "with fur, meat, hides or berries" (36). But after the institution of the reservation system and then passage of the Dawes Act, Fleur is forced to scramble for ways to earn the money to pay the taxes the government imposes on each parcel of allotted land. If she does not pay, she is told by both the Indian agent and the Catholic priest, her land will be put on the auction block and sold to the highest bidder. When Fleur falls behind in her payments, the young priest, Father Damien, travels to Matchimanito Lake to inform her that a group of whites is interested in buying the Pillagers' allotted lands and building a fishing lodge for tourists.

But Fleur refuses to sell out. In a desperate bid to raise money, she and her family strip every bush around Matchimanito Lake for the cranberry bark they sell weekly to the white tonic dealer. The hard physical labor changes Fleur and degrades the vegetation on her land. "Though she traveled through the bush with gunnysacks and her skinning knife, though she worked past her strength, tireless, . . . Fleur was a different person than the young woman I had known. She was hesitant in speaking, false in her gestures, anxious to cover her fear" (177). Thrust into a wage economy she only partially understands and in which she is ill-prepared to operate, she remains unrewarded for her tireless labors; her worst fears are realized when she is unable to keep Matchimanito Lake from being sold to the Turcot Lumber Company or to prevent her family from being dispossessed. Her situation illustrates, as cultural critic Nancy Hartsock expresses it, that the dominant class, race, and gender actively structures and envisions "the world in a way that forms the material-social relations in which all parties are forced to participate; their vision, therefore, cannot be dismissed as simply false or misguided. In consequence, oppressed groups must struggle for their own vision, which will require both theorizing and the education that can come only from committed political struggle to change those material and social relations."[16] Realizing that she cannot fight the dominant culture solely based on a Chippewa vision of the world, Fleur enters the struggle to change power relations between her people and the voices of officialdom by sending Lulu to boarding school, a wrenchingly difficult decision that leaves her scarred and grieving and that makes Lulu resentful and bitter.

Nanapush depicts Fleur as courageous, and her story conveys an attitude of resistance to control of Indian people. At the same time, he clearly shows that domination and marginalization rarely, if ever, create better people; on the contrary, people are often defeated and scarred by the large-scale political, economic, and religious forces operating outside their local communities and environments. Upon Lulu's return to the reservation after her damaging boarding school experience, Nana-push gathers her into his arms, tells her Fleur's story, and invites her to look around at the bureaucratic, official grid imposed on Indian peoples and their lands by government agents and religious authorities. The Chippewa, he observes, are becoming a "tribe of file cabinets and tripli-cates, a tribe of single-spaced documents, directives, policy. A tribe of pressed trees" (225). He recognizes that the Chippewa will never again live in the world into which he was born; therefore, the struggle for alternate visions of the world will require his people to gain some manner of access to the power to change material, social, and environ-mental relations. This is the reason, he tells Lulu, that he has learned to read newspapers and government reports, to write letters, and to wade through a "blizzard of legal forms," and the reason why he later enters politics and is elected tribal chairman (225). It is also the reason, he implies, why Fleur decides to send Lulu to a government school: she hopes her daughter might acquire additional tools to help herself and her people enter the official landscape and effect change.

Struggling for alternative visions of the world, then, requires a knowl edge not only of the vernacular landscape but of the official one as well. Moving intelligently and cautiously between these two landscapes, Nanapush opens both to the possibility of reinterpretation and resig-nification, and finds tools to create new ceremonies and new knowledges in both places. He ushers Lulu into a middle place between the two, saving her with a story, by showing her the power and significance of her mother's experiences at the same time that he is showing her how she might use her boarding school education to fight for justice. The story of Fleur's tireless struggle to change the material and social relations be-tween her people and officialdom, and of her eventual dispossession exposes an injustice. By describing this injustice, Nanapush finds ground for critique of dominant institutions and ideologies that benefit only the elite few, and offers his insight to his granddaughter.

In *Tracks,* Louise Erdrich illustrates that those who are not a part of the dominant race, class, or gender, not part of the minority that rules the world, need to know how that world works in order to change it. They need to understand how and why they are systematically excluded and marginalized. Their survival depends on doing more than simply ignoring power relations or resisting them; they must engage in the historical, political, theoretical process of making the significance of their own experience visible. Once this significance is understood, they can name themselves from their own perspectives, speak for themselves, and insist on their right to participate in naming the terms of their interactions with the dominant culture. In a compelling, accessible, narrative form that marks the transformability of existing social arrangements and the possibility for a different social organization, Erdrich exposes relations among people that are inhuman and thus calls readers to action. Unlike Pauline's version of Fleur's story, which is told for Pauline's benefit alone and which fails to explicate how systematic practices of exploitation work and how they might be changed, *Tracks,* like Nanapush's version, is cultural critique that calls for change and participation in altering the power relations at the root of social and ecological problems.

Erdrich writes *Tracks* for people like Lulu, people like my Med-Start students and their families, people who still have ties to the vernacular landscape. She is not writing specifically for academics, although no one is excluded. Her novel is entertaining literature that appeals to kids on the reservation *and* to college professors, but it should be taken as seriously as academics take theory because it is cultural critique that makes accessible to large audiences of people some complex ideas about the connections between history, politics, economics, culture, and the environment. Erdrich writes in a language that makes us laugh and *care* and begin to see how these concepts operate in our lives. Just as if we were at a storytelling session, she calls us into the interpretive process, inviting us to explore other ways of knowing, other modes of theorizing, and to participate in building alternate visions of the world.

Practicing Local Pedagogy

Nanapush's insistence that transformative change requires an understanding of both the vernacular and official landscapes suggests the reasons why we much eschew academicism for the sake of academicism or theory for the sake of theory and learn to map shared connections between literature and local peoples and places. The official landscape is built on the notion that progress is inevitable, that we must shut the door on the vernacular landscape and move relentlessly forward. But Nanapush contests this notion by practicing what might be thought of as a local pedagogy, which swings open the door between vernacular and official landscapes, allowing Lulu (who represents the community) to move back and forth between both places, searching for the tools and theories she needs to answer urgent questions that face her community. She cannot simply dismiss dominant culture because it structures the social-material relations in which all parties are forced to participate, but she can use what she learns in both landscapes to improve the condition of her people and to contest authoritarian and discriminatory practices.

If our goal as writers, teachers, and scholars is to move away from a valorizing academicism and teach readers, students, and community members how to read themselves and the world critically, with the goal of changing both, then we need to know who is sitting in our classrooms and enough about the local landscapes we inhabit to render both the vernacular and official problematic as well as comprehensible. We must transform the social and natural world outside the classroom into the subject matter of education. We might think of our classrooms as something of a middle place or door between landscapes, where students move back and forth, honing the tools and critical theories they will need to work for a more socially and environmentally liveable world.

As I noted at the beginning of this chapter, Med-Start students often enter the classroom in touch with knowledges and forces that fall outside their instructors' knowledge and academic specializations. In discussions focused on a novel such as *Tracks* and aimed at making connections between literature and their own communities and their future professions in the medical arts, it becomes very clear how describing the significance of each student's cultural and historical experiences gives us more and better tools to build alternative visions of the future. For example, in a discussion of Nanapush's use of story and song to heal Fleur, a Diné student might point out that unlike Western medicine, which treats the symptom, traditional songs and ceremonies are aimed at healing the whole person, body and spirit. An Anglo student might call our attention to the considerable contributions that Western science and technology have made in improving our lives, adding that a diabetic patient experiencing kidney failure will most likely die without dialysis even if that person is given a traditional Diné healing ceremony. A Tohono O'odham student might observe that experiments with traditional foods such as mesquite-bean flour are being conducted to see if diet might help prevent adult-onset diabetes. A Mexican/Yaqui student might suggest that the doctor she is shadowing at the University Medical Center should know more about the kinds of herbs her grandmother, a traditional medicine woman or curandera, successfully uses to treat various illnesses suffered by members of her community. These students might then write essays discussing the great potential that lies in combining elements of traditional healing practices with elements of Western medical practices.

In these discussions, the classroom becomes a place where students discover shared situations (diabetes, for example, is a disease that affects all races). The official university landscape becomes a more welcoming place where students not only tap into thousands of years of Western culture and technology, but where they bring their own valuable knowledges and make important contributions. What students discover is that where we are located in the social structure as a whole does affect how we understand the world. But finding common ground is possible. By mapping the local and theorizing our various experiences, we can come to understand how we are similar (not the same) and how we are different, which social and environmental issues we share, and which issues affect different groups differently.

Moreover, taking the issues that a novel such as *Tracks* raises into the world students actually inhabit is absolutely crucial to the development of a shared sense of responsibility for the future. A Tohono O'odham student may feel no responsibility for the toxic contamination of the aquifer beneath a Mexican American barrio in South Tucson until he discovers that the same political, economic, and social forces that removed the Tohono O'odham from their floodplain gardens along the Santa Cruz River later forced the removal of Mexican Americans from their barrios along that same river and subsequently placed them at a contaminated locale in an industrial section of Tucson.[17] An earnest Anglo student may justifiably and resolutely refuse to assume responsibility for her great-great-grandfather's relation to the removal of American Indians to reservations only a fraction of the size of their former territories or to the forced removal of Indian children to government boarding schools. However, she will be hard-pressed to abjure all responsibility for the cultural politics that give the dominant culture the power to deplete aquifers to keep her campus mall green, and she will have a difficult time accounting for the large-scale forces that still contribute to an underrepresentation of the Tohono O'odham at the University of Arizona, despite the proximity of their reservation to the campus.

The development of a deeply felt sense of connection to local people and places is often the first step in the development of a sense of responsibility, which in turn can lead to the formation of alliances with others who are committed to finding solutions to the urgent problems that face us as we move into a new century. Used in the practice of a local pedagogy, a multicultural novel such as *Tracks* becomes common ground on which readers, students, community members, and others can come together to explore their connections to and responsibilities for shared situations.

CHAPTER 5

And the Ground Spoke

Joy Harjo and the Struggle for a
Land-Based Language

The great struggle is to make whatever language you have really
speak for you.
—Leslie Marmon Silko, interview by Laura Coltelli, *Winged Words*

During the six years that I taught American Indian students both on
and off the University of Arizona campus, the subject of traditional
languages came up often. The few students who spoke both English and
a traditional language were held in high regard by their peers. But most
students did not speak the languages of their grandparents and placed
much of the responsibility for language loss at the feet of the U.S.
government's boarding school system. Having heard many stories about
their forebears' experiences in the boarding schools, they knew of the
humiliation and physical punishment their relations suffered if they
attempted to speak their languages. They understood that the reason
why many of them had not been taught tribal languages was that their
parents believed that speaking English to their children would help
them succeed in school. However, many students were keenly interested
in learning their tribal languages and were taking university classes in
Hopi, Navajo, or O'odham and spending as much time as possible with
their grandparents.

The subject of language also comes up often in the interviews, poetry,
fiction, and prose of American Indian writers. They repeatedly comment on the difficulty of expressing tribal perspectives in English, a
language that Joy Harjo, in the title of her 1997 anthology of contemporary American Indian women's writing, refers to as "the enemy's language." In this chapter, then, I examine how and why American Indian
writers are engaged in the process of transforming English into what

Harjo describes in her poetry collection *She Had Some Horses,* as "a land-based language" that would "break up" the hard, dichotomous foundation of English and infuse it with the moral force of tribal perspectives and traditions that would promote beneficial changes in the attitudes of individuals toward their responsibilities as members of larger human and ecological communities.

Language and A Sense of Place

In an interview with Laura Coltelli, Louise Erdrich points to the "concerted efforts" of the infamous boarding schools as one of the reasons why most writers from Indian communities work primarily in English.[1] Erdrich was referring to the more than fifty-year period (1879 to the 1930s), when Indian children were literally kidnapped by the U.S. cavalry and sent long distances from their homes and families to schools where teachers insisted they give up their cultures and languages, and accept new identities as members of a foreign culture.[2] In the 1940s and 1950s, children were sometimes able to attend day schools closer to their homes, but native languages were still forbidden within the walls of the school. Recalling his own kindergarten experience in the 1940s at a Bureau of Indian Affairs Day School, Acoma Pueblo writer Simon Ortiz remembers that he quickly learned "how language was used . . . against us, really to identify us but more than that, to keep us in our place. . . . I mean, you need to get punished and embarrassed and humiliated just about once and then you learn to speak English pretty well."[3]

Ortiz observes that "Some would argue that this means that Indian people have succumbed or become educated into a different linguistic system and have forgotten or have been forced to forsake their native selves. This is simply not true. Along with their native languages, Indian women and men have carried on their lives and their expression through the use of the newer language."[4] Pointing to the linguistic history of indigenous peoples, Ortiz notes that before European colonization, native peoples often spoke not only their mother tongue but that of sister nations and cultures. After colonization, they added French, English, and Spanish to their repertoire of languages, sometimes against their will and often to ensure their own survival. Ortiz insists that the use of English must be seen as one of the strategies Indian peoples have used to survive, and for this reason, it cannot be argued that the use of

English is somehow "inauthentic." He is not arguing that traditional native languages are not important to the communities that speak those languages or that English should replace native languages. He speaks the Acoma language and incorporates Acoma into his poetry and prose. Rather, he is arguing that American Indian uses of English have been among the ways that native peoples "have creatively responded to forced colonization."[5] In their efforts to survive as distinct peoples and cultures, Ortiz observes, American Indians "necessarily utilize English *as* a Native American language."[6]

In discussions of their work, Louise Erdrich, Simon Ortiz, and Joy Harjo have described the process by which they see English being transformed into an American Indian language. Erdrich notes that her own use of English finds its roots in a "different heritage, background, a different worldview, a different mythology."[7] As the child of a Chippewa mother and German American father, her primary language was English, but her perspectives and use of language were shaped within a family that she characterizes as "probably a microcosm of tribal traditions" because family members with mixed tribal and European backgrounds were always "sitting around and telling stories" that had "evolved out of a set of shared memories."[8] Erdrich believes that her experience mirrors that of many other American Indian writers who grew up in multiethnic families and communities listening and talking to some people whose first language was English, some who were fluent in a tribal language, and others who spoke a mixture of English and a tribal language.

Linguist Muriel Saville-Troike notes that within multilingual communities, there is often a variety of language codes and ways of speaking available. Some members of the community have learned about certain topics in one language and other topics in a second language. Some may know the vocabulary to discuss a topic in only one of their languages or feel it is more "natural" to use another language for a particular topic. Saville-Troike adds that in conditions where group members may be bilingual in their own ethnic language and the dominant language or where group members are monolingual in the dominant language but wish to remain identified with their cultural group, linguistic markers such as choice of lexical items and syntactic forms are often developed and maintained.[9]

However, as Ortiz's experience of being punished for speaking Acoma in his government-run day school illustrates, people who do not speak

English as a first language and people who are bilingual or whose speech is linguistically "marked" are often singled out by members of the dominant culture as the targets of racism or educated away from their first languages or both. Joy Harjo experienced both. As a result of her tribe being forcibly moved on the Trail of Tears from Alabama to Oklahoma, Harjo was not raised traditionally Creek. She grew up in northern Tulsa, Oklahoma, and attended school with other mixed-blood, multilingual Indian children who were not allowed to speak their tribal languages. Consequently, she is not fluent in Creek and struggles to articulate tribal perspectives in English.[10] Writing from a place she describes as a "brutal border," she reaches back into the "wealth of memory" possessed by her family and tribe, and draws on their oral traditions, constantly thinking about what she, as a person with a Creek heritage, "can add to the [English] language."[11]

Mikhail Bakhtin's discussion of the process of "hybridizing language" helps to explain the linguistic struggle that Harjo describes. The language of the dominant culture always exists in "other people's mouths, in other people's contexts, serving other people's intentions . . . [and] it does not submit easily to seizure and transformation."[12] However, living language always exists in what Bakhtin has termed an "elastic environment" where the languages of differing social and linguistic groups and the languages of oral and written genres, past and present, come into contact. "It is precisely in living interaction with this specific environment," Bakhtin adds, that a writer encounters the "multilanguagedness surrounding and nourishing his own consciousness" and finds the necessary materials to adapt language to his own expressive intentions. By putting language into a "new situation," the writer begins "to liberate himself from the authority of the other's discourse" (348).

In his essays on American Indian oral and written literatures, Simon Ortiz does not use words or phrases such as "multilanguagedness" and "elastic environment," but his observations about why and how a language might be seized and transformed parallel Bakhtin's. In the mouths of soldiers, missionaries, settlers, and boarding school teachers, the English language did suppress indigenous voices. But American Indian people are seizing and transforming English and making it meaningful in their own terms because the stake in the process of "liberating" language is survival. For those who no longer speak traditional languages but are committed to carrying on their traditional cultures and lifeways, there is no other recourse but to proceed with the search for a transformed language.

Ortiz sees place—which he defines as the "spiritual source" of "who you are in terms of your identity"—as key to this transformation.[13] A sense of place, he explains, is strongly rooted in a people's culture and expressed in their oral traditions, which, in turn, are inextricably bound to specific geographies. He insists, however, that "oral tradition" not be defined too strictly. American Indian oral traditions do include ancient creation and emergence stories, stories of trickster's outrageous behavior, tales of the interactions between gods and humans, ceremonies, songs, and legends.[14] But the oral tradition is a continuously growing body of stories that also speak crucially about the last five hundred years in the Americas, stories about social protocol, jokes, and even everyday stories about events that occur in the community.[15] Ortiz argues that American Indian writers are transforming English for their own expressive purposes by incorporating elements from their tribal narratives (along with their cultural expectations, structural patterns, linguistic peculiarities, and association with specific geographical locations) into their contemporary fiction and poetry.[16]

A Land-Based Language

Many ethnic and minority groups in the United States whose first language is not English nevertheless use this language everyday. Their children often grow up "marking" English in ways that are distinct to their particular group. So what would make Native American transformation of English in any way unique or different? In a 1985 interview with Laura Coltelli, published in Coltelli's book *Winged Words: American Indian Writers Speak,* Joy Harjo gives some insight into how this question might be answered. In her own poetry and prose, Harjo is struggling to create what she calls a "land-based language," or a language capable of expressing "the spirit of place recognized" (63). The American Indian experience is different than that of other groups in that Indian peoples have not chosen to immigrate to other countries and take up other languages. Unlike other ethnic and minority groups, many American Indian tribes still inhabit parts of their ancestral homelands, or in the case of tribes such as Harjo's, they have been dispossessed and removed but remain connected to what Harjo calls a "larger tribal continental memory" of the American Indian experience in both their traditional homelands and in the places to which they were removed (57). Harjo herself feels a spiritual connection to both Alabama and Oklahoma but no longer possesses the language through which her grandparents once spoke of their cultural and historical experiences in those places.

When she seeks to articulate in her poetry something of her Creek heritage or of her American Indian culture and history, she finds English too emotionally and spiritually limited. English, she argues, is a language that denies "anything other than that based on the European soul" (63). In a sense, it is a language that has been used, she tells Coltelli, to "pave over" the indigenous sense of the landscape as a place where humans live in a reciprocal relationship with the natural world (63). Euro-American people, notes Harjo, looked at the North American continent and named it "wilderness," something to be afraid of, something to be "conquered because of fear" (64). Their fear drove them, with great rigor, to use language to "pave over" or rename everything non-European they encountered. In this way, they fundamentally changed perceptions of human relation to the natural world, paving over all sense of a land "alive with personality, breathing. Alive with names, alive with events"(64).

Thus, when Harjo speaks of "reinventing the enemy's language" so that it might convey the "spirit of place recognized," she is not speaking simply of finding the words in English to articulate a creation story or folktale.[17] To understand what she means, we must understand something about the inextricable connection between myth, history, culture, moral expectations, and place in American Indian oral traditions. Although stories from the oral tradition are often associated with specific geographic locations, storytellers rarely dwell at length on detailed descriptions of the natural world. Ethnographer Keith Basso explains that because the people listening to the story are already familiar with the mountain or spring or boulder mentioned in the story, because they may live in the shadow of the red sandstone ship rock or not far from the ancient ruins mentioned in the story, the storyteller has no need to provide the audience with a detailed description of place. In the Western Apache historical narratives or folktales that Basso studies, a story may begin simply with a phrase such as "It happened at . . . ". The storyteller then goes on to relate the events of the story, describe the characters, tell what happened in that place, and detail how the character's behavior either conforms to or fails to conform to moral and cultural expectations vis-à-vis human relations to other humans and to the land. The stories are morality tales, pure and simple, notes Basso, "compact commentaries" that "are 'about' historical events and their geographical locations" and, at the same time, "'about' the system of rules and values according to which Apaches expect each other to organize and regulate their lives."[18] Although grandmothers and uncles must perish, unique geographical features of the landscape and the stories about them serve as a kind of "omnipresent moral force," Basso says, promoting beneficial changes in the attitudes of individuals toward their responsibilities as members of larger cultural and ecological communities (46).

Because English is a language that has been built on the dichotomous separation of nature and culture, argues Harjo, English erases the layers of mythological and historical significance that blanket the land, paving over all sense of the moral force of American Indian stories, which depict a reciprocal relationship between humans, nonhumans, and the natural world. Therefore, when Harjo observes that she is struggling to transform English into a land-based language, she is speaking of her search to find ways to speak of a world in which nature and culture, event and place are not separate. She is seeking to infuse her primary language—English—with the moral force of American Indian oral traditions, to speak not just of places but of the ancient and historical events that occurred in those places.

Speaking Navajo, in English

The transformation of language, then, is essentially an act of the imagination. It is a collaborative process, Harjo tells readers in "We Must Call a Meeting," in which the "spirits of old and new ancestors perch on my shoulders," holding conversations long into the night, leading Harjo out into a landscape alive with event, teaching her to "walk this thin line between the breathing / and the dead."[19] In "For Alva Benson and Those Who Have Learned to Speak," Harjo envisions a transformed, land-based language with roots so strong that it would fragment what she metaphorically describes as the "mortar and concrete" of colonizing language.

The poem begins with the birth of a Navajo child near the end of the twentieth century. The child's female ancestors crouched near the ground to give birth, but the child is born in the Indian Hospital in Gallup, a stark, linear structure built on a foundation of "mortar and concrete" and symbolizing a modern world that paves over the living landscape of the Navajo by constructing nature as separate from culture. In this world of towns and cities, the child grows up surrounded by people who no longer know the names of the plants and the birds, no longer know the stories connected to the land, and no longer care about the people who lived and died in those places.

However, from the time she is born, the child is nurtured by an extended family of Navajo speakers and speakers of a combination of Navajo and English. Listening, she learns to speak "Navajo, in English," to "speak / both voices," to carry on her Navajo life and traditions through the use of both languages.[20] Despite being educated in schools where her teachers attempt to pave over her tribe's language and stories with the mortar and concrete of an authorized Euro-American vision of history, science, and religion, she has listened to elders who tell about the voices of the earth in creation stories, historical narratives, and contemporary stories associated with specific geographic features within her tribe's homelands. Each day, she sees the red sandstone cliffs and boulders referred to in the stories and is familiar with the "compact commentaries" on the moral and cultural expectations of her community embedded in them. The stories give her ways to think about her relationship to her community and her environment that are different than the ways of the culture she is learning about in school. Unlike most members of the dominant culture, she and her family do not simply dwell in a place; they inhabit a landscape so alive with myth, history, and event that the child can "hear the ground talking" (18).

"For Alva Benson" illustrates that Harjo is interested in how the continued use of the oral tradition, whether it is conveyed in a traditional language or in English, provides evidence that resistance to those colonizing forces that would suppress the Native American voice is ongoing. The child in the poem hears the ancient stories and the ancient names "in her sleep" (18). She is not able to speak her traditional language, so the names must necessarily change into other words and names, like "the harmonic motion of a child turning / inside her mother's belly waiting to be born / to begin another time" (18). Even in the new language, these words and stories and names have the power to help her think about the place in which she finds herself in the late twentieth century. The stories provide her with the tools to struggle actively against the constraints of those oppressive institutional practices, including the reservation and educational systems, that are the legacy of Euro-American colonization of North America.

When the child becomes an adult and gives birth to her own daughter, she "strains against the metal stirrups" in the Indian Health Service Hospital, and medical personnel restrain her by tying her hands to the bed (18). Harjo's dramatic juxtaposition of metal stirrups and hand restraints with the image of indigenous women crouching to the earth to give birth represents the ways in which Euro-Americans implicitly symbolize those governmental and educational practices that have attempted to bind, restrain, and suppress native cultures and lifeways. However, Harjo implies that through the use of both traditional languages and languages transformed by the colonial experience, the mother will teach her child to resist those forces that would suppress her culture and voice. Together, mother and child will speak not only about survival but of "another time" in which people deliver their children into a place beyond domination and control (18). Clearly, the child/woman/mother of Harjo's poem privileges the survival of her child and thus of her people and culture over any notion of a pure, original language or an "authentic" culture or myth. The poem implies that as long as the stories continue to be told—in Navajo, in English, or in some combination of the two—the ground will "[go] on talking." Both mother and child will pass away, but the unique features of the land and the stories attached to them will endure, serving as omnipresent moral forces that resist the dichotomous nature/culture binary of Euro-American languages by constantly reminding community members of the inextricable connections between humans and the natural world. "[W]e go on," the poem concludes, "keep giving birth and watch / ourselves die, over and over. / And the ground spinning beneath us / goes on talking" (19).

Gazing into the Abyss

In "Resurrection," from *In Mad Love and War,* Harjo illustrates that the stake in the process of transforming language is survival. By setting the poem in the Nicaraguan mountain village of Esteli during the time of the Reagan administration's covert activities in support of Contra soldiers, she insists that the oppression of indigenous peoples in the Americas is ongoing. Like people everywhere, Estelian villagers desire peaceful and fully lived lives: the poem depicts lovers touching and planning to meet, people laughing in a cantina undulating with the sound of calypso, and women lighting candles in a barrio church. But there is an undercurrent of gunfire. Young Contra soldiers watch over what they fear, and despairing mothers give "away the clothes of their dead children" (17). And beneath it all, it is possible to hear the dead calling "out in words that sting / like bitter limes" (17). The bitter words of the dead, the stories of their deaths and the places in which they died become part of a landscape alive with event; as the words emanate from the ground, they break through the mortar and concrete of colonizing languages— Spanish and English—used by Nicaraguan government officials, Contra soldiers, and Reagan administration military strategists to construct abstract policies that justify genocide. There are "no damned words to make violence fit neatly / like wrapped packages / of meat," observes the narrator of the poem (17). So "we all watch for fire / for the fallen dead to return / and teach us a language so terrible / it could resurrect us all" (18).

In a 1992 seminar she conducted at the University of Arizona, Harjo explained that she uses the word *terrible* to describe the reimagined language she is struggling to create because, for five hundred years, Native Americans have witnessed a horrifying "destruction of our home. . . . [I]t's an evil that is destroying land, creatures, . . . human beings, [and] cultures, . . . at mass levels."[21] From the Spanish colonial decimation of the peaceful Arawok tribe to the Trail of Tears to the covert activities of the United States in Nicaragua, the atrocities committed against the indigenous peoples of the Americas "are not spoken," and this gaping "abyss" of silence enables the continuation of the destruction and bloodshed.[22] The American education system, Harjo asserts, "come[s] directly out of this . . . silence," this agreement that "We're not going to talk about [the genocide]."[23]

But what happens, Harjo asks, when you look into the abyss of genocide, hear the dead calling out, and decide to speak, to end the silence? What happens if the only language in which you can articulate this vision is the colonizers' language? For the dispossessed and marginalized, the difficulty of transforming English is not only that it has been used to pave over a landscape alive with myth and event, but that it is a language used to perpetuate a deadly silence that veils the incredible destruction and horrifying bloodshed of the last five hundred years. Those who wish to rent the veil must enter into the silence and voice the unspoken in the language of the enemy. Consequently, for those who seek not only to survive but to move their people and cultures beyond domination, there is no other recourse but to imagine a language powerful enough to articulate the stories of the dead *and* the people determined to live.

The process of transforming language *is* "terrifying," declares Harjo. "But what the hell, I'd rather be alive and walk through it terrified than to sit around anymore and just keep my mouth shut about it. [The United States] is stunted until everyone . . . addresses that abyss in their own way and walks through it. . . . This has to do with everybody . . . not just Indian people. It's not just our loss, it's the loss of everyone in this country. And that has to be walked through in some way."[24] Walking the thin line between the breathing and the dead, Harjo looks into the abyss in order to tell stories that might promote beneficial changes in the attitudes of individuals toward their responsibilities as members of larger cultural and ecological communities. Readers from the United States, for example, cannot claim to be unconnected to Nicaraguan mothers or to their dead children because their own government aids and supports Contra soldiers. Harjo makes clear that what has been lost, with deadly consequences, is something at the very heart of the oral tradition: a sense of how an individual's behavior either conforms to or fails to conform to moral expectations vis-à-vis human relations to other humans and to the community. In a sense, Harjo's search for a land-based language is the search for a middle place where deadly silences give way to voices that speak of the values by which individuals and communities organize and regulate their lives in relation to each other and to the places they inhabit.

In chapter three, I wrote of Pueblo gardens as a middle place in which people, guided by their oral traditions, think carefully and responsibly about the reciprocal relationship between humans and the land. Focusing on Simon Ortiz's poem "To Change in a Good Way," I examined how Mary teaches Ida to break up the hard red clay in her garden with sheep dung, an act that results the next spring in the abundant growth of corn, chili, lettuce, and tomatoes. Like the gardener engaged in the act of cultivating her garden, Harjo is engaged in the act of imagining a language that would break through the mortar and concrete of colonizing languages and become, for those who no longer speak the language of their ancestors, a middle place between their traditional cultures and the contemporary cultures in which they find themselves as they look toward a new century. Like the gardener who gives something back to the earth so that it might continue to sustain life, the speaker of a land-based language would continually ask what he or she could add to the language so that life might go on. He or she would dare to gaze into the abyss of our loss and search for a language that would help us survive.

CHAPTER 6

A Place to See

Self-Representation and Resistance in Leslie Marmon Silko's *Almanac of the Dead*

No one who would truly understand American literature may by any means turn away, in lofty literary scorn, from the almanac,— most despised, most prolific, most indispensable of books, which every man uses, and no man praises; the very quack, clown, pack-horse, and pariah of modern literature.
—Moses Coit Tyler, *A History of American Literature,* vol. 2

Throughout the five hundred years . . . each time we have tried to speak, it came as a surprise for many people of the outside world, because it was as if we Indians should not do so, or could not do so. . . . But we Indians have resisted . . . because we are the ancient owners of this continent.
—Rigoberta Menchú, on the quincentenary celebration of Columbus's voyage to the Americas[1]

The Literature of Environmental Justice

On New Year's Day 1994, a dramatic world event lent Leslie Marmon Silko's *Almanac of the Dead* the quality of prophecy. Mayan insurgents calling themselves the Zapatistas burst out of the great Lacandon rain forest straddling the border of Mexico and Guatemala and took control of four sizeable towns in the Mexican state of Chiapas.[2] Because *Almanac of the Dead* tells the story of an indigenous army that gathers in Chiapas and begins marching north, demanding the return of tribal lands, reporters were clamoring within the week for Silko's opinion on the matter. In an interview that aired on the 10:00 news in Tucson, Arizona, reporter Lupita Murrillo asked Silko if she considered her novel a "prophecy" of recent events.[3] Silko explained that Chiapas was once an important region in the ancient Mayan Empire, but today, it is the poorest state in Mexico. By calling themselves Zapatistas, the predominantly Mayan rebels were honoring Emiliano Zapata, the hero of the Mexican Revolution who called for land reform and redistribution, and associating their uprising with an indigenous fight for land that has been ongoing since the Spanish conquest of the Mayan Empire. It should come as no surprise, Silko observed, when a people who have experienced some of the harshest repression in Central America but who have always exhibited a "strong fighting spirit" arise once again to resist oppression.[4] Stopping short of claiming that her novel predicts the rebellion, Silko acknowledged that, at the very least, it anticipates the issues brought to the table by the Zapatistas.

Almanac of the Dead is not the first U.S. novel to explore what it would mean for a racially or culturally marginalized group to rise up and resist state and corporate actions that put their families and environments at risk. Since the 1980s, a number of writers—predominantly writers of color—have begun to write novels, poems, and plays that redefine environmental issues as social and economic justice issues and that address these concerns as basic human rights. In previous chapters, I discussed works by Ofelia Zepeda, Simon Ortiz, Louise Erdrich, and Joy Harjo that grapple with many of the same issues raised by groups such as the Dinéh Alliance and the Zapatista rebels. To the list of these literary works, which might be described as the literature of environmental justice, we could add other novels, poems, and plays by U.S. writers from diverse backgrounds and cultures—such as Octavia Butler's *Xenogenesis* series, Ana Castillo's *So Far from God,* Jonathon Harr's *A Civil Action,* Linda Hogan's *Solar Storms,* Winona LaDuke's *Last Standing Woman,* Cherríe Moraga's *Heros and Saints and Other Plays,* Helen Maria Viramontes's *Under the Feet of Jesus,* and Karen Tei Yamashita's *Through the Arc of the Rainforest* and *Tropic of Orange.*

This literature differs somewhat from other U.S. literary works written since the 1980s that reflect what ecocritic Cynthia Deitering terms a "toxic consciousness." Deitering notes that novels such as John Cheever's *Oh What a Paradise It Seems,* Don DeLillo's *White Noise,* and John Updike's *Rabbit at Rest* depict the United States as a "postnatural" land defined no longer by what it produces but by its waste. In each, a main protagonist struggles in some way with the consequences of himself as a producer of waste and with his culture's "shifting relation to nature and to the environment at a time when the imminence of ecological collapse was, and is, part of the public mind and of individual imaginations."[5] The paradox of these characters, Deitering concludes, is that they still dream of a "pastoral homesite associated with innocence and harvest" at the same time they acknowledge they are living in a society "that has fouled its own nest" (201, 200).

In this chapter, by threading my discussion of *Almanac of the Dead* with observations about Subcomandante Marcos, the Zapatista's most visible, non-Mayan spokesperson, and about Rigoberta Menchú, a Mayan woman who was recently accused of misrepresenting the details of her life in *I, Rigoberta Menchú*, I explore why the main protagonists of the literature of environmental justice must do more than reflect on the postnatural landscape while dreaming of a pastoral homesite. More specifically, I examine why these characters must be persons of action capable of representing themselves and their people from their own perspective, persons who are not afraid to cross boundaries, make decisions, confront authority figures, and contend with violence. I begin by noting some of the parallels between critics' reception of *Almanac of the Dead* and the Mexican government's response to the Zapatistas.

The "Authentic" Native American Novel

Early reviews of *Almanac of the Dead* generally judged the novel a failure in terms of the reviewers' own expectations for the genre of the Native American novel. Novels in general, these reviewers insisted, must be brief, have fully developed characters, a linear narrative, and avoid controversial political rhetoric.[6] *Almanac of the Dead* failed on all counts. Reviewers were aghast at the intimidating length of Silko's book, its seemingly disjointed plot and subplots, and its daunting cast of Mayan revolutionaries, Yaqui medicine women, ecowarriors, politicians, military generals, prostitutes, biotechnologists, murderers, and mafiosos. Most reviewers admitted their disappointment at finding the novel so different from Silko's previous works, *Storyteller* and *Ceremony*. Melody Graulich, for example, critiques the style of *Almanac of the Dead* for having "little of the sensuous lyricism of Silko's early work or its rich treatment of tradition."[7] Alan Ryan of *USA Today* was not so generous. He was so incensed about Silko's narrative style that he impugned her credentials as a Native American writer. Silko's reputation, he railed, is based on the "special insight into the lives and minds of Native Americans" she demonstrated in earlier works. *Almanac of the Dead,* however, is nothing more than a "teetering truckload of politically correct themes, from racial oppression to ecology," proving that "more than just the novel itself needs remedial help."[8]

A parallel might be drawn here between Ryan's criticism of Silko, one of America's most celebrated Native American authors, and the Mexican government's response to the Zapatista rebellion and its most visible leader. To understand that response, we must understand something of the history and politics surrounding the events of 1 January 1994. The Zapatista rebellion occurred on the borders of a rain forest that the Maya have inhabited for millennia and that, in an official decree, the Mexican government pledged to protect. But in the last few decades, the government has looked the other way while the Lacandon has been shorn (for mahogany, highways, farms, oil, resettlement, even airstrips for drug traffickers) to the bare minimum necessary to keep its ecosystems from collapsing. With the expropriation of lands that once provided the basis of their subsistence economy and with the disappearance of the rain forest plants and animals that once supported them, the Maya have been forced to abandon their villages to work as wage laborers in the countryside or to seek work in cities, where they often live in poverty.[9]

So when Subcomandante Marcos, one of the masked leaders of the Chiapas revolt and its most prominent spokesperson is asked, "What is behind this revolution in Mexico?" and answers that the rebels want their "land back," he is not referring to a fight to preserve pristine rain forest ecosystems.[10] He is referring to the fight to save lands that have been the basis of Mayan cultural and economic survival since ancient priests carved the first "American" histories and calendrical systems into the stone pyramids and stelae that dot the states of Chiapas and Oaxaca.

From the beginning of the rebellion, the Mexican government represented the Mayan Indians as if they were unable to speak for themselves or to work actively for a future of their own making. On 7 January 1994, the government issued a bitterly worded statement to the media alluding to the Zapatista's fair-skinned, non-Mayan leader, Subcomandante Marcos: "This is not an indigenous or peasant movement but actions by a radical group directed by professionals who are tricking and even forcing the participation of Indians."[11] The implication of this statement is that if the Maya practice their traditional culture, then they can be considered purely "Indian," but if they don the mask of rebellion, insist they cannot practice their traditional culture without a land base, send communiqués out over the Internet, give interviews to the U.S. news media, or form alliances with non-Mayan people, they must be tainted, corrupted by outside influences, unauthentic, less than Indian. Ignoring government allegations, the Zapatistas have continued to use Marcos as their spokesperson. In an interview published in *Vanity Fair,* Marcos responded to the government's claims this way: "The government says that this is not an indigenous uprising, but we think that if thousands of indigenous people rise up in protest, then it is indeed an indigenous uprising."[12]

At the initial round of peace negotiations in February 1994, Marcos made it absolutely clear that the Zapatistas saw gaining a voice in government as a primary aim of their movement and insisted that election reforms would be a crucial first step toward that goal. This demand for representation in Mexico's political system highlights one of the most important issues articulated at the First National People of Color Environmental Leadership Summit, which convened in Washington, D.C., in October 1991. There, three hundred grassroots environmental leaders from people-of-color communities in the United States, Canada, and Latin America came together to debate mainstream environmentalist definitions of "nature" and to contest the institutionalized practice of environmental racism.

But the issue that came to the fore as foundational to all other social and environmental concerns was the issue of self-representation. For too long, observed the delegates, indigenous people have been represented as people with an ancient wisdom that alone can save the planet while simultaneously being represented as part of a wild, untamed nature that must be exploited and controlled. These paradoxical representations have had grave social and environmental consequences for people of color all over the world, including genocide and the toxic contamination of the communities where they live. Delegates insisted that these problems can be addressed only when people of color rise up, speak with their own voices, and demand recognition of and respect for "their cultures, languages, and beliefs about the natural world."[13]

There are some notable similarities between the Mexican government's disdain for an indigenous movement because its most prominent leader is non-Mayan and Ryan's dismissal of *Almanac of the Dead* because its author seems to him to be speaking unauthentically. Ryan's criticism of Silko is based, in part, on the fact that *Storyteller* and *Ceremony* placed Silko among the ranks of nationally recognized American Indian writers because they mirrored and helped to construct the expectations many readers bring to their reading of works by American Indians. Such readings are linked to the processes of canonization that American Indian texts have undergone in the United States since the publication of N. Scott Momaday's Pulitzer Prize–winning *House Made of Dawn* in 1968. Momaday is often referred to as the "father" of contemporary Native American literature, and his novel is frequently put forward as the first in a line of creative works that signal a contemporary literary "renaissance" among American Indians. Over the past three decades, predominantly non-Indian and Euro-American critics and readers of Native American literature have determined the hallmarks of this literary renaissance to include, in Ryan's words, some kind of "insight" into the "lives and minds" of American Indians (read: some kind of insight into the ancient traditions and sacred ceremonies of tribal people).

In a sense, *Almanac of the Dead* dons the mask of rebellion to confront the ways in which a largely Euro-American academic community and readership have participated in the process of canonization of certain American Indian–authored works. But, as I show in the next section, Silko weaves elements of the most ancient "American" literature—the Mayan almanacs—into her novel, thereby rejecting the notion of a renaissance in American Indian writing and insisting that indigenous peoples have been writing and articulating their cultures and beliefs for hundreds and even thousands of years. In lectures and interviews, Silko has repeatedly observed that those who would understand her project must put aside ambiguous notions of "novelistic merit" and read her book—as the title clearly indicates—as an almanac.[14]

Almanacs are loose compilations of astrological, calendrical, meteorological, agricultural, historical, literary, and other miscellaneous information. For more than two thousand years, when people of various cultures—Egyptian, Roman, Chinese, Mayan, European, and early colonial American—wanted to understand changes in the weather and the earth, ascertain how these changes would affect them personally, and predict how they might bring themselves and their lands into a more positive, harmonious relationship with the universe, they consulted their almanacs. By imagining her novel as an almanac, Silko also embraces the debate and dialogue that are key characteristics of the genre. Almanacs have a long history of challenging those who claim the privilege and authority to represent "reality" from only one perspective. In early colonial America, for example, almanacs were compiled by colonial elites, but authors of both genders and different races participated in their production, and the contents were dictated more by the common people who purchased them than by the people who produced them.[15] Although colonists might not dare dispute the scriptures they found in their Bible or add their own personal histories to that authoritative Christian text, they often felt free to record the events of their daily lives on blank pages of their almanacs or to scribble in the margins any objections they had to what they were reading.[16] So, although authoritative texts attempt to maintain hegemony over representational space, almanacs challenge the very notion of authoritative discourse. As Silko observes, almanacs are "designed so that you don't have control when you confront [them]."[17]

However, those whose power and position depend on entrenched racist categories of representation, whether newspaper reviewer or politician, often respond with linguistic and physical violence to perceived boundary violation. Ryan implies that when Silko speaks of indigenous oral traditions and spirituality, she can be considered an "Authentic Native American Author," but when she confronts expected literary conventions, constructs her novel in ways that challenge hegemony, or speaks of genocide, resistance, and revolution, her status as "Authentic Native American Author" must be revoked. Ryan reacts to Silko's perceived literary transgression by attacking her personally, pronouncing her in need of "remedial help," and warning readers to avoid her novel altogether. And this is where a parallel between Ryan's vitriolic review and the Mexican government's violent response to the Zapatistas might be drawn. Within a week of the rebellion, the Mexican government sent in its military to crush the rebellion they termed not "purely" Indian. Their actions left more than four hundred mostly civilian people dead.[18]

Despite the violence of some reviews of *Almanac of the Dead,* Silko is unapologetic about writing a novel so confrontational that it immediately commanded the attention of the popular press. In a seminar conducted shortly after the novel's publication, Silko told her audience that she was pleased that Ryan, her *USA Today* reviewer, was driven "so berserk" that he himself was forced to abandon the newspaper's usual practice of keeping book reviews on "the sunny side." *Almanac of the Dead,* she observed, was calculated to "shake people up," to tear them out of their comfort zones and make them see things differently. If the novel drove the critics a little "berserk," Silko laughingly asserted, then she was achieving her aim.[19]

Similarly defiant, Subcomandante Marcos showed no signs of backing down from his own statements or his group's actions. Dubbed Mexico's "Poet Rebel" by the Mexican media, Marcos made this statement in his first communique in the early days of the rebellion: "Here we are, the dead of all times, dying once again, but now with the objective of living."[20] Later, in a savvy act of twentieth-century political articulation aimed at garnering international sympathy for the Zapatistas, he agreed to be interviewed by Ann Louise Bardach, a reporter for the popular magazine *Vanity Fair.* After five hundred years of repression, Marcos explained, the Mayan people in the mountain villages of Chiapas were no longer willing to be brutalized and exploited. The Zapatista National Liberation Army was born "as a self-defense force. . . [,] we have to take up arms to defend ourselves . . . to protect the villagers, not to attack" (132).

But to demonstrate to the government that they were serious in their demands for political representation and agrarian reforms, the Zapatistas also armed themselves with electronic technology, speeding communiqués (which the Mexican government attempted to suppress) out on the Internet to the world community. Highly conscious of international opinion, the Mexican government was constrained from using the full force of its military to put down the rebellion. Consequently, a technology that might be termed "nontraditional" or "non-Indian" was used successfully by the Mayan rebels to link the Zapatistas to networks of sympathizers all over the world. As a result, the Mexican government was forced to loosen the purse strings in Chiapas to build new houses for corn farmers and to improve the infrastructure in the poorest Indian communities.[21]

Like the Mexican Poet Rebel's communiques, Silko's novel transgresses conventions—literary and political—in order to focus a spotlight on the most glaring consequences of five hundred years of genocide, be-

trayal, and exploitation in the Americas. The implication of her boundary violation is that she and other authors of an emerging literature of
environmental justice, like environmental justice activists all over the
world, have as their objective the survival of their peoples and communities. In the next section, I focus on the pre- and post-Columbian Mayan
and colonial American almanacs on which Silko patterns her novel in
order to examine the story she is telling of indigenous peoples who
deliberately transgress all manner of imposed boundaries in their search
for the texts and tools they will need to battle for their own survival.

From Early "American" Almanacs to
Almanac of the Dead

Almanac of the Dead centers around and tells the story of a fictional
almanac given to Lecha and Zeta Cazador, sixty-year-old, twin, mixed-
blood Indian women. The twins receive the almanac from their grandmother, Old Yoeme, a Yaqui Indian who has participated in the Mexican Revolution and survived imprisonment for "high treason against
the federal government" (exploits that associate her with Emiliano Zapata and his involvement in the 1910–19 Mexican Revolution).[22] She has
also acted as a "keeper of the almanac," one of the many men and
women who, throughout the course of hundreds of years, have protected with their lives the sacred, secret record of their people's history,
traditions, and cultural knowledge. Sensing she is nearing her death,
Old Yoeme passes the almanac down to Lecha and Zeta, explaining that
the ancient stories, historical narratives, and other miscellaneous information contained in the almanac tell the people "who they were and
where they had come from" (246).

When Lecha and Zeta open up the wooden ammunition box contain-
ing the almanac, they discover fragments of parchment covered with
strange hieroglyphic markings, several old, dilapidated notebooks,
stacks of newspaper clippings, yellowed papers scrawled with an unfamiliar, classical Spanish script, and blank pages, one of which has been
recently filled with Yoeme's own personal testimony of her miraculous
escape from a Mexican prison and her journey to Tucson, Arizona.

In an interview with Laura Coltelli, Leslie Silko explains that the
fragmented parchments covered with strange hieroglyphic markings
that Lecha and Zeta find in the ammunition box are modeled on the

four Mayan books—or codices—that survived the bonfires of ardent Spanish missionaries who followed in the wake of the Spanish conquistadors, burning the great Mayan libraries.[23] Mayan priests once used the information in these brightly inked books as mnemomics to teach Mayan children about mathematics, history, royal lineages, rituals, prayers, hymns, and the astonishingly accurate Mayan 260-day calendar. Today, the four surviving fragments are housed in museums in Dresden, Paris, Madrid, and Mexico City.

What interested Silko specifically about Mayan almanacs and history, is that, as she tells Coltelli, from the beginning of the colonial period, European peoples claimed the right to "tell the story," to speak for indigenous peoples, and to represent reality from only one perspective (151). Yet the Maya consistently resisted those representations, fought for their communities and lands, and, like their ancestors before them, continued to record their histories and stories in sacred books they kept hidden from their oppressors. But after their books had been destroyed and the Spanish were committing genocide on an unimaginable scale, Mayan elders realized they could not maintain their traditions orally for very much longer. It was at this point, Silko tells interviewer Coltelli, that the elders must have gathered secretly to plan their resistance (152).

To understand the Mayan resistance Silko celebrates in *Almanac of the Dead,* we must understand something about ancient Mayan history. Archaeologists, anthropologists, and contemporary Mayan elders tell us that the Maya were an ancient people whose culture had developed over several thousands of years. Having faced challenges to the survival of their culture many times before, they viewed Spanish conquest in light of the innumerable military invasions, social upheavals, and ecological crises they had already suffered and survived. The Mayan elders whom Silko imagines gathering and planning their resistance would certainly have had an understanding of their long history. They would have known that during what anthropologists now call the Classic Period of Mayan civilization, from 300 to 900 A.D., their city-states had flourished, and their ancestors had built massive pyramids and dotted their cities with stone monuments inscribed with hieroglyphic "almanacs" detailing their calendars, gods, religious ceremonies, and royal genealogies. Hieroglyphic texts in great quantities were also painted on pottery and door lintels, and inked on long strips of paper folded like screens to make books.[24]

But around 900 A.D., Mayan civilization mysteriously collapsed. There is still considerable debate about what happened to the Maya and about why their cities were suddenly and rapidly depopulated. However, a series of dramatic archaeological and anthropological breakthroughs in the last thirty years have led Mayanists to an emerging consensus about factors that may have contributed to the collapse. Archaeologist T. Patrick Culbert has discovered evidence of overpopulation and an accompanying overexploitation of the rain forest ecosystem on which the Maya depended for food. Culbert adds that there is evidence this ecological crisis led to water shortages, a disintegrating agricultural system, and malnutrition.[25]

The most startling new information, however, learned when scholars began deciphering the Mayan writing system, is that the Maya were not the peaceful people scholars once assumed. Indeed, they were a militaristic people, and warfare played a key role in their civilization.[26] Before 761 A.D., explains Arthur Demarest, the leading archaeologist of Mayan civilization, the rulers of competing Mayan city-states conducted very well-orchestrated battles to seize dynastic power and to procure royal captives for very public and ornate executions. But after 761 A.D., "wars led to wholesale destruction of property and people, reflecting a breakdown of social order comparable to modern Somalia."[27] By the end of the Classic Period, ferocious competition, fueled by a ruling elite grown large enough to produce intense rivalries, may have exploded into a civil war that triggered full-fledged, vicious wars and turned once proud city-states into abandoned ruins.

But despite this deepening vortex of overpopulation, environmental degradation, malnutrition, tribal warfare, and rapid depopulation of cities, the Maya continued to record their histories and to compile their almanacs. After the Classic Period, they no longer inscribed their texts on monuments and buildings, but scribes went right on making books for another six centuries. Ethnologist-linguist Dennis Tedlock explains that the survival of Mayan literature was not dependent on outward forms. During and after the crisis at the end of the Classic Period, what seems to have been important to the Maya was not so much the medium—stone or paper—in which their almanacs were recorded, but simply that their knowledges and histories would continue to be recorded. Mayan priests tenaciously refused to let crisis deprive them of the books they so highly valued, and this tenaciousness served them well in the sixteenth century, when Europeans arrived in Mesoamerica determined to dominate the Maya and destroy their culture.[28]

Whereas the story of Mayan conquest, told from the conqueror's perspective, ends in smoke and flame, the much more interesting and important story from Silko's point of view—the one around which she builds *Almanac of the Dead*—is the story of how the Mayan people resisted domination, held on to their culture, and survived into the twentieth century. She tells this story by imagining the almanac in Yoeme's possession to include a fifth, undiscovered Mayan codex, one that has been kept secret from anthropologists and museum directors, and protected for hundreds of years by keepers of the almanac, who have deciphered, transcribed, and translated the red-and-black glyphs inked onto ancient parchment.

When Lecha inspects the fragmented fifth codex, she finds the ancient glyphs still clear. She also finds that previous keepers of the almanac have completed phonetic Mayan transcriptions of the fragments and translated their transcriptions into an often misspelled, archaic Spanish (569, 134). One of the Spanish translations of the Mayan glyphs, now retranslated into English, reads as follows: "Ik is three. Ik is wind on the edge of the rain storm; deity of the rain carries pollen; Lord of the night of the hollow drum, God of caves and conch shells. Earthquake is a scale off the back of earth monster Crocodile" (572). Another translation on the same page reads: "Kan is four. Kan is lizard from whose belly sprang all the seeds for grain and fruit" (572). "Ik" and "Kan" are the names for two of the days of the ancient Mayan 260-day calendar, but Silko does not provide the reader with any other clues to the meaning of either of these passages or with any hints as to how they may fit together. By not providing any sense of the meaning of the fragments Lecha is reading, Silko starkly reminds readers that European colonization of the Americas violently fragmented ancient, pre-Columbian cultures and that many elements of those cultures have been forgotten or irretrievably lost to fire and treachery.

But Silko's purpose in drawing historical materials for *Almanac of the Dead* from texts such as the Mayan codices is not to portray ancient Mayan history, culture, science, or religion accurately, and she is clearly not interested in any romantic notions about recovering an "authentic" or "pure" Mayan culture that has been brought to the brink of extinction. Rather, she is interested in how the Maya struggled in the face of violence and loss to continue as a people. In the chapter "From the Ancient Almanac," Lecha finds translated passages of the ancient Mayan codices on the same page of the almanac where she also finds passages referring to post-Columbian events. She reads: "1560. The year of the plague—intense cold and fever—bleeding from nose and coughing, twisted necks and large sores erupt" (577). In another passage on this page, she reads about the Maya still carrying on their daily lives three decades later: "1594. Today, September 23, a land dispute between the Xevacal Tuanli is decided according to law" (577). Both of these passages allude to historical events recorded in books that the Maya made secretly *after* colonization, books such as the Popol Vuh, the Quiché Mayan creation story, and the eighteen surviving Books of the Chilam Balam, which were written by a class of priests called the Chilam Balam, or "Jaguar Priests," who continuously copied, recopied, and expanded their histories from the sixteenth to the nineteenth centuries.[29]

The fragmented and miscellaneous documents that Lecha and Zeta find in the ammunition box with the fifth codex, then, are patterned on books like those compiled by the Jaguar Priests. According to historian Ronald Wright, these books, which were part bible, part community charter, part almanac, and part chronicle, were continuously updated and expanded, making them, in a sense, "living books," and every "Yucatec town of any size possessed one."[30] Ironically, the Spanish friars who were so determined to disengage the Maya from their surrounding discursive and nondiscursive environments provided the means for the people to transform their ancient knowledges into new languages and thus to create these living books.

Catholic priests determined that if the Spanish were ever to convert indigenous peoples to Catholicism, they themselves would have to learn something about the languages and cultures of the people they had subjugated. So the friars worked out the problems of adapting their own alphabet to the sounds of indigenous languages and set to work teaching young boys of royal descent how to read and write the Mayan language phonetically. The boys were also taught Latin and classical Spanish. Very little time passed, Silko tells interviewer Coltelli, before it dawned on native elders that the alphabets and languages acquired from the missionaries—the burners of ancient books—could be used for political and religious applications other than those of Rome (152). Mayan priests and elders instructed the boys to use their new skills to

record and preserve their own ancient stories and systems of knowledge, and to add to those ancient texts a record of their continuously
unfolding history.

Like the Mayan priests who were no longer able to record their
almanacs on stone but who kept right on making books for another six
centuries, these young royal writers placed more importance on the
survival of their culture than on the outward forms in which their books
would be written. In the Popol Vuh and the Books of the Chilam
Balam, they left a literary legacy that is both more extensive than the
surviving hieroglyphic codices and more open to modern interpretation
and understanding because the books were usually recorded in both
alphabetic Mayan and classical Spanish. Also, books such as the Popol
Vuh are important, Tedlock argues, because they tell "us something
about the conceptual place of books in the pre-Columbian world."[31]
The writers of the Popol Vuh describe the book they are composing as a
"seeing instrument," "a complex navigation system for those who wish
to see and move beyond the present," and, even more poetically, a "place
to see."[32]

This background helps to explain why Silko's fictional keepers conceptualize their almanac as a place in which to "foresee the months and
days and years to come" (137). Despite Spanish claims to have conquered and reduced indigenous peoples to the permanent status of
childlike, "natural" beings who must be tutored and spoken for, the
keepers of the almanac are collecting evidence in their living books to
prove that indigenous peoples have always actively worked to undermine the powers of domination. Their books provide them with many
of the details of their ancient culture and systems of knowledge as well
as a comprehensive interpretation of the past, thus giving them a solid
foundation on which to view the present and a "place to see" how they
might move intelligently into the future.

Not only does Silko imagine the almanac in Lecha and Zeta's keeping
as a living book that has been continuously updated and expanded, she
also imagines how such a text—originally compiled by the Maya—
might have found its way to Tucson, Arizona, and ended up in the
hands of twin Yaqui sisters. Old Yoeme tells Lecha and Zeta that in the
sixteenth century, Mayan elders instructed those skilled in the colo-
nizer's languages to write down their ancient stories and systems of
knowledge on horse-gut parchment. These parchments were guarded

and continuously expanded until the late 1800s, when Mexican colonialist dictators and landowners began forcing indigenous peoples to work
on large plantations and in silver mines. Many indigenous peoples sick-
ened or died of disease, and others were being literally worked to death.
After much debate over whether the almanac should be allowed to fade
from existence along with the people or they should fight to save both
the people and the almanac, the keepers of the almanac decide that an
effort should be made to save the "book of days" (575). The elders decide
that if "even part of their almanac survives they as a people would
return" (246).

They select four children—three girls and a boy—to escape to the
north with the sacred almanac. The children's flight alludes to the actual
historical contact between the Maya of the Yucatán Peninsula and the
Yaqui people of Sonora, Mexico. After one of Mexico's cruelest dictators, Porfirio Díaz, came to power in 1876, the Yaqui people—who had
always been known for their resistance to unjust Spanish and, later,
Mexican oppression—were deported en masse from their traditional
homelands along the U.S.–Mexico border in the state of Sonora to the
Yucatán Peninsula, where they were enslaved in chain gangs on large
estates and plantations. Silko implies that the four children are Maya
who are seeking members of their own tribe who may have already fled
with escaping Yaqui back to "the high, arid mountains" of Sonora
(246).[33] Once having returned home to Sonora, however, many of these
Yaqui found that to escape continuing Mexican persecution, they would
need to flee still further north. Crossing the U.S. border, the Yaqui
established several pueblos in and around Tucson, Arizona.

Though parts of the "book of days" are lost during the children's
desperate flight, many of the missing stories are remembered by the
young girls and passed down by word of mouth to successive keepers of
the almanac, who write them down in their own imperfect Spanish and
add them to translations of ancient Mayan texts already a part of the
almanac. Sometime later, because of deterioration and wear, the keepers
copy and recopy as much of the sacred almanac as they can into new
notebooks to keep the stories from being lost. These notebooks are the
ones that Old Yoeme delivers into Lecha's and Zeta's hands, thus explaining how members of the Yaqui tribe might have come into the
possession of an almanac chronicling the history of the Maya and the
history of the Yaqui, as a result of their later alliance with the Maya.

However, the almanac does not consist of indigenous tribal histories and knowledges alone. Yoeme and other keepers feel free to add accounts of such devastating events as the influenza epidemic of 1918; their own personal testimonies about those events; newspaper articles detailing crimes, atrocities, and indigenous uprisings all over the world; and even sections of old colonial American farmer's almanacs (570). By mentioning farmer's almanacs among the documents that the keepers add to their almanac, Silko taps into the animate cosmos of the colonial American farmer, a world that is unfamiliar to most twentieth-century readers, but one that would be familiar and recognizable to tribal people who make no distinction between nature and culture. Farmer's almanacs, notes environmental historian Carolyn Merchant, were first published in colonial America in 1639, a time when most colonists—educated and uneducated alike—believed that "Nature, personified as animate mother, carried out God's dictates in the phenomenal world."[34] Colonists believed that land was a living thing that had to be nursed and humored, and that the sun, moon, and stars influenced both the human body and the earth's body. A good farmer needed to understand and work within the celestial cycles and to approach nature mimetically so that the land could be made to yield and the soil could be kept fertile. By mimicking nature's actions—watching the seasons closely, observing changes in plants, predicting rain by watching ants carry eggs out of their nest, dancing in the fields to encourage fertility—colonists hoped for a sympathetic response to their entreaties. This is precisely why the slim, four-by-seven-inch, sixteen-page almanacs were so popular; they were the main printed source of the astrological information colonists needed to bring themselves and their land into a more positive, harmonious relationship with the cosmos.[35]

Those sections of late-seventeenth-century American almanacs that employ earth mother imagery in profusion or advise colonists about how to make healing herbal remedies would be useful to the keepers of the almanac because they support the keepers' own beliefs about the earth as animate, responsive "Mother" (625). But sections of late-eighteenth- and early-nineteenth-century almanacs that advise colonists to see the earth as commodity and to master nature's processes for profit would also be useful to the keepers because they show how European consciousness about nature has been deliberately constructed over time to support colonialist objectives. As the Apache elders of one of the narratives included in the almanac assert, one of the most dangerous qualities of Europeans is that they suffer "a sort of blindness to the world. To them, a 'rock' was just a 'rock' wherever they found it, despite obvious differences in shape, density, color, or the position of the rock relative to all things surrounding it" (224).

By refusing to acknowledge the role that rocks and other nonhuman complexes play in the ecology of a place, Euro-Americans reduce every-thing that is not European to a resource to be utilized in whatever way they deem necessary for profit and "progress." The irony is that all during the seventeenth, eighteenth, and early nineteenth centuries, as colonists were transforming nature from an animate, responsive mother into an inert commodity, the earth *was* responding to human-induced change. But as colonists rejected their own mimetic traditions, they became increasingly unable to understand the languages in which the earth responds to long-term overexploitation—depletion, species extinc-tion, pollution, and famine. The keepers of the almanac understand that this reduction of and "blindness" to the world, this refusal to interpret the earth's responses to domination and control, is driven by greed and deliberately constructed over time in the colonizing effort to claim power over nature and society. Yoeme, a twentieth-century witness to the long-term damage done to the earth by the greedy "Destroyers," observes that if humans continue to misinterpret and fail to respond to the earth's languages of depletion and extinction, they "might not sur-vive," but the "earth would go on, the earth would outlast anything man did to it" (719, 718).

By creating a living book from fragments of pre- and post-Columbian "American" almanacs, personal testimonies, and other miscellaneous information, Silko's keepers are creating a text that insists that indige-nous peoples and their environments are not the ground and matrix of Euro-American action, but alive, responsive, resistant, and capable of articulating their own perspectives about the world and their place in it. Thus, the sacred almanac that Yoeme has passed down to Lecha and Zeta provides support for the keepers' claim to the right to "tell their own story" and to determine their own futures. In the next section, by drawing some connections between the Mayan Nobel Peace laureate Rigoberta Menchú and Silko's Mayan character Angelita, I explore why those who rise up and claim their right to self-representation and self-determination must be prepared to respond to threats to their survival and how these people are preparing themselves to enter into dialogue and debate with international politicians, bankers, corporate executives, developers, and environmentalists over what it means to "protect indigenous peoples" and to "save nature."

Rigoberta Menchú, Angelita, and the Search for New Forms of Expression

In the Popol Vuh, the gods of the sea and the gods of the sky make four attempts to create human beings who will be capable of speaking intelligibly to each other and to the gods. What they want, notes Dennis Tedlock, is "beings who will walk, work, and talk in an articulate manner."[36] What they get on the first try is beings who have no arms with which to work and who can only squawk, chatter, and howl. These beings become the animals who walk the earth today. On a second attempt, they try making a solitary person of mud, but with the first rain, it is washed away. Amidst an ever-widening conversation that continually calls other gods into their deliberations, they fail on their third attempt as well, creating beings from wood who look and talk and multiply something like humans, but who forget to call on the gods in their prayers. These beings become the monkeys who inhabit the forests. Before describing the fourth attempt, the authors of the Popol Vuh turn their attention to the heroic deeds of two sets of twins, whose "adventures make the sky-earth a safer place for human habitation."[37] Then, turning back to the problem that confronted the gods at the beginning of the text, the authors describe a fourth attempt to create articulate beings. Having failed with mud and wood, the gods grind white and yellow corn into a fine flour that they mix with water, forming the first four humans. These beings are all the gods had hoped for and more; they are articulate, respectful, and see everything perfectly in the earth-sky. The gods, however, are fearful of humans with such powerful, godlike capabilities, so they put a fog in the humans' eyes. From this time forward, humans will need the Popol Vuh as a "seeing instrument" to help them see through the fog, remember the past, and move beyond the present into the future.

Having created her novel in the tradition of a Mayan "seeing instrument," Leslie Silko ends *Almanac of the Dead* on the brink of an event that will occur sometime in the future: either the arrival in North

America of an army from Chiapas, the violent overthrow of national and state governments by the mafia or ecoterrorists, the interruption of the national electrical power system, or the collapse of the international computer networking system, and possibly more than one of these events. By leaving readers on the cusp of such ominous possible events, Silko implies that those who are interested in working for human and nonhuman survival must look into the "book of days," remember the past, make some prognostications about the future, and plan the days and months ahead accordingly. In a gathering that echoes the ever-widening conversation among the gods of the Popol Vuh, many of the characters of *Almanac of the Dead* meet for an International Holistic Healers Convention where they begin to discuss possibilities for forming alliances that will work to transform the conditions that threaten the survival of their communities and lands.

Between scheduled speeches and workshops, participants at the convention hear news reports and rumors about the adventures of two sets of twins who are attempting to make the earth-sky a safer place for human habitation. The first set of twins, who have already been introduced, are Lecha and Zeta. The second set are charismatic Mayan brothers named Tacho and El Feo, who live in the Mexican state of Chiapas. Both brothers possess the godlike ability to divine signs in the heavens and the earth, and have read numerous signs indicating that the time has arrived to begin gathering an army and reclaiming their stolen lands.

Initially, the army forms in reaction to the illegal appropriation of Mayan lands that "the people had cleared for farming" but that "had later been claimed by the federal government" and "resold to German coffee planters" (468). This governmental-corporate appropriation and the Mayan people's resistance to it are only the most recent actions in a long history of such events that can be traced back through Emiliano Zapata's resistance to Mexican dictatorship and Mayan resistance to Spanish colonization. The twin brothers believe that with "the return of Indian land would come the return of justice" (513). But they have no grandiose visions of world domination. They are "fighting for their way of life," for the lands where their clans and tribes once practiced sustainable agriculture and where their shrines and temples are located (513). The brothers see their movement as peaceful, hoping that an "army as big as theirs would not need weapons" (710). The members of their army are overwhelmingly indigenous, but the brothers invite people of all races to join them. To be inducted into this army, men and women need "only to walk with the people and let go of all greed and selfishness in their hearts" (710).

Nevertheless, the twin leaders understand that, historically, justice has been constructed quite differently by different political, cultural, religious, corporate, and tribal groups, so it will be almost impossible to "fight a war for such a big change without the loss of blood" (532). Preferring to keep their focus on peaceful actions that will restore the land to the people, they leave the politics, the fund-raising, and the details of supplying their army to those with an inclination for it—the women, which is where the twin Yaqui sisters, Lecha and Zeta, and a fierce Mayan woman, Angelita, come in. Lecha, a psychic who can see murders, rapes, and massacres before they happen, and Zeta, an arms dealer, travel to the International Holistic Healers Convention because the almanac in their keeping points to the Mayan brothers as the fulfillment of tribal prophecy. They are determined to do whatever they can to aid the brothers and their army. Knowing that Angelita—the brothers' political representative, security officer, army recruiter, and organizer— is planning to attend the conference, they decide to attend as well. They hope to meet the Mayan woman who has amassed "one of the largest and most sophisticated arsenals" in the Chiapas region by working with "a dozen foreign governments" and "underground groups," including the one headed by Zeta (310).

Whereas the brothers advocate peace, Lecha, Zeta, and Angelita embody agency, intelligence, and strength—and allow for the possibility of violence. Silko's focus on the activism of these strong, capable women reflects the fact that the overwhelming majority of activists in the environmental justice movement are women and predominantly women of color.[38] Moreover, by repeatedly emphasizing in many of the novel's narrative lines the sexual intimidation and violation that Lecha, Zeta, and Angelita have all experienced, Silko implies that to understand the most troubling aspect of *Almanac of the Dead* and the most disturbing aspect of indigenous resistance to domination—the willingness to use violence as a defense against violence—readers must make some connections between the sexual violation of women, the historical objectification of people of color, and the objectification and violation of the body of Mother Earth. There is the sense in the novel that women will stand for such personal and environmental violation no longer.

To gain an even deeper understanding of why Silko might portray her female characters as being prepared to fight violence with violence, one need only set the novel into a context with the murders, rapes, and torture depicted in a contemporary Quiché Mayan text, *I, Rigoberta Menchú,* and with the controversy that broke over possible inaccuracies in Menchú's accounting of the atrocities committed against her people. A descendent of the same ancient Quiché Mayan people who learned to write phonetic Mayan and Spanish so that they could transform their ancient codices into texts such as the Popol Vuh, Rigoberta Menchú clearly places her book within the tradition of Mayan almanacs and Latin American *testimonios* in the first lines of her book. "This is my testimony," she tells Argentinian anthropologist Elisabeth Burgos-Debray, who taped and transcribed Menchú's narrative, then transformed it into a written narrative. "I didn't learn it from a book," Menchú adds, "I didn't learn it alone. I'd like to stress that it's not only *my* life, it's also the testimony of my people."[39]

A testimonio, notes John R. Beverly, a professor of Spanish and Latin American literature, "is a personal story that also contains a message from a subordinated group involved in a political struggle." Rigoberta Menchú is not a transparent reporter to us, Beverly adds; she is a "person with an ideological agenda. Her book wants to create solidarity" for the Quiché people, who, at the time Menchú was interviewed by Burgos-Debray, were being murdered and tortured by the Guatemalan military in horrifying numbers.[40] It is estimated that more than one hundred thousand people were murdered and that forty thousand are still missing. Certainly, if Menchú's purpose in allowing her story to be told was to bring attention to the genocide of her people, she was successful. Her book and later the attention that came to her as a result of her Nobel Prize helped raise money for the Guatemalan Indian peasantry and played a role in bringing thirty-six years of civil war to an end.[41]

Burgos-Debray notes in her introduction to Menchú's narrative that when they met in Paris, Menchú was an anonymous, twenty-three-year-old political exile, invited to Europe by a number of solidarity groups as a representative of the 31 January Popular Front, which was a Guatemalan alliance of six organizations that came together in January 1981 to commemorate the massacre of a group of Quiché Indians who occupied the Spanish embassy in Ciudad Guatemala in order to draw attention to their plight. Two years after the death of her father in the embassy, Menchú agreed to tell her story to Burgos-Debray.

I, Rigoberta Menchú tells of Quiché Mayan life in the Guatemalan highlands and recounts the ways in which Quiché customs and beliefs are still very much shaped by the words of the ancients, which have been preserved through oral traditions and written texts such as the Popol Vuh. In Menchú's detailed description of her people's customs, we hear the echoes of the religious, cultural, and astronomical lessons taught by ancient priests to Mayan children—the same echoes of past, present, and future that Silko attempts to reflect in her fictional "book of days" and in the personal testimonios that her character Old Yoeme and other keepers add to the almanac. As Burgos-Debray expresses it, Menchú's testimony proudly and quietly leads us into "a world in which the sacred and the profane constantly mingle, in which worship and domestic life are one. . . . Within that culture, everything is determined in advance; everything that occurs in the present can be explained in terms of the past and has to be ritualized so as to be integrated into everyday life, which is itself a ritual" (xii).

Menchú's story illustrates how the continued practice of ancient birthing, marriage, planting, and funeral customs and the continued adherence to the ancient 260-day Mayan calendar (despite five hundred years of being forced to recognize the Christian calendar) is a powerful form of resistance to colonial domination. Indeed, Burgos-Debray heads many of the chapters of Menchú's story with epigraphs from the Popol Vuh that correspond to the Quiché customs described therein. This small, but important literary flourish helps to emphasize how the struggle of the ancient writers of the Popol Vuh to record their most sacred stories and beliefs has energized the contemporary struggle of Menchú's people.

However, Menchú clearly shows that her people are not fighting in the name of a romanticized or mythical past. She allows the atrocities committed against her family and people to break violently into the narrative, a strategy that reminds her audience of what will be lost if the Guatemalan military remains unchecked and the civil war is allowed to continue. To her description of traditional Quiché customs, she unflinchingly adds the story of how U.S.–backed Guatemalan "security forces" use torture, murder, and rape to terrorize, degrade, and control. In some of the most horrifying accounts of this savagery, she recounts how her father, mother, and brother were killed by the military. To battle this barbarity, the villagers begin "looking for texts" that they could relate "to our Indian culture" and use in the fight to survive (131). In their ancient oral and written traditions, Menchú's people discover that the weapons of their ancestors—stones, salt, and chili—could be hurled skillfully into their enemy's eyes. From the Bible, they learn not to "turn the other cheek" but that the stories of Judith, Moses, and David teach resistance to "injustices which are committed against our people" (134). And from an educated *ladino compañero,* a person from a class and a mixed Latin-indigenous race that Menchú had formerly hated because she believed that they all oppressed Indians, Menchú learns to speak Spanish and to "think more clearly about some of my ideas which were wrong, like saying all *ladinos* are bad" (165). He teaches her the history of other Indian groups and helps her see that many ladinos also live in terrible conditions, just as the Indians do. Menchú's point in recounting what she has learned from both Mayan and non-Mayan sources is to emphasize that Indian people are not quaint, unlearned people. They are intelligently able to select new knowledges relevant to their lives and to incorporate new texts and languages into their struggle. This ability does not mean that they are accepting "a condition, or abandon[ing] our cultures," writes Menchú. "It was more like another way of expressing ourselves" (139).

Menchú's search for new forms of expression that would aid the Indian peasantry in their struggle to survive a brutal civil war ultimately swept her into international prominence upon the publication of her story in 1983. By 1992, Menchú's book had become a best-seller, and she had become a spokesperson for and a symbol of indigenous people's resistance to injustice. That year, in recognition of her long years of activist work for social justice and ethnocultural reconciliation, the Nobel Committee awarded her with a Prize for Peace.

But by 1999, Menchú and her testimony were in the eye of a storm. In his book, *Rigoberta Menchú and the Story of All Poor Guatemalans,* North American anthropologist David Stoll accuses Menchú of embellishing the details of her history in order to gain sympathy in the West for a communist guerilla movement she backed and that aimed to topple

Guatemala's government. Basing his charges on interviews conducted in Menchú's village, Stoll writes that key events in Menchú's narrative did not take place. Conceding that her father, mother, and brother were killed by military forces, Stoll painstakingly details the inaccuracies in Menchú's account of her brother's death. He was not burned to death before her eyes as Menchú claims; indeed, she did not even witness her brother's murder at all. Although Stoll's conclusions are not based on conversation or dialogue with Menchú herself, he establishes himself as the ultimate authority on her experience and her narrative of that experience by suggesting that members of the Guerrilla Army of the Poor who were advising Menchú may have encouraged her to make her story more typical of the oppression of the Guatemalan peasants so that it would have a broader appeal to the world community and thus garner support for their leftist, guerilla cause.[42]

Stoll's suggestion that Menchú is probably being directed by others to misrepresent herself so that she can bring attention to her cause is interesting in light of my earlier discussion of reviews that dismissed *Almanac of the Dead* because of its supposedly unauthentic voice and of the Mexican government's suggestion that the Maya who joined the rebellion in Chiapas were being "tricked" by "professionals." But, as I explain in the remainder of this chapter, the charges also point to wide cultural differences between the ways that the Maya perceive of their books and testimonios as "seeing instruments" that help us better understand the present and move intelligently into the future and the way that Anglo-Europeans perceive of their books as a place for a Voice of Authority to pronounce Truth.

In interviews she has given since the publication of Stoll's book, Menchú concedes that she wove the testimony of other victims of the civil war into her own story, but defends her book as an accurate depiction of the suffering of her people. In defense of her narrative, she uses words that might have been used by the royal writers of the Popol Vuh to describe their project: "I was a survivor, alone in the world, who had to convince the world to look at the atrocities committed in my homeland."[43] She counters the charges against her by accusing her critics of attacking her to strike at indigenous people who dare to add "to the official story our own story."[44]

If, in situating her narrative within Mayan and Latin American literary traditions that place more emphasis on the survival of the group than on the details of an individual's story, Menchú breached Western scholarly conventions, I believe that Leslie Silko's character, Angelita, can help us understand why; and conversely, Menchú's testimonial can help us better understand Angelita's "leftist" organizing activities and her willingness to employ new texts, tools, and forms of expression to defend her people against violence. In speeches urging local Mayan villagers to organize and defend themselves, Angelita reminds her audience that the ancient makers of living books understood that stories of genocide, murder, rape, and torture powered resistance to oppression and that the "most complete history was the most powerful force" (316). Europeans attempted to crush the fighting spirit of the people, in part, by attempting to erase a long history of indigenous uprisings and rebellions. "Here's what the Europeans don't want us to know or remember," Angelita declares, rattling off a list of hundreds of indigenous resistance fighters—including Hateuy, Simón Bolívar, and Emiliano Zapata—and naming the uprisings they led (527–30). Angelita urges her people to solidarity and calls them to action by detailing the atrocities committed against their ancestors and recounting the history of their resistance.

Making further connections between their history and the threats they are facing in the modern world, Angelita explains that international politicians, bankers, and environmentalists are telling a story of "pristine rain forests" and representing the people who live there as unable or unfit to take responsibility for such a dazzlingly valuable global treasure. But like the keepers of the almanac who utilize both ancient texts and sections of the early American colonizers' almanacs to support their resistance to dominant culture, Angelita urges her people to resist categorizations that represent them as a "traditional" people with a primitive or quaint ancient knowledge that inadequately prepares them to live in the "modern" world. She understands that, in a world dominated by large-scale forces centered in the capitals of foreign states and in the boardrooms of multinational corporations, ancient texts and local traditions alone will not protect her people and their lands. So she practices a syncretic resistance by following ancient Mayan traditions at the same time that she is adding Spanish and English to her repertoire of languages and attending a Marxist Freedom School in Mexico City, where she learns to obtain aid from foreign governments and underground groups (310).

Those closest to Angelita fear she has been "converted" to Marxism, but she asserts that she "is no communist" (313). Rather, she is searching for tools that can be related to Indian culture and used in the struggle to survive. But her search is always done with an intelligent, critical eye. Making distinctions between Marxist, Stalinist, and Maoist styles of communism, she condemns the "immense crimes" of Stalin and Mao, who allowed millions of "human beings to starve while others ate" (316). However, she finds much in the writings of Marx that can help energize her people's struggle. "For hundreds of years," she explains, "white men had been telling the people of the Americas to forget the past; but now the white man Marx came along and he was telling people to remember" (311). Marx backs his assertions with evidence, filling his essays with descriptions of children worked to death in European factories. These descriptions are consistent with the experiences Angelita's people have remembered in their oral traditions and recorded in their living books. "Tribal people had had all the experience they would need to judge whether Marx's stories told the truth. The Indians had seen generations of themselves ground into bloody pulp under the steel wheels of ore cars in crumbling tunnels of gold mines. The Indians had seen for themselves the cruelty of the Europeans toward children and women" (312).

Angelita sees herself as fighting for her people's right to practice their traditional culture and religion, and to derive a sustainable living in the places where they were born. However, her organizing activities, her readings of Marx, her travel to foreign countries, and her fund-raising illustrate her growing understanding that the fight against modern state and corporate exploitation will require her to search continually for new ways to express herself in a world dominated by national and international voices urging that she and her people be ignored or silenced.

Angelita and the Problem of Violence

Silko makes it clear that Angelita does not seek violence, but she will not allow her people to be ground under the wheels of any kind of single-minded ideology that silences their voices or authorizes their suffering or displacement. In a scene surely judged shocking by critics who lamented Silko's failure to write a novel as "authentic" as *Ceremony,* Angelita presides over the trial and execution of Bartolomeo, a handsome blond Cuban Marxist whose ambition for promotion to the "central committee in Havana" leads him to betray the twin brothers, Tacho and El Feo, and other members of the people's army who are hiding in the mountains (510, 514–15). By scattering handbills through-out the capital of Chiapas that link the twin brothers to the people's army, Bartolomeo exposes both the members of the army and the people in the highland villages where they are hiding to the Mexican federal army, which has a long, violent history of crushing indigenous upris-ings. Bartolomeo, Angelita's former instructor at the Marxist Freedom school, is also threatening to have all foreign aid to the local people cut off because he has "received unconfirmed reports that these mountain villages were hotbeds of tribalism and native religion. Marxism did *not* tolerate these primitive bugaboos!" (515). Thus, his greed, ambition, and dogmatic readings of Marx lead Bartolomeo to justify actions that would silence the twin brothers and result in the hardship and suffering of the people he dismisses as "primitive."

However, from Angelita's perspective, Bartolomeo's worst crime is that he believes that "history did not exist" before Fidel Castro (316). Bartolomeo is unaware that "Marx had been inspired by reading about certain Native American communal societies," and he knows nothing of the cultural histories of indigenous American peoples, of their experi-ences with genocide and oppression, or of their long history of resistance (519). He willfully ignores the fact that Marx's stories of "depravity and cruelty were the driving force of the revolution, not the other way around" (316). Bartolomeo bases his authority to speak for indigenous peoples not on any connections to the local people or place, but on his elite education in a distant city, his Marxist training, and his appoint-ment by the Havana central committee to a position in which he is charged with "reeducating" the Indians. Thus authorized, he appoints himself judge and jury, blithely dismissing whole tribes as incapable of self-representation and self-determination simply because they are In-dian. But his cruelty, betrayal, and "attempted annihilation of tribal histories" catch up to him when Angelita brings him before a "people's assembly for crimes against the revolution" (515).

There is an interesting parallel between the creation of the mud being in the Popol Vuh and the trial and execution of Bartolomeo—one that suggests that Silko may not be writing simply a scene in which a treach-

erous man is caught up in his own machinations, but in the tradition of
the almanac she is challenging the very notion of authoritative discourse
or a Voice of Authority claiming the right to speak for others. As Dennis
Tedlock, the translator of the Popol Vuh has noted, when the Quichéan
gods create the being of mud, it is their only experiment with singularity
because all other beings have been created in groups of two and four.
The creation of this solitary shape results in the only being in all the
Popol Vuh to utter such inarticulate sounds that they cannot even be
quoted through onomatopoeia.

Early anthropologists noted many similarities between this passage
and the passage in the Christian Bible that tells the story of God's
creation of Adam, the first man, from mud. Some of these anthropologists speculated that this passage from the Popol Vuh was possibly a
syncretic paraphrase of Genesis. Some implied that the Popol Vuh may
have been tainted, unauthentic, possibly even written by a friar dis-
guised as an Indian. However, in his consultations with contemporary
Quiché Mayan elders about the Popol Vuh, Tedlock began to suspect
that the passage is probably not simply a paraphrase of a Christian text
but a "negation of Adam," a comment on the superimposition of Christianity on Quichéan peoples, "even a criticism of the Bible."[45] It seems
likely that in washing away a being who is very similar to the one
created by the Christian God, the writers of the Popol Vuh are claiming
the right to speak from their own perspective about the culture of the
conquerors and to get into the conversation about who has the right to
tell the story.

With or without the intentional negation of Adam, notes Tedlock,
the failure of the solitary and inarticulate mud being points clearly to the
rift that separates European and Mayan religion and philosophy. In
Genesis, God creates the world through monologue. No other voice is
heard until Adam, in a monologue of his own, names the first animals
and Woman. But in the Popol Vuh, dialogue is a positive force, necessary before the creation can even be conceived. Creation proceeds, observes Tedlock, not through "unities or solitudes, but from dualities. . . .
Here are primordial world *and* divinity, light *and* darkness, sky *and* sea,
female *and* male, and the creation moves not according to the gusty
wind of God's will and the clandestine questioning of a miserable ser-
pent, but according to the increasing light of a widening dialogue.

When, on just one occasion, the gods attempt an experiment with singularity, a monad of mud, it disintegrates without even having uttered something so quotable as an animal cry."[46]

If read in context with the story of the mud being, Angelita's conclusion that Bartolomeo had "outlived his usefulness" (532) might be read as a comment on the grave social and environmental consequences— especially for poor, marginalized, and people-of-color groups—of European philosophies that give solitary beings the right to name everything and that presuppose the existence of a position of power from which one has the right to speak, rule, and control other human and nonhuman species. In the middle place, Silko implies, beings who can speak only in the language of monologue, declaration, and command are of little use. What we need are beings who are articulate in the midst of dialogue, questions, and speculation. What we need are beings who are not afraid to act, who are capable of speaking intelligibly to each other, and who recognize their partnership with the natural world.

Making it clear that Bartolomeo is a type or symbol of something larger, Silko writes that there is only one thing both Angelita and Bartolomeo jointly understand: "the trial wasn't really a personal matter or about personal dislike of Bartolomeo. The Committee for Justice and Land Redistribution had no time for mere personal matters. This was the trial of all Europeans" (526). Bartolomeo represents not one man or "white people" per se, but an entire history of relations between Europeans and indigenous people. His execution is not only a comment on the superimposition of a controlling culture on indigenous cultures, but a negation of reductive relations. From this time forward, the writer of the *Almanac* suggests, indigenous people will speak with their own voices and determine their own political, economic, spiritual, and ecological futures.

A Politics of Articulation

The authority of Angelita, El Feo, and Tacho (and of Rigoberta Menchú) to speak for their people is not derived from their status as members of an elite class or specific race, or from distant educational institutions or powerful political ideologies. Nor does their authority derive from their ontological "natural" status as Indians. Rather, their authority stems from their relationship to each other and to the local environment. They are working to reclaim lands to which they clearly have a *social* relationship. In other words, their rain forest home is not just a place; it is their partner in a communal struggle to survive. They have never viewed their "home" as the Garden of Eden, that pristine place where no one works and where a single mistake will result in expulsion by a vengeful god who speaks for all. They see their home as a middle place where lives and ways of life are absolutely dependent on work and collective cooperation. Survival requires individuals and groups to listen, to articulate their own positions, to interpret and reinterpret the languages of other humans and of the natural world continually, and to enter into a conversation to find enough common ground on which to take a stand and effect change.

As the diverse, interracial groups represented at the International Holistic Healers Convention and by the interracial people's army illustrate, there is nothing in the concept of the world as middle place that rules out articulations by nonindigenous peoples who are committed to protecting indigenous peoples or to "saving nature." Indeed, in a world controlled by powerful and often greedy national and international politicians, corporate executives, bankers, and developers, like and unlike actors have a responsibility not to speak *for* "Others" or for nature, but simply to speak up—to enter into dialogue about how we might work to save ways of life not only for humans but for all the creatures who live in the ever-changing, relentlessly historical middle place.

Because all the actors in the middle place are acknowledged to be articulate and capable of articulation, everyone who enters this conversation must think carefully about his or her own location and position in relation to threatened environments and to the humans and nonhuman species who live there. As Donna Haraway expresses it, with the exchange of a politics of representation for a politics of articulation, all the "patterns, flows, and intensities of power are most certainly changed."[47] Moreover, as the gods of the Popol Vuh illustrate, because articulation is hard work and sometimes fails, necessary conditions for joining the conversation include commitment, engagement, and a willingness to keep working until a goal is met.

Haraway adds that to articulate "is to put things together, scary things, risky things, contingent things" (324). Certainly, in representing themselves and in determining their own futures, characters such as Angelita, Lecha, and Zeta (and historical figures such as Rigoberta Menchú) do seemingly incongruous, scary things, things that critics of "Authentic Native American Writing" and "Accurate Scholarly Texts" may find disturbing. Their work as active defenders of their traditional cultures places them in the realm of the modern: they travel to conventions, obtain foreign aid, are familiar with electronic and military technologies, and read and speak multiple languages. Consequently, they are engaged in a seeming contradiction: they are working to preserve an unmodern way of life with the aid of both ancient and modern texts, and with traditional and contemporary practices and technologies. But from the perspective of a "politics of articulation," we might see these powerful, articulate women as forging innovative collectives of land, plants, animals, near and distant allies, and old and new texts and technologies in a world that has, as Haraway puts it, "always been in the middle of things, in unruly and practical conversation" (304). In this world, no boundary violation is involved because strict categories such as *traditional* and *modern, authentic* and *unauthentic, primitive* and *civilized, pure* and *tainted,* and *natural* and *cultural* no longer make sense.

When we place Angelita, Lecha, and Zeta into a context with the Zapatista rebels, Subcomandante Marcos, and Rigoberta Menchú, we begin to see exactly why characters in the literature of environmental justice must do more than simply reflect on a postnatural landscape and muse about the possibility of a pastoral homesite. To be sure, they must understand the philosophical roots of our current ecological crisis, but the historical experiences of their peoples teach them that any program to protect indigenous peoples or to save nature must be based on social justice—an end to murder, rape, discrimination, illegal appropriation of lands, and unethical exploitation of the earth's natural resources. To achieve their aims, they must be able to think and analyze problems as well as to enter into conversation and debate, be capable of making decisions and taking action, and, most importantly, be able to take responsibility for the consequences of their own and others' actions. These characters clearly illustrate why the issue of self-representation is key to the still emerging environmental justice movement and why grassroots, multicultural activists all over the world who are engaging in transformative actions for spiritual, political, economic, and environmental justice often challenge our most cherished notions about indigenous peoples, people of color, or other groups of people who have been stereotyped as "close to nature."

A Place to See

Silko roots her novel in the writings of both ancient Mesoamericans and early American colonists because the histories of both these peoples illustrate what can happen when humans refuse to pay attention to the earth's cacophonous human and nonhuman voices. As Ronald Wright explains in *Stolen Continents,* the Maya and Aztecs understood that humans took a toll on the earth and that the earth would respond to human-induced change, so they repaid the earth for the existence they enjoyed at the expense of other life through a form of sacred personal bloodletting by kings and priests and through an occasional high-stakes ball game that may have served as a substitute for war.[48] But, as Wright notes, scholars speculate that environmental fluctuations, overpopulation, ever-increasing competition for shrinking resources, and a ruling elite torn apart by rivalry may have played a role in the dramatic abandonment of cities and in the instability and militarism that were characteristic of Mesoamerican cultures (34). Scholars believe that the ruling class may have tried to prolong the survival of their civilization by feeding the sun with more and more human blood, which led to the wholesale immolation of war captives. "Human sacrifice was therefore not the persistence of an old 'savage' practice among civilized people who should have known better," argues Wright, "but rather a hypertrophy of sinister elements in the culture, which in more gracious times had been kept in check" (34).

Silko's character Old Yoeme uses far more strident words than Wright's to castigate a powerful Mesoamerican ruling elite for their "ignorance of the prophecies and warnings" in their sacred almanacs and for their violent practices. "Those who worshiped destruction and blood," observes Yoeme, "secretly knew one another. Hundreds of years earlier, the people who hated sorcery and bloodshed had fled north to escape the cataclysm prophesied when the 'blood worshipers' of Europe met the 'blood worshipers' of the Americas. Montezuma and Cortes had been meant for one another" (570). Yoeme studies the ancient writings in the almanac for clues that will help her people survive, but she refuses to romanticize her Mesoamerican ancestors. Unflinchingly, she notes that among this ancient people there were those who ignored the responses of the "earth's forces" to exploitation of both people and land. The will to dominate and control, she concludes, is the connection between the violent "blood worshipers" of all cultures.

Yoeme links the blood worshipers of Mesoamerica to those in North America by adding sections of old farmers' almanacs to the keepers' living book. The almanacs of early colonizers of North America advised farmers to dominate and exploit American lands for profit by practicing ever and ever more pervasive technologies. As a result of the continuing practice of these kinds of technologies (one might even say, this "hypertrophy of sinister elements" in Euro-American culture), modern humans, like the ancient Mesoamericans, are facing an age of intense competition for shrinking resources in a world that has been made unstable and militaristic by the discursive and nondiscursive practices of powerful elites who claim the right to represent less-powerful people, countries, cultures, and ecosystems, and to appropriate their resources.

By linking Mesoamerican Indian cultures to North American Anglo-European cultures and by ending *Almanac of the Dead* on the brink of social-ecological crisis, Silko raises this question: What will happen if we do not come together in dialogue to work for a more socially and environmentally just world? Angelita gives readers a clue. While attending the Marxist Freedom School, she walks for hours around downtown Mexico City, "in a daze at what she was seeing—at the immensity of wealth behind the towers of steel and concrete and glass built on this empire for European princes" (312). This was the end of what the white man had to offer the Americas, she thinks: "poison smog in the winter and choking clouds that swirled off sewage treatment leaching fields and filled the sky with fecal dust in the spring. Here was the place Marx had in mind as 'a place of human sacrifice'" (313). The phrase "place of human sacrifice" reiterates the connection that Silko makes repeatedly throughout all her writings between the violent blood worshipers of all cultures and social and ecological injustices.

Further exploring the question of where the earth and its people are headed, Silko writes that Old Yoeme believes that the "earth would have its ups and downs; but humans had been raping and killing their own nestlings at such a rate [that] humans might not survive" (718–19). Yoeme clearly understands that the earth has no stake in human survival. Therefore, those who cognitively, emotionally, and politically care for the beleaguered earth and its people will need to engage in innovative kinds of actions and practices. If, like Yoeme, Lecha, Zeta, and Angelita, we wish to make the middle place safer for both humans and nonhumans, then we must come together to articulate our various positions, negotiate, compromise, and seek better ways of interpreting the litany of voices in the natural world. By insisting that we must take seriously our responsibility to learn to converse with and respond to all the actors in an articulate world, Leslie Silko has created an unruly, uncategorizable almanac that provides us with a "place to see."

CHAPTER 7

Reinventing Nature

Leslie Marmon Silko's Critique of Euro-American "Nature Talk"

All around us we see life "dying back"—in nature, in our families, in society. Homo sapiens are literally killing their own seed and the seed of other life forms as well. One cause of this suicidal violence is greed. And that greed feeds on the philosophy that Earth is not our Mother, but an "it" that can be used and consumed. This philosophy even extends to the "conquest" of outer space. History shows that when the people in power call Earth "it," they consider all connected with her to be its, too—objects to be dominated, controlled, consumed, forgotten. Vanished. They are—*we* are—expendable.
—Marilou Awiakta, *Selu: Seeking the Corn Mother's Wisdom*

Every summer, on the first day of their six-week stay at the University of Arizona, the seventy-five students participating in the Med-Start Program not only unpack their suitcases and take a tour of the campus, but also take a short diagnostic writing test so their instructors will have a better sense of what skills they bring to their composition courses and what skills they need to improve. After administering this test for several years, I noticed a trend in the students' essays that I think is significant. Each year I asked students to write a brief, well-organized essay arguing the relative strengths and weaknesses of their local high schools. In the first years, most students, who were from rural areas and reservations, wrote essays criticizing high school administrators for not offering them the same college preparatory courses or honors courses offered to students from better-funded, urban high schools. But as the years went by, I noticed that students were becoming increasingly concerned about a single issue: violence. I read fewer essays focusing on scholastics and college preparation, and an increasing number of essays criticizing school administrators for not doing enough to keep students safe from classmates intent on bringing guns and knives to school. The recent mass murders in high schools across the United States illustrate that their fears were well founded.

After each of these mass murders, which have occurred in high schools attended by mostly white, middle-class students, there is a glut of media attention, an outpouring of national soul-searching. In contrast, little media attention has been focused on the steady increase in violence occurring in and around the high schools attended by students like the ones who participate in Med-Start. In the last decade, in South Tucson (a section of the city populated by mostly low-income, predominantly Mexican American, Native American, and African American people), many young people have lost their lives walking or driving to or from their schools, the victims of stray bullets or gang-related violence. But even if these children have absolutely no ties to a gang, the nation's attention is not focused on the problem, which gives one the sense that this violence is dismissed as inevitable and unpreventable, the irrational acts of a dispensable people.

This discrepancy raises several questions: Why is it that a barrage of media attention follows when white, middle-class suburban boys go on a rampage, killing in numbers that admittedly are larger than the random but repeated individual shootings that occur in and around high schools located in low-income neighborhoods? In the aftermath of an event such as the one that occurred at Columbine High School near Denver, Colorado, pundits point their fingers at the "culture of alienation" in the United States and talk of improving school curriculums, controlling guns, regulating the Internet, and installing V-chips on TVs.[1] But in the wake of violence that occurs in and around low-income, barrio, ghetto, or reservation schools in the United States, politicians talk about the need to crack down on tough teenage gangsters; sociologists blame negligent parents who fail to instill good values in their children; and police, prosecutors, and judges promise to make more arrests, prosecute more minors as adults, and send more teens to adult penal institutions.

Why are responses to violence in different places so different, and what has this to do with our concerns for the environment? In this chapter, I suggest that *Almanac of the Dead*—which author Leslie Marmon

Silko describes as an extended meditation on the "death orientation that . . . permeates the times we live in"[2]—offers some important insights into how we might answer these questions. By juxtaposing the story of Sterling, a Laguna Indian man who returns home to his Pueblo after many years away to find his people living amidst radioactive tailings piles and drinking contaminated water, and the story of Serlo, a wealthy white "scientist" building a steel-and-glass enclosure for endangered plants and animals, Silko explores the philosophical bases of environmental racism and implicitly suggests that those who wish to keep their children from becoming what she terms "Destroyers" must analyze and critique Euro-American discourses on nature that sanction the sacrifice of people and their surrounding environments.

Sterling's Exile and Return

As already noted, *Almanac of the Dead* immediately commanded the attention of the popular press when it was published in 1991. Some reviewers were optimistically puzzled, and others were scathingly critical. Elizabeth Tallent of the *New York Times* acknowledged that the novel is pervaded with bloody and violent images, but argued that it "is a form of meditation" on the "cruelty of contemporary America."[3] Alan Ryan of *USA Today,* whose review gave me much to discuss in the previous chapter and from which I tease out just a little more here, pulled out all the stops, warning readers to stay away from this "unholy mess" of narratives about "society's misfits: . . . rapists, murderers, gun-runners, people who make films of dissections and abortions, . . . and opportunistic real-estate developers."[4]

Ironically, by beginning his catalogue of Silko's "unholy" characters with rapists and ending with opportunistic real-estate developers, Ryan unwittingly links those who commit murder and sexual violence to those who do violence to the earth. This connection is exactly the one that Silko wants her readers to make. In a 1992 seminar, she explained that she wants readers to see rape and murder "side by side with what's been done to cultures and populations and geography."[5] Adding a personal note, she told seminar participants that the ten years she spent grappling with genocide and displacement and trying to understand how violence against people and the destruction of the environment "are intertwined" were extremely difficult for her both psychically and emotionally (52). After sending her manuscript off to the publisher, she tried to rest, to avoid television and newspapers, and to reestablish a sense of personal balance by "dragging out [her] Buddhism books" (21).

But, she said, "around the time . . . when I was reading Buddhism and . . . thinking about the larger picture and the long haul, almost as if in answer to me there was the killing of the [nine] Buddhists up near Phoenix, [Arizona]" (22).[6] The senseless execution-style murders, committed by two teenagers seeking to steal the monastery's rumored riches, confirmed for Silko what she had been thinking about while writing *Almanac of the Dead:* that we are living in a time of violence so pervasive that even our children are becoming "Destroyers," the term she uses in both *Ceremony* and *Almanac* to describe those whose greed drives them to justify bloodshed and destruction. The deaths of the Buddhist monks, observed Silko, illustrate that we "can't just closet ourselves with our Buddhist books and expect it to get any better. We need to try to find ways to deal with this violence and to try to see ways in which people can live though this . . . time of great, great upheaval" (22).

For many American Indian writers, understanding how one might live through this time of great upheaval involves a process of looking into what Joy Harjo calls a "terrifying abyss of violence and loss" to see where we have been and ascertain where we are going. Many Native writers depict this process in their poetry and fiction as the process of "coming home." A main protagonist—having been forcibly dispossessed or relocated or sent away to boarding school, or having been drafted to fight in a foreign war or forced by economic need to search for employment in places far from the reservation—must somehow resist oppressive practices, gather fragments of his or her traditional culture, and find his or her way home. For example, in Silko's first novel, *Ceremony,* the main protagonist, Tayo, joins the military and leaves Laguna Pueblo with his brother Rocky to fight in World War II. After surviving the Bataan Death March in the Philippines but seeing his brother lose his life, Tayo returns to the reservation and tries to make sense of the death and destruction he has witnessed. With the help of his grandmother and the medicine man, Betonie, he begins to gather fragments of his cultural and personal past and to put them together in ways that have meaning in the present. In the process, he comes to stand at the edge of a uranium mine, gazes into the terrifying abyss, and pieces together the strands of what he terms a "monstrous design"[7] of death and destruction: finally, he understands the connections between the historical oppression of his people, the mining of a deadly, yellow mineral, the work of scientists in a top-secret laboratory deep in the Jemez Mountains, the testing of a nuclear bomb at Trinity Site in New Mexico, and the incineration of twelve thousand Japanese people in two repulsively beautiful clouds of heat and light.

In *Almanac of the Dead,* Silko again uses the motif of a character returning home to Laguna Pueblo and finding himself drawn to the gaping abyss of the open-pit uranium mine near his village. Upon retiring from a job working for a railroad in Barstow, California, Sterling looks forward to spending his remaining years taking care of his ninety-year-old Aunt Marie. But shortly after his return, he runs afoul of the elders of his tribe when they ask him to oversee a Hollywood film crew that has come to shoot a movie near the Pueblo. Because of his years at the boarding school and his years of employment in California, Sterling does not clearly understand his tribe's culture and history. This lack of understanding leads him to unwittingly allow the movie crew to film a sandstone formation that has recently emerged from a tailings pile at the open-pit mine. Laguna villagers believe this formation to be the embodiment of Maahastryu, an ancient snake god who once lived in a beautiful lake near the Pueblo and protected the people and their water sources. The elders, who have long experience with the ways in which "anthropological research" and "scientific studies" are used to rob the tribe of sacred cultural artifacts or to justify the appropriation of their lands and resources, fear the possible outcome of the movie crew's activities. They see Sterling's mistake as one that may have terrible consequences for the tribe and for the sacred snake they are protecting because they believe it has returned to protect them and their natural resources. So the Tribal Council banishes Sterling from the Pueblo.

The year Sterling spends in exile in Tucson, Arizona, as the gardener for Lecha and Zeta, his twin Yaqui employers, forces him, first, to reexamine his own relationship to his culture and to the stories his Aunt Marie told him as a boy, and second, to confront the increasing social and environmental violence of the twentieth century. It is no accident that Sterling finally begins to gather fragments of his cultural past and to make them meaningful in his contemporary present while he is working as a gardener. As he rakes and digs in the soil that has become "almost a stranger to him," he smells breezes blowing off the blue mountain peaks surrounding the Yaqui sisters' ranch. He remembers that his aunt taught him that the sacred kachina gods visit humans in the form of rain clouds that can be smelled long before they are seen.[8] Bitterly, he blames his boarding school education and the U.S. government's Relocation Program for taking him to California in the 1950s and thus preventing him from learning more about "the kachinas and the ways to pray or greet the deer, other animals, and plants" (87).

While working the earth, his mind wanders back to the lifeways and stories of his ancestors, who cultivated corn, beans, and squash in flood-plain gardens located close to the place of emergence. He begins to see the connections between his separation from his people when he was a child and the inability of the few elderly people left in the village during the 1950s to stop the U.S. government from mining uranium near the Pueblo. "The old-timers had been dead set against ripping open Mother Earth so near to the holy place of emergence" (34), Sterling remembers, but a whole generation of young people torn away from their language, stories, and gardens by the boarding school system, the same generation who served the government as soldiers during World War II, "had come home looking for jobs, for a means to have some of the comforts they had enjoyed during their years away from the reservation" (34). Realizing their children could no longer survive in the U.S. market economy by means of their traditional subsistence farming practices, the "Tribal Council had gone along with the mine because the government gave them no choice, and the mine gave them jobs" (34). As a result, "They were the first of the Pueblos," Sterling observes, "to realize wealth from something terrible done to the earth" (34).

When Sterling returns home after his year of exile, he is compelled, as was Tayo, to crawl under the fence surrounding a multinational corporation's now abandoned uranium mine and to stand at the edge of the abyss. Everywhere he looks he sees virulently radioactive tailings that funnel and swirl in breezes carrying them to water sources once protected by Maahastryu. He remembers that when the government began sinking test holes in the fields where the Laguna people, acting in accordance with nature's patterns, were cultivating corn, squash, and chili, the old-timers protested, but scientists and government officials, positioning themselves as the perfectly objective representatives of nature, determined that in the interest of progress and development, the United States must cordon off Pueblo land so that clandestine testing could be conducted, and eventually the land could be opened up to extract uranium. The dangers of radiation contamination were already known at the time, but the U.S. government determined that the lives of desert-dwelling Pueblo people and the lands where they lived were dispensable.

U.S. history is replete with acts of state that sanction the targeting of a minority group within U.S. territory as dispensable. But since the 1980s, those incidences that involve the deliberate targeting of people-of-color communities for toxic waste facilities, mining, or heavy industry and the official sanctioning of the presence of life-threatening poisons such as radiation and other pollutants in communities inhabited by poor and minority peoples have come to be termed environmental racism. By juxtaposing Sterling's story of the U.S. government's deliberate sacrifice of his people and their gardens with Serlo's story of an elite group's secret scientific plan to protect rare plants and animals, Silko's wildly dystopian novel explicitly questions and critiques those Euro-American discourses on nature that are used to support and justify the practice of environmental racism. As I argue in the next section, the novel suggests that those who are interested in building a more socially and environmentally just world must understand and critique Western forms of "nature talk" that split humans from nature and environmental from social concerns.

Serlo and the Vivisectional Imperative

A distant cousin to the living kings of Europe, Serlo is raised in Columbia, the place to which his wealthy family fled after World War II. He heads a clandestine group dedicated to preserving the *"sangre pura"* or "blue (pure) blood" of a fast-disappearing European nobility (542). For that purpose, the group has established a "research institute" where they are busily freezing and storing the sperm of kings and aristocrats, and racing against time to research, design, and build "Alternative Earth Units," which will orbit high above the earth and be capable of remaining cut off from the upheaval and violence perpetrated by "swarms of brown people" who threaten those of "superior lineage" (543).

Serlo and his fellow "biosphere tycoons" conceive of the Alternative Earth Units as "orbiting paradise islands" where the richest people on Earth can "bail out of the pollution and revolutions" and retreat to glass-and-steel-enclosed rain forests filled with rare and endangered plants and animals (728). By referring to Serlo as a "biosphere tycoon," Silko clearly alludes to Biosphere 2, a glass-and-steel enclosure built in 1987 in the Sonoran Desert just north of Tucson, Arizona, by Texas billionaire Ed Bass and cofounder John Allen. In 1991, eight "biospherians" and thousands of rare and exotic plant and animal species from the rain forests, oceans, and deserts of the world were sealed into the enclosure to demonstrate how humans might survive if Earth, or "Biosphere 1," should become hopelessly contaminated. The biospherians and their "mission" captured the world's attention, but many questioned the value of the project given the frequently whispered rumor that Bass and Allen were simply rich, white, authoritarian cult leaders looking for a way to survive the coming environmental holocaust with a few chosen followers.[9]

Serlo's Alternative Earth Units clearly parody the glass-enclosed Biosphere 2 and at the same time allow Silko the opportunity to critique those Euro-American scientific and philosophic discourses on which mainstream environmentalists base their argument for creating wilderness preserves where some species are viewed as "contaminants" and targeted for removal, but other species are viewed as "endangered" and targeted for protection. Serlo's claim to be "protecting" the earth's scarce resources from swarms of brown people (728) also raises all sorts of questions about what and who counts as an endangered species and contests that form of Euro-American discourse that posits certain people as superior to nature but specifies "other" humans, usually humans of non-Caucasian ancestry, as part of nature and therefore less than human and expendable. This form of discourse, which environmental and cultural historian Giovanna Di Chiro terms Euro-American "nature talk," opposes an Edenic or sublime nature to a fallen culture, categorizing people of color as identical with nature, a move that throughout the colonial period entitled those of "superior lineage" to exploit and have dominion over "other" humans in the same way they claimed to have dominion over nature.[10]

By depicting Serlo's philosophies in such extreme terms, Silko leaves little doubt that she is critiquing romanticized discourses that characterize nature's "fallen children" as overbreeding, border-overflowing, slashing and burning, whale-killing, toxic, ecologically incorrect third worlders or illegal immigrants. Serlo's project to remove himself and his followers from an Earth "contaminated" by brown people may strike some readers as exaggerated and implausible, even for a novel, but Silko could not have more clearly articulated the contrasting view of many people of color whose forebears were removed from traditional homelands and who, as a result, may live in polluted and impoverished cities or rural areas. From the perspective of these people, the obsession with preserving biodiversity ignores the poverty and suffering of the poor and marginalized, and willfully obscures the history of colonization and its related social and environmental consequences.

The research institute in which Serlo and his followers are developing the technology to launch the Earth Unit into space also illustrates how the removal, displacement, or poisoning of humans is rooted in Euro-American forms of "nature talk" that construct nature as a "laboratory" in which man objectively performs experiments that teach him how to gain greater control over his environment. Serlo prides himself on embodying the objectivity of the scientist who exhibits complete indifference to "the fate of insignificant beings" (550). It does not bother him in the least that his subordinates are helping to finance his creation—a clean, well-ordered world—by selling police torture, live autopsy, and child pornography videos on the black market. Here, Silko explicitly calls attention to the ways in which scientific discourses empower, even mandate, the modern scientist, state, or multinational corporation to engage in what anthropologist Shive Visvanathan has called "social triage." As Visvanathan explains, *triage* is the silent term mediating between the still influential ideas of Francis Bacon, Rene Descartes, and Thomas Hobbes.[11]

Often referred to as the "father of modern science," Bacon envisioned the creation of "totally artificial environments created by and for humans" in which decisions would be made "for the good of the whole by scientists, whose judgment was to be trusted implicitly for they alone possessed the secrets of nature."[12] To Bacon's call for a state committed to science, Descartes put forward the notion of the scientist's need for complete objectivity and indifference. He assumed that a problem could be simplified by abstracting it from its complicating environmental context, then dividing it into as many parts as needed to resolve the problem, a notion he tested through the practice of vivisection. Indeed, he considered the dissection of living animals more enlightening than the study of conventional books. Thus, he gave vivisection—the inflicting of pain on "lesser animals" for the purpose of scientific research—its imprimatur.[13]

The philosophical foundation of the modern state committed to science was complete only with the work of Thomas Hobbes, who posited that nature was a state of anarchy, a chaos of meanings, emotions, and hallucinations, and that in a state of nature, man is an enemy to every other man. Hobbes believed that the new political and moral order could not be established until all dark places of sedition—including such unscientific and irrational beliefs and practices as primitive Christianity, Aristotelianism, witchcraft, occult sciences, and all other bacchanalia of the mythopoetic imagination—were eradicated. He defined progress linearly as a moving away from a past replete with seditious beliefs and practices, and toward modernity.[14]

As an experiment, argues Visvanathan, vivisection has inherent in it the idea of indifference, and "progress implies obsolescence. Triage interweaves these ideas as the obsolescence of those one is indifferent to" (48). Triage is a concept that has come to be associated with the sorting and allocation of treatment to patients on the battlefield according to a system of priorities designed to maximize the number of survivors. Examining how this concept is applied within the borders of the modern state committed to science and development, Visvanathan notes that nonscientific civilizations or tribal cultures come to be associated with the past. Set up to benefit an elite, progress-oriented culture and race, the state sorts out Others and judges them expendable based on a system of priorities that does not allow for the "treatment" of those categorized as incapable of progress. Because obsolescence is encoded in the notion of progress, the Other must either acculturate, assimilate, or disappear.

Silko puts her critique of the vivisectional imperative of the modern state in the mouth of an activist known as the Barefoot Hopi. Though he heads an organization with the primary goal of working to ensure the human rights of people being held in prisons all over the world, the Barefoot Hopi has formed an alliance with a radical environmentalist group whose objective is to fight large state and corporate development projects. If the goal of the environmental justice movement is to form activist alliances that critique modernist and colonial philosophies of unlimited progress, unchecked development, and the privileging of

Western scientific notions of objective truth and control of nature, then the Barefoot Hopi must certainly be considered an environmental justice activist, although Silko does not refer to him by that term.

In speeches he travels all over the world to deliver, he argues that the majority of those incarcerated in the world's prisons are people of color—a fact, he points out, not unconnected to environmental exploitation and degradation. Just as Serlo and his wealthy, white partners are seeking to remove the last of the earth's clean air and water, leaving the planet a virtual prison for people of color, European countries and the United States have been extracting natural resources from the homelands of indigenous people for more than five hundred years. The direct result has been the deaths of millions of people due to their removal and displacement. Those who survived have experienced the loss of their communities, cultures, languages, and homelands; as a result, they have experienced a disenabling alienation that sometimes leads to acts of violence or desperation judged "crimes" by the dominant culture. Thus, the history of colonization, the Barefoot Hopi concludes, factors heavily in the staggering numbers of people of color crowding prisons all over the world.

In his speeches and lectures, the Barefoot Hopi repeatedly raises these questions: Why are people of color imprisoned for acts of social violence that can be linked to their historical experiences with state-sanctioned removal and displacement when government officials and corporate executives are not jailed for the violent social upheaval caused by giant governmental and corporate development projects such as hydroelectric dams and their accompanying resettlement programs? Why are state and corporate executives never jailed for extracting uranium or constructing nuclear power plants, the operation of which poisons both human and nonhuman species for miles around the places in which they are operating? These projects, the Hopi insists, though cloaked in a rhetoric of scientific progress and development said to benefit "all of mankind," must be considered violent acts, even terrorism. "Poisoning our water with radioactive wastes, poisoning our air with military weapons' wastes—*those* are acts of terrorism! Acts of terrorism committed by governments against their [own] citizens" (734).

Although pointing to the state and corporation committed to scientific development and progress as the prime antiecological force in the world, the Hopi does not discount science or advocate that we all "go back to nature" or "precontact" times. The members of his alliance utilize computers, satellite dishes, and air travel in their struggle to protect their communities and environments. He understands that science and technology work extraordinarily well and effectively help humans meet many of the goals they set for themselves. However, by observing that nations all over the world are practicing social triage in the name of progress, he reveals that the problem with all hegemonic discourses—science, law, religion, philosophy, anthropology—is not the contents, methods, or concepts they produce but their effects once they are centralized, linked to institutions, and used to claim a mandate to set national borders, determine reservations boundaries, cordon off wilderness areas, or initiate massive development projects that displace or completely destroy entire communities.

The Oral Tradition and Alternate Visions of the Human/Nature Relationship

With the emergence of the sacred sandstone snake into the open-pit uranium mine, Silko symbolically represents place-based community resistance to the vivisectional imperative of the modern state and corporation. To a mining corporation executive, the snake might look like a simple sandstone formation, like any other in the desert Southwest, slowly emerging from the slag heap under which it has been buried as the wind blows tailings away from the mine toward the community and their water sources. But the shape and the color of the stone suggest to the Laguna people that the formation is Maahastryu, the water snake who once lived in a beautiful lake near the Laguna place of emergence. According to Laguna oral tradition, the snake took care of the community and protected their water sources. But neighbors jealous of the Laguna's peaceful, healthful existence disturbed the sacred snake, and it disappeared, leaving only a dry lake bed.

The implication of the neighbors' actions is that when greed or jealousy drives people in the pursuit of their own interests, they exhibit little respect for the sacred and accept no responsibility for their own communities or for the surrounding environments. The emergence of Maahastryu is an implicit criticism of the actions of a mining corporation that puts its own greedy pursuit of profit before any concern for the health of the community. Like the neighbors in the story, these corporate "neighbors" deliberately fail to acknowledge that the activities conducted at the mine will have an impact on the community in which the mine is located.

Juxtaposed with the story of Serlo, the story of the sandstone snake also draws attention to the ways in which Serlo and his group are caught up in a greedy pursuit of their own interests. Although couching their professed interest in the environment in the scientific language of endangered species, they refuse to give up any of the comforts or luxuries they enjoy, thus failing to acknowledge the ways in which their own existence contributes to the impoverishment and extinction of other human and nonhuman species and to the degradation of the environment. Their project enacts a kind of Cartesian vivisection because it abstracts a single environmental issue—saving endangered species— from its surrounding contexts, cloaking the profound historical interconnections among human and nonhuman species, and obscuring the related social and environmental problems that contribute to the destruction of all species, including humans.

By exposing the historical and ecological effects on humans and the nonhuman world of dominant ideologies that invent nature as a place where some humans are separate from and superior to Others, and as a laboratory in which Man may inflict pain on "lesser animals" in the interest of "progress," Maahastryu's emergence offers an alternate vision of what might constitute proper human/environment interrelations and practices. The snake suggests that it is unwise, even immoral, to separate the nonhuman natural world from the nonnatural human community. The story of Maahastryu clearly illustrates that everything humans do affects every other living thing in the community. If out of jealousy or greed you do something harmful to the environment, you might lose a valuable resource, and the entire community—including plants, animals, and humans—will suffer.

Stories about the snake also symbolically illustrates that for the Laguna, ideas about nature cannot be separated from ideas of community, history, ethnic identity, and cultural survival. Silko is not implying that by learning stories from the oral tradition we will all be inspired to cease our polluting ways and live ecologically ever after. Everything she has ever written conveys a sense of how monumental the task of fighting the vivisectional imperative of the Destroyers will be. Rather, she is imaginatively illustrating that the power of the oral tradition lies in the way the stories confront and critique Euro-American forms of nature talk by intimately associating nature with everyday social and cultural life.

The story of Maahastryu suggests that we will not solve the historical problems of particular Euro-American capitalist dominations of nature by saving a rare bird here or an exotic fish there or by removing humans as "contaminants" from the few remaining spaces of relatively intact wilderness left on earth. Rather, if we want to solve our most complex environmental problems, we must critique those forms of nature talk that support and justify environmental racism; we must also recognize our connections and responsibilities to our natural and social communities.

A Model for Community Activism

While she was growing up, Silko observed how the notion of community conveyed in stories from the oral tradition might have implications in the contemporary world. At her government-run day school, she was separated from the Keresan language of her grandmother and aunts by teachers who insisted that Laguna culture was obsolete and that progress demanded assimilation. But, as she mentioned in the "Poetics and Politics" seminar, at home she was continually surrounded by people "talking and telling, relating incidents and stories" from the ancient oral traditions, from Laguna historical and cultural experiences, and from everyday occurrences in the community. The stories her relatives were telling, however, were often focused on the "fact that their land had been stolen" (23). Silko later learned that her father and Aunt Susie, among others, were telling and retelling these stories not only because they were entertaining and laden with cultural information, but because they were gathering evidence to support the Laguna community's legal claims to the lands where they had lived for hundreds of years.

Before the United States Congress approved the creation of the Indian Claims Commission in August 1946, no tribe could bring a land-claim suit against the United States without special permission from Congress. But after the commission began its proceedings in the 1950s, people from many diverse cultures and various professions—lawyers, folklorists, anthropologists, tribal storytellers, and healers, among others—came together to create the documents that would establish each tribe's claim to its traditional lands. Silko's father and Aunt Susie were two of the people working with the Indian Claims Commission to gather stories about the place of emergence; about ancient shrines; about the places where the people lived, planted corn, hunted, and worked. Once incorporated in official U.S. government reports, these stories became the crucial foundation of the Laguna peoples' land suits against the U.S. government, the state of New Mexico, and others who had unjustly appropriated their land (24–25).[15]

Listening to her relatives tell stories and talk about the court proceedings, Silko learned that the old stories were not just incidentally entertaining; they "were important in terms . . . of getting the land back" (24). But in illustrating how like and unlike people could come together to form a community (though contingent and based on the issue at hand), the Indian Claims Commission proceedings also present a model for the kinds of community-based activism that might be utilized in the fight against the vivisectional imperative of state and corporation.

Silko incorporates the insight she gained from her father's and Aunt Susie's involvement in the Indian Claims Commission proceedings into the International Holistic Healers Convention at the end of *Almanac of the Dead*. The convention is attended by people of all races and cultures who are members of different groups and various backgrounds and professions. They are all interested in working for better communities and in protecting the environment, but because of their different cultural histories and experiences, they have no natural or immediate bond. Many are even suspicious of some of the others' motives and political views, and question whether or not there can be a positive outcome to the proceedings. Silko implies that if they want to succeed in achieving a set of agreed-upon goals, they will need to tackle the hard work of trying to understand one another's specific social and environmental experiences. Just as the Barefoot Hopi's organization finds common cause with a radical environmentalist group, the diverse peoples attending the Holistic Healers Convention must find common ground, a middle place, by framing their different experiences in ways that mobilize them to work together.

Silko does not depict the outcome of the convention and does not speculate about whether or not a socially and environmentally just society is even possible, but the novel clearly indicates that "working for the environment" cannot simply mean working for endangered species. Working for the environment must mean working with interested others for the entire social and biophysical community. A first step in that direction would require us to gain an understanding of how particular Euro-American discourses on nature have brought us to this point and how the discourses of Others might offer alternatives. We must stand at the edge of the abyss of genocide, massive displacements, and species extinction, and try to understand how social and environmental injustices are connected. Then we must go home to the places where we live, work, and play, roll up our sleeves, and get to work.

Cultivating Community in the Middle Place

In essays decrying the increasing violence in and around their high schools, many of the Med-Start students I worked with for many years called on their school administrators to build fences around the perimeters of the schoolyard or to install metal detectors at the entrances to their schools. They insisted that more and better college-prep courses could not help them gain entrance into U.S. institutions of higher learning if they were so worried about violence inside and outside the school that they couldn't concentrate on their studies. But as the killing of the Buddhist monks and the shooting of thirteen innocent people at Columbine High School illustrate, we are living in a time of such great upheaval that our children themselves are becoming Destroyers, and there are few, if any, places safe from violence.

As we move into a new century, it is time to acknowledge that cordoning off barrios, ghettos, and reservations will not render white middle-class neighborhoods safer from crime and that removing humans as contaminants from wilderness will not necessarily move us closer to a sustainable future. If we want to give our children the bright futures they are asking us for, we will need to do more than build fences around our neighborhoods, install metal detectors at the entrances of schools, and establish wilderness areas for endangered species.

Much has been made of the fact that the young shooters at Columbine High School were loners, alienated from their high school peers and from their community. In *Almanac of the Dead,* the Barefoot Hopi addresses the subject of alienation, and his observations have some relevance to this horrifying incident. For five hundred years in the Americas, he explains, the indigenous peoples who survived genocide and disease experienced a profound sense of loss as a result of being removed from their homelands, detached from their communities, and forced to live in impoverished, often polluted environments where hopelessness produced a disenabling sense of alienation.

The Hopi's words resonate with media pronouncements, following the school massacres, about the "culture of alienation" in the United States. I cannot pretend to know the motivations of teenage boys who take the lives of innocent people, and certainly I am not excusing what they did, but it might be worth speculating about the environment in which these boys live, one so impoverished by the demands of capitalist market forces that children rarely have extended families close by, feel little connection to their communities, know little about the natural world from which all the materials of their survival derive, and have no developed sense of place. However, these children are exposed daily to violence in the media and can easily access information on the Internet about how to make bombs. *Almanac of the Dead* makes much of the fact that the majority of mass murderers in the United States have been of Euro-American descent, and there is a sense in the novel of "chickens coming home to roost" in a culture that justifies violence in the language of science and that breeds alienation on a massive scale while calling it "progress."

Sterling's return to his home and to the gaping abyss where the Pueblo people once cultivated corn and chili suggests that if we want to build a better future, we must reinterpret and reinvent nature and the environment to mean something that looks more like a Pueblo garden, that place where community members move from one field to the next helping each other ready the soil for planting. What makes this environment so rich and hopeful is the deeply felt sense of connection between the people and the land, and the strong sense of community and place they develop in working with the earth and with each other to provide for their children and to ensure their own survival. Perhaps we caught a glimpse of this kind of community building in the protests held after the Columbine shootings on the Capitol steps in Washington, D.C., and at the National Rifle Association's 1999 National Convention. Like gardeners, parents, activists, and concerned others from all across the country were coming together to protest violence and, hopefully, to transform their environment in positive ways; in the process, they were extending their sense of alliance and connection beyond the boundaries of their local communities.

As we move into the twenty-first century, pundits are suggesting that gun control could be a "hot-button" election issue as Americans begin seeing their own children as an endangered species and begin caring more about their communities than they do about an individuals' right to keep and bear arms. If this happens, it could be a small step toward ending the violence that now seems so much a part of modern existence. Certainly, when children are destroying children, it is time to gaze into the abyss, make some connections, and come home to the middle place.

Conclusion

To San Simon and Back

Everywhere it was green. They grew flowers and vegetables. And
oh! the flowers! The perfume was everywhere in the summer
breezes. His father, Don Enrique, sold vegetables from a cart. All
of us children would run after the cart. He gave us free sugar cane.
Now the river is dry. The milpas are gone and the people are gone.
(The river had water then! Can you believe the Santa Cruz had
water?!)
—Patricia Preciado Martin, "The Journey,"
Days of Plenty, Days of Want

At the end of our day teaching at Tohono O'odham High School,
Adrienne and I walked to our car conscious of a palpable silence. There
is a quiet that blankets the saguaro forest in the late afternoon, but in
San Simon it is punctuated with the calls of cactus wren and quail and
the voices of school children running to catch their buses. Two hours
later, after passing Baboquivari Peak and crossing the bridge on Ajo
Way over the dry bed of the Río Santa Cruz, we drove into South
Tucson, which was alive with the noise and motion of rush-hour traffic.
From there, we turned onto Interstate 10 and passed by the downtown
Convention Center. I can never pass this place without thinking of
Patricia Preciado Martin's short story "The Journey." Preciado Martin
writes of a woman who meets her aged *tía* at the Martin Luther King Jr.
Apartments, a public-housing unit for the elderly. After visits to a cherished cathedral and a small, neighborhood grocery, they walk by the
new Convention Center. Standing in the middle of the asphalt parking
lot, the aunt points to the ground and says to her niece, "*Aquí estaba mi
casita*. Here was my little house. . . . I was born here. It was a good house,
a strong house. When it rained, the adobes smelled like the good clean

earth." Then, looking toward the dry riverbed, the elderly woman muses about her neighbor Don Enrique, who once terraced the banks of the Santa Cruz to grow vegetables and flowers. Almost as if she does not believe it herself, she says, "The river had water then. Can you believe the Santa Cruz had water?!"[1]

Don Enrique's small, terraced *milpa* connects Preciado Martin's story to other multicultural works (such as Simon Ortiz's *Fight Back,* Rudolfo Anaya's *Bless Me, Ultima,* and most recently, Leslie Marmon Silko's *Gardens in the Dunes*) in which the garden is a powerful symbol not only of nature but of livelihood or the right of humans to derive a living from the earth. This perspective has been largely silenced in mainstream environmentalism as a result of an unequal distribution of power in society that favors certain social constructions of nature at the expense of others. Mainstream environmentalism often treats nature more like a wilderness where humans are intruders than like a garden where humans are an active and appropriate part of nature. By incorporating the garden into their work, multicultural writers confront and problematize the dichotomization of people and nature that pervades contemporary environmentalism and much American nature writing. They also illustrate that there are kinds and degrees of use: Don Enrique's vegetables and flowers help sustain a community, whereas the Convention Center and its parking lot are part of and help to authorize patterns of use that contribute to widespread environmental degradation.

The garden metaphor is not necessarily a romanticization of earlier, simpler times. It is often a powerful symbol of political resistance. Preciado Martin's story, for example, emerges from the dust that settled over Tucson in the 1950s and 1960s, when Mexican American barrios were condemned and bulldozed so that Interstate 10 and the Tucson Convention Center could be built. Residents of the barrios, among the most impoverished in Tucson, were relocated away from their homes and gardens to the southside of the city near the airport and heavy industry. These were the same years that Tucson, which is completely dependent on groundwater wells, pumped its water table so low that the Río Santa Cruz sank into the ground and disappeared. Once the water was gone, the towering cottonwoods and the song sparrows that had sheltered in the canopy disappeared along with the gardens. Today, when you stand on the edge of a once docile Santa Cruz and look down, the banks are steep and in many places lined with concrete in order to contain the roaring torrents of water that occasionally rush by the Convention Center after heavy summer rains. Once, monsoon floods were controlled by the cottonwoods and other vegetation growing along the riverbanks, but now torrential rains race over miles of paved surfaces in downtown Tucson and surge angrily into a deeply eroded and still eroding riverbed.

By 1981, the Mexican American people that Preciado Martin writes about had suffered a two-fold tragedy. At the same time that their barrios were being demolished and that the gardens and cottonwoods were disappearing, groundwater wells located in South Tucson were being contaminated with high levels of trichloroethylene, or TCE, a toxic industrial cleaning solvent used by Hughes Missile Systems Company. The people were never adequately compensated for their barrio homes and then, after being moved to neighborhoods near Hughes, were exposed to toxic chemicals that had been released for decades into the open environment and allowed to seep into the aquifer.[2] Twenty years later, in the 1970s and 1980s, when increasing numbers of people living near Hughes began experiencing high rates of cancer, birth defects, and genetic mutations, the Environmental Protection Agency discovered TCE in the people's tap water and traced the contamination to wells fed from a massive plume of groundwater that spans the distance between the Hughes plant and the bridge on Ajo Way over the Santa Cruz.

Consequently, the people of South Tucson are connected to the people of Sells and San Simon by more than just Ajo Way. Indeed, Ajo Way might be read as a symbol of the jarring connection between social inequities and environmental degradation in rural and urban areas: both occur most often in the places inhabited by the poor and marginalized. The problems experienced by southside barrios of Tucson, the communities of the Tohono O'odham Nation, the Black Mesa community on the Navajo Nation, and the Acoma and Laguna Pueblos in the Four Corners Area (and even further south, the Mayan peoples living in the great Lacandon rain forest) illustrate how the support and maintenance of social inequities undermine the environment by creating sacrifice zones where it is considered acceptable to discount people and poison the earth. But since the 1980s, the people of these communities have been rising up, forming small place-based alliances with a larger international movement, and demanding an end to interconnected social and environmental injustices. This movement found its way to

Tucson when lawyers for the grassroots, community-led group Tucsonans for a Clean Environment filed a lawsuit against Hughes Missile Systems on behalf of southside residents who had been exposed to TCE-contaminated water. In June 1991, they won their case, with Hughes settling out of court for $84.5 million, a sum currently being used to fund neighborhood centers and health clinics.[3]

Preciado Martin writes that when the niece points out a flower growing up through the asphalt of the Convention Center parking lot, the elderly woman declares that, now, her niece has discovered the secret of their journeys. "What's the secret, Tía?" her niece asks. Her aunt replies, "*Que las flores siempre ganan.* The flowers always win" (65). Both the aunt's weekly return to the place of her birth and the flower that recalls Don Enrique's garden make the Mexican American experience in South Tucson the ground for critique of dominant institutions and ideologies that are detrimental particularly to communities of the poor and working classes and to people of color. Like the American Indian literature that has been the focus of this study, Preciado Martin's story illustrates that when we put aside strict generic conventions about what counts as nature writing or environmental literature, we discover that writers of diverse ethnic, racial, and class backgrounds are making interconnected social and environmental issues the focus of their poetry, fiction, and creative nonfiction.

In many of these works, the garden becomes a metaphor for the values and concerns of multicultural groups that fall outside mainstream American environmentalism. However, I do not think that multicultural writers are urging readers to shift their energies from one landscape to another—from the wilderness to the garden. As Simon Ortiz's, Leslie Silko's, and Ofelia Zepeda's work illustrates, not all of nature is wilderness, but not all is garden either. The Sonoran Desert, which is the setting for Zepeda's poetry, for instance, is a continuum of landscapes, from a college campus to thoroughly humanized areas where people raise livestock or grow gardens, to exploited areas where people extract minerals, and to barely humanized reaches of saguaro, ironwood, and desert poppy.

Rather than calling for the creation of literal gardens, the garden metaphor calls our attention to the world as a middle place, a contested terrain in which dispute arises from divergent cultural ideas on what nature is and should be, and on what the human role in nature is and should be. Like the garden where the gardener endeavors to understand how nature's large-scale patterns work in specific places, multicultural writers are inviting readers into an ever-widening discussion focusing on the large-scale economic, political, cultural, historical, ecological, and spiritual forces affecting both the places where people live and where they do not. The garden metaphor calls us to an awareness that if we want to work toward the creation of a more livable world, we must assess, understand, and critique these forces; come together to discuss differently situated human practices and perspectives on nature; and arrive at some consensus (however contingent and based on local people, situations, and places) about what our role in nature will be.

As Silko shows in her depiction of the International Holistic Healers Convention, the world is so fraught with divergent interests and un-equal allocations of power that coming to any kind of consensus about human relation to the natural world will not be easy. But if, as I and other critics have argued, environmental crisis involves a crisis of the imagination, then writers, teachers, environmentalists, and literary and cultural critics have a key role to play in these conversations and debates. But to enter these conversations and to work effectively for transforma-tive change, they must have a clear sense of who they are writing and working for so that they can speak intelligibly to their audience(s). As the writers of the Popol Vuh suggest, those who speak only to others like themselves are rarely heard, and their work might ultimately be washed away with the first rain.

Demographers tell us that by the year 2020, the face of America will look something like the faces of the diverse American Indian, Mexican, African, Asian, Anglo, and Other American students who were mem-bers of my Med-Start classes. If we determine that we are writing and working for this diverse audience, for the places in which they/we live, *and* for the treasured, barely humanized places where they/we do not live, then that determination must guide the orientation we take in our creative, critical, pedagogical, and activist work. It must also determine the language we use and the purpose for which our work is intended.

This book has been an experiment in opening up the newly emerging field of ecocriticism to the voices, challenges, and imaginative visions of the multicultural students with whom I work and of the multi-cultural writers whose poetry, fiction, and creative nonfiction we read. My weekly trips with Adrienne took me outside the campus gates and into some of the landscapes and communities where they live. When I returned, I returned with the insights and experiences my journeys afforded me. Like the gardener who sees humans as an active and appropriate part of nature, I have conceived of my experiences as an appropriate element of my literary and cultural analysis, and have made them the ground for critique of dominant institutions and ideologies that authorize interrelated social and environmental injustices. It is my hope that I have created a place to see or a middle place, where writers, academics, teachers, students, activists, and members of their communities are free to travel back and forth from the official landscape to the vernacular, from the universal to the local, from scholarship to narrative, and from theory to practice. My goal has been to theorize a way of reading that provides us with the tools we need for building a more satisfying multicultural ecocriticism and a more inclusive, multicultural environmentalism that can be united with other social movements to create a more liveable world for humans and nonhumans alike.

Notes

Where clear in the text, subsequent references to cited sources are given parenthetically by page number.

Introduction: Entering the Middle Place

1. In their own language, the Navajo people call themselves *Diné,* which means "the people," and I use that term when referring to them. Formerly known as the Papago, the tribe whose homelands are located to the southwest of Tucson, Arizona, recently reclaimed their identity as the Tohono O'odham or Desert People. The terms *Native American, native,* and *Indian* are heavily laden with colonial history and political controversy. Joy Harjo and Gloria Bird note in *Reinventing the Enemy's Language* that *Native American* is a term invented in academe to replace *American Indian.* They write that in "our communities we first name ourselves by tribe, but the general term commonly used is *Indian* in the United States" (20). Some American Indian authors—Simon Ortiz, for example—do use the term *Native American.* Throughout the introductory essay of *Woven Stone,* Ortiz uses the term *Native American* when referring to Indian people as an increasingly empowered political group and *Native American literature* when referring to the growing body of poetry, fiction, and nonfiction by Indian writers. In this book, I use *Indian* or specific tribal names when referring to individual students or authors, *American Indian* when referring to groups that include more than one tribal group, and *Native American* when making references to the academic fields of Native American studies or Native American literature.

2. Chavis is quoted in Giovanna Di Chiro, "Nature as Community," 304.

3. Di Chiro, "Nature as Community," 306. All seventeen Principles of Environmental Justice are reprinted in this article.

4. Scott Slovic, "Ecocriticism: Storytelling, Values, Communication, Contact."

The Road to San Simon:
Toward a Multicultural Ecocriticism

1. The Tohono O'odham recently took a term from their own language—*Tohono O'odham* or "Desert People"—as their official tribal name.

2. Private communication with Claudia Nelson, program coordinator of the University of Arizona's American Indian Studies Office of Community Development.

3. James S. Griffith, *Beliefs and Holy Places,* 14.

4. Laura Coltelli, "Interview with Joy Harjo," in *Winged Words,* 64.

5. Griffith, *Beliefs and Holy Places,* 17.

6. Kent C. Ryden, *Mapping the Invisible Landscape,* 45.

7. Terry Tempest Williams, *An Unspoken Hunger,* 116.

8. See Gary Nabhan, "The Creosote Bush Is Our Drugstore," in *Gathering the Desert,* 11–19.

9. Ofelia Zepeda, "Bury Me with a Band," in *Ocean Power: Poems from the Desert,* 40.

10. Cheryll Glotfelty, "Introduction: Literary Studies in an Age of Environmental Crisis," in *The Ecocriticism Reader,* ed. Cheryll Glotfelty and Harold Fromm, xix.

11. Glen Love, "Revaluing Nature: Toward an Ecological Criticism," 230.

12. Patrick Murphy, *Literature, Nature, and Other,* 127. Murphy accuses the editors of *On Nature: Nature, Landscape, and Natural History* (Daniel Halpern), *This Incomparable Lande: A Book of American Nature Writing* (Thomas Lyon), and *The Norton Book of Nature Writing* (Robert Finch and John Elder) of "literary genocide." He concedes that the editors would "deny that they ever intended anything of the sort, and I would believe them. I am not speaking of the intentions of these men, but of the effects of their decisions on the perceptions and understanding of their audiences in the increasing number of nature writing courses that are being taught around the country" (127).

13. See both "Voicing Another Nature" and "Let the Survivors of Contact Speak," in Murphy, *Literature, Nature, and Other,* especially 125–29.

14. Terry Tempest Williams, *Refuge: An Unnatural History of Family and Place,* 287.

15. Lawrence Buell, *The Environmental Imagination,* 2.

16. O'odham villages could once be found as far north as the Gila River near Phoenix, as far east as the Santa Cruz River near Tucson, as far south as

Pitiquito in Sonora, Mexico, and as far west as the Colorado River near Yuma. See Griffith, *Beliefs and Holy Places,* 14–30.

17. In 1951, the Tohono O'odham petitioned the federal Indian Claims Commission for compensation for lands wrongly taken from them. In 1976, the tribe accepted $26 million for the lost lands. For more about copper mining on Arizona reservation lands, see Winona LaDuke and Ward Churchill, "Native America: The Political Economy of Radioactive Colonialism," 108.

18. William Kitteridge, *Owing It All,* 156–57.

19. Sherman Alexie's character Adrian should not be confused with my friend and colleague Adrienne.

20. Sherman Alexie, "Imagining the Reservation," in *The Lone Ranger and Tonto Fistfight in Heaven,* 49.

21. James S. Griffith, "Native Christianities," in *Beliefs and Holy Places,* 75–76 and 85–87. Although the relationships between the archaeological Hohokam—whose ceremonies were derived from central Mexico and who lived for several hundred years in the regions now occupied by the Desert People—and the living Tohono O'odham have not been settled to the satisfaction of most archaeologists, Griffith speculates that in practicing their traditional folk Catholicism, the "Tohono O'odham may be keeping faith with a very ancient part of their heritage" (87).

Abbey's Country: Desert Solitaire and the Trouble with Wilderness

1. Edward Abbey, *Desert Solitaire,* 4.

2. Black Mesa sits at the center of what has been termed the Navajo-Hopi Land Dispute, a one-hundred-year-old controversy over land granted by the federal government to the Hopi people because of their longer tenure on the land, but previously inhabited by both peoples for hundreds of years. I do not intend to discuss this controversial and complex issue at length, but it is the Dinéh Alliance's position that what has been represented as a dispute between Diné and Hopi peoples "turns out to be a commercial hunt for the natural resources in the area." In other words, they believe there would be no dispute if the intense competition for natural resources in the area did not pit one tribal government against the other over the issues of mineral leases and annual royalties to the two tribes from the proceeds of Peabody's Black Mesa mine. See "Dinéh Alliance Press Statement" and "Black Mesa Decision."

3. All information in this chapter about the residents of Black Mesa and their experiences with the Peabody Coal mine are based on conversations, from 1991 to 1999, with Michelle and Alexandra Tsosie, Diné sisters who live at Rough

Rock, located near the base of Black Mesa, and with other former students in my freshman composition courses. I also base my discussion of the mine's effects on Black Mesa community members' health on an interview conducted on 12 February 1999 with Carl Etsitty, a Black Mesa resident who recently graduated from the University of Arizona with a master's degree in environmental science. All Etsitty's brothers work at the mine, and as a Peabody scholarship recipient, he has worked for Peabody, testing groundwater in the area for toxicity levels.

4. Abbey, *Desert Solitaire,* 42.

5. Don Scheese, *"Desert Solitaire,"* in *The Ecocriticism Reader,* ed. Glotfelty and Fromm, 306.

6. William Cronon, "The Trouble with Wilderness," 76.

7. Peter Wild, "Edward Abbey: The Middle Class Maverick," 18.

8. Simon Ortiz, introduction to *Woven Stone,* 188. All Ortiz quotes in this chapter are from *Woven Stone,* a University of Arizona Press reprint of Ortiz's *Going for the Rain, A Good Journey,* and *Fight Back.*

9. Scott Slovic, *Seeking Awareness,* 18.

10. For a discussion of indigenous Kayapo people and their use of fire in the Amazon rain forest, see Susanna Hecht and Alexander Cockburn, *The Fate of the Forest.* In "Whose Nature?" James Proctor observes that the Pacific Northwest "was shaped to some extent by the land-use practices of Native Americans long before Europeans arrived; for example, their common practice of burning grasslands often prevented incursion of the forest into the river valley floors" (276). In "Human Impacts on Arizona Grasslands," Conrad Bahre notes that "The accidental or intentional commuting of fire to the grasslands by Amerindians—through fire drives, mescal roasting, smoke signals, abandoned campfires, fire during warfare, and so forth—may have contributed to the largely brush-free state of the grasslands when the first Europeans arrived" (234–35).

11. E. Adamson Hoebel, "Zia Pueblo," 407–8.

12. Leslie Marmon Silko, "Interior and Exterior Landscapes: The Pueblo Migration Stories," 37.

13. Each culture refers to the place of emergence and the place where they established their village by a different names. In their emergence story, Zuni Pueblo storytellers often refer to the place where they established their first village and where they planted corn for the first time as the "Middle Place"; see Dennis Tedlock, trans., "The Beginning," in *Finding the Center,* 275–98. According to Simon Ortiz, the Acoma refer to the place where they established themselves on a high mesa, one of the oldest continuously inhabited cities in North America, as "Which Is Prepared," see *Woven Stone,* 338.

14. Alvin M. Josephy Jr., "The Murder of the Southwest," 55.

15. Carl Etsitty, personal interview by the author, Tucson, Arizona, 12 Feb. 1999.

16. In *Woven Stone*, 289.

Simon Ortiz's Fight Back: *Environmental Justice, Transformative Ecocriticism, and the Middle Place*

1. See "Black Mesa Decision."

2. Carl Etsitty, personal interview by the author, Tucson, Arizona, 12 Feb. 1999.

3. Simon Ortiz, introduction to *Woven Stone*, 31. All quotations from Ortiz in this chapter are from *Woven Stone*.

4. Richard White, "Are You an Environmentalist, or Do You Work for a Living?" 175.

5. Michael Pollan, *Second Nature*, 214.

6. William Cronon, "The Trouble with Wilderness," 89.

7. For discussion of place as "space humanized," see Edward Relph's *Place and Placelessness* and Yi-Fu Tuan's *Space and Place: The Perspective of Experience*.

8. Kent Ryden, *Mapping the Invisible Landscape*, 38.

9. Lawrence Buell, *The Environmental Imagination*, 261, 264.

10. David Harvey, *Justice, Nature, and the Geography of Difference*, 303.

11. This is Benjamin Chavis's definition, quoted in Giovanna Di Chiro, "Nature as Community," 304. For more about the three incidents of environmental racism I discuss, see Di Chiro, "Nature as Community," 303–9, and Harvey, *Justice, Nature, and the Geography of Difference*, 369–71.

12. Don Scheese, *"Desert Solitaire,"* 318.

13. Qtd. by Harvey in *Justice, Nature, and the Geography of Difference*, 357.

14. Kent Ryden, "Landscape with Figures," 24.

Cultural Critique and Local Pedagogy: A Reading of Louise Erdrich's Tracks

1. The Med-Start Program—which works to increase the number of minority and economically disadvantaged students in medical schools and, ultimately, the number of health professionals on reservations and in rural areas of Arizona—has been sponsored by the University of Arizona's College of Medicine for close to thirty years. I supervised the composition instructors and writing tutors for this program from 1990 to 1997. During those years, some of the writers who accepted invitations to speak to Med-Start students as part of the English Department's annual Summer Multicultural Writers Series (in addi-

tion to those already mentioned) included Ai, Gloria Bird, Pat Mora, Denise Chávez, Louis Owens, Janice Gould, Greg Sarris, Luci Tapahonso, and Demetria Martinez.

2. See John Brinckerhoff Jackson, *Discovering the Vernacular Landscape.*

3. See Eric Zencey's discussion of cosmopolitanism and the role that "rootless professors" play in educating us away from place in *Virgin Forest,* 60–71.

4. Houston A. Baker Jr., "Local Pedagogy; or, How I Redeemed My Spring Semester," 402.

5. See Gloria Anzaldúa, "*Haciendo caras, una endrada:* An Introduction," in *Making Face, Making Soul,* ed. Gloria Anzaldúa, especially xxiii, xxv; and Barbara Christian, "The Race for Theory," 335.

6. Teresa L. Ebert, "Ludic Feminism, the Body, Performance, and Labor," 7.

7. Barbara Christian, "The Race for Theory," 336.

8. Interview with Laura Coltelli in *Winged Words,* 47.

9. The Chippewa are also called the *Ojibwa* but are more correctly called *Anishinabeg,* which is a collective name referring to those who speak the same woodland language. See Gerald Vizenor, *The People Named the Chippewa,* 13. In this chapter, I use *Chippewa* because that is the term Erdrich uses in *Tracks.*

10. Kay Bonnetti, "An Interview with Louise Erdrich and Michael Dorris," 98.

11. Ruth Landes, *Ojibwa Religion and the Midewiwin,* 199.

12. Louise Erdrich, *Tracks,* 18.

13. A. Irving Hallowell, "Ojibway Ontology, Behavior, and World View," 173; also see Mary Douglas, *Purity and Danger,* 90–91.

14. Hallowell, "Ojibwa Ontology, Behavior, and World View," 172, 173.

15. Richard M. Dorson, *Bloodstoppers and Bearwalkers,* 27.

16. Nancy Hartsock, "Rethinking Modernism: Minority vs. Majority Theories," 206.

17. I discuss and document the experience of Tucson's Mexican American communities with toxic contamination of the aquifer at more length in the conclusion of this book.

And the Ground Spoke: Joy Harjo and the Struggle for a Land-Based Language

1. Laura Coltelli, "Louise Erdrich and Michael Dorris," in *Winged Words,* 47.

2. See Kirk Kickingbird and Lynn Kickingbird's "A Short History of Indian Education" (Parts I and II).

3. Simon Ortiz, reading for "Poetics and Politics," 7. Ortiz made the statement quoted here in a seminar conducted by Larry Evers and Ofelia Zepeda at

the University of Arizona, Tucson, Arizona. I am quoting from the as yet unpublished and unedited transcript.

4. Simon Ortiz, "Towards a National Indian Literature," 10.

5. Ibid.

6. Coltelli, "Simon Ortiz," in *Winged Words,* 110.

7. Coltelli, "Louise Erdrich and Michael Dorris," in *Winged Words,* 47.

8. Kay Bonnetti, "An Interview with Louise Erdrich and Michael Dorris," 87.

9. Muriel Saville-Troike, *The Ethnography of Communication,* 51, 53, 85, 86.

10. Coltelli, "Joy Harjo," in *Winged Words,* 62; Joseph Bruchac, *Songs from This Earth on Turtle's Back,* 92.

11. Joy Harjo, seminar discussion for "Poetics and Politics," 11. Harjo made the statement quoted here in a seminar conducted by Larry Evers and Ofelia Zepeda at the University of Arizona, Tucson, Arizona. I am quoting from the as yet unpublished and unedited transcript.

12. Mikhail Bakhtin, *The Dialogic Imagination,* 294.

13. Coltelli, "Simon Ortiz," 105.

14. Coltelli, "Simon Ortiz," 104–5; Ortiz, "Poetics and Politics," 9.

15. Ortiz, "Towards a National Indian Literature," 10.

16. Coltelli, "Simon Ortiz," 109.

17. Harjo and Gloria Bird titled their 1997 anthology of contemporary Native women's writing *Reinventing the Enemy's Language.*

18. Keith Basso, " 'Stalking with Stories,' " 36.

19. Joy Harjo, "We Must Call a Meeting," in *In Mad Love and War,* 9.

20. Joy Harjo, "For Alva Benson and Those Who Have Learned to Speak," in *She Had Some Horses,* 18.

21. Harjo, "Poetics and Politics," 29.

22. Harjo, "Poetics and Politics," 22.

23. See Coltelli, "Joy Harjo," 63–64; and Harjo, "Poetics and Politics," 22, 23.

24. Harjo, "Poetics and Politics," 22.

A Place to See: Self-Representation and Resistance in Leslie Marmon Silko's Almanac of the Dead

1. From an interview with Rigoberta Menchú in Ronald Wright's *Stolen Continents: The Americas Through Indian Eyes Since 1492,* 272.

2. In Spanish, the rebels call themselves the Ejercito Zapatista de Liberación Nacional.

3. NBC, KVOA, Tucson, Arizona, 6 Jan. 1994.

4. For more on an ongoing history of rebellion against European conquerors

that dates back at least to 1697 when the Maya arose against the Spanish and were defeated at Tayasal in what is modern-day Guatemala, see Wright, *Stolen Continents,* 173–76. For an account of Emiliano Zapata's life and death, see Wright, *Stolen Continents,* 248–51.

5. Cynthia Deitering, "The Postnatural Novel," in *The Ecocriticism Reader,* ed. Glotfelty and Fromm, 196.

6. John Skow, "People of the Monkey Wrench," 86.

7. Melody Graulich, introduction to *Leslie Marmon Silko's "Yellow Woman,"* 24.

8. Alan Ryan, "An Inept *Almanac of the Dead,*" D6.

9. Since 1982, the trees of the Lacandon jungle have been cut down at the rate of 3.5 percent a year, falling to the international market for mahogany. Just 30 percent of the original five thousand square miles of the rain forest remain. Chiapas provides 60 percent of Mexico's hydroelectric energy, but in towns such as Ocosingo, Altamirano, and Las Margaritas—the towns where the Zapatistas burst into prominence on New Year's Day—only one-third of the households have electricity. Discoveries of petroleum deposits in Chiapas in the 1960s and 1970s did little to improve the lot of many of the state's inhabitants. Where oil was found on Indian communal land, the land was expropriated. Profits from the drilling of oil were directed away from Chiapas residents and toward the more prosperous center of Mexico. Today, 80 percent of the families in Ocosingo, Altamirano, and Las Margaritas earn less than $245 a month, and 48 percent of the adults are illiterate. See Daniel Dombey, "Chiapas Uprising Surprises a Mexico in Denial," A16; and Homero Aridjis, "Chiapas Revolt Rooted in Repressive History," A13.

10. Ann Louise Bardach, "Mexico's Poet Rebel," 73.

11. See Tim Golden, "Peasant Groups, Church Members Accused of Rebel Aid," A16.

12. Bardach, "Mexico's Poet Rebel," 70. According to anthropologist Gary Gossen, "The Zapatistas' collective Indian leadership itself—said to consist of a directorate of Tzeltal, Tzotzil, and Tojolabal Mayans, and other elders, male and female, from [the twenty-two] various Maya-speaking communities—has thus far remained relatively silent and invisible insofar as any direct contact with the media is concerned. Whatever the political, pragmatic, or symbolic reasons for the low profile of the Indian leadership in this movement, there can be little doubt about its strong Indian constituency, both within Chiapas and outside." See Gossen, "From Olmecs to Zapatistas," 553–54.

13. This phrase is taken from the Principles of Environmental Justice drawn up at the Leadership Summit. All seventeen principles are included in Giovanna Di Chiro's article, "Nature as Community," 307–9.

14. On 6 April 1992, in a seminar conducted by Larry Evers and Ofelia

Zepeda at the University of Arizona, Tucson, Silko insisted her novel must be read as an almanac. Her statement can be found on page 32 of the unpublished transcript, "Poetics and Politics: A Series of Readings by Native American Writers: Leslie Silko."

15. Two women and one African American man were among the numerous producers of colonial American almanacs. See Marion Stowell, *Early American Almanacs,* 102–11, 155.

16. Ibid., 44, xii.

17. Silko, "Poetics and Politics," 43.

18. Bardach, "Mexico's Poet Rebel," 71.

19. Silko, "Poetics and Politics," 43.

20. Qtd. in Bardach, "Mexico's Poet Rebel," 71.

21. Joel Simon, "Zapatistas Caution Against Election Fraud," A11.

22. Leslie Marmon Silko, *Almanac of the Dead,* 579.

23. Laura Coltelli, "Leslie Silko," in *Winged Words,* 151.

24. Dennis Tedlock, introduction to *Popol Vuh: The Definitive Edition,* 24–25.

25. Qtd. in Michael Lemonick, "Secrets of the Maya," 48.

26. Michael Coe, *Breaking the Maya Code,* 65, 270.

27. Qtd. in Lemonick, "Secrets of the Maya," 47. See also Coe, *Breaking the Maya Code,* 20, 270.

28. Tedlock, introduction to *Popul Vuh,* 24–27.

29. In the novel, Silko makes specific reference to The Book of Chilam Balam of Chumayel, a "Jaguar Priest" book that was compiled in the Yucatec Maya village of Chumayel, located on the Yucatán Peninsula. ("Error in translation of the Chumayel manuscript: 11 AHU was the year of the return of fair Quetzalcoatl" [572]). See G. B. Gordon's introduction to *The Book of Chilam Balam of Chumayel,* 5, 9.

30. Wright, *Stolen Continents,* 165.

31. Tedlock, introduction to *Popul Vuh,* 31.

32. Ibid., 32, 71.

33. For a discussion of the deportation of the Yaquis to the Yucatán Peninsula, see Wright, *Stolen Continents,* 247.

34. Carolyn Merchant, *Ecological Revolutions,* 114.

35. Ibid., 116–17; Jon Butler "Magic, Astrology, and the Early American Religious Heritage," 321.

36. Tedlock, introduction to *Popol Vuh,* 46–47.

37. Ibid., 35.

38. See Di Chiro, "Nature as Community," 300.

39. Rigoberta Menchú, *I, Rigoberta Menchú,* 1, emphasis Menchú's.

40. Beverly is quoted in Robin Wilson, "Anthropologist Challenges Veracity of Multicultural Icon," n.p.

41. On 29 March 1994, Guatemala's government and rebel leaders signed three breakthrough agreements aimed at ending more than three decades of civil war. See Hector Rosada Ganados, "Guatemala, Rebels Sign Rights Accords Aimed at Ending 33 Years of Civil War," A4.

42. Stoll's charges are corroborated in Larry Rohter, "Rigoberta Menchú: Tarnished Laureate," and the controversy surrounding *I, Rigoberta Menchú* is summarized in Wilson, "Anthropologist Challenges Veracity of Multicultural Icon."

43. Qtd. in Associated Press, "Menchú Admits Inaccuracies in Her Book," n.p.

44. Qtd. in James Poniewozik, "Rigoberta Menchú Meets the Press," n.p.

45. Dennis Tedlock, *The Spoken Word,* 270, 264.

46. Ibid., 271, emphasis Tedlock's.

47. Donna Haraway, "The Promises of Monsters," 314.

48. Coe, *Breaking the Maya Code,* 65–66, 270.

Reinventing Nature: Leslie Marmon Silko's Critique of Euro-American "Nature Talk"

1. In April 1999, two senior students at Columbine High School, near Denver, Colorado, entered the school and murdered twelve students and a teacher before turning their guns on themselves.

2. Leslie Marmon Silko, seminar discussion for "Poetics and Politics," 27.

3. Elizabeth Tallent, "Storytelling with a Vengeance," 6.

4. Alan Ryan, "An Inept *Almanac of the Dead.*"

5. Silko, "Poetics and Politics," 52.

6. "Teen, 19, Receives 264 Years for Killings at Buddhist Temple," B1, B2.

7. Leslie Marmon Silko, *Ceremony,* 246.

8. Leslie Marmon Silko, *Almanac of the Dead,* 36.

9. See Jim Erickson, "The Man Who Ran the Biosphere," 1A+.

10. Giovanna Di Chiro, "Nature as Community," 311.

11. See Shive Visvanathan, "From the Annals of the Laboratory State," 49.

12. See Carolyn Merchant, *The Death of Nature,* 169–81.

13. See ibid., 231, and Visvanathan, "From the Annals of the Laboratory State," 43.

14. See Merchant, *The Death of Nature,* 206–15 and Visvanathan, "From the Annals of the Laboratory State," 38–40.

15. Many of the original documents on the history and anthropology of American Indian tribes who were involved in the Indian Claims actions are presented in the *American Indian Ethnohistory* series published by Garland. Reports on the history of Laguna land claims as well as their anthropology,

emergence stories and stories of shrines, ceremonies, traditions, and hunting practices, which were recounted orally and collected by scholars as the basis of Laguna land claims, have been published by Garland in the following documents: Myra Ellen Jenkins, "History of Laguna Pueblo Land Claims," which mentions a letter written by Aunt Susie's husband, Laguna governor Walter G. Marmon, about encroachment on Laguna land (117–18); Robert L. Rands, "Laguna Land Utilization," which addresses Laguna shrines and hunting practices (68–70); and Florence Hawley Ellis, "Anthropology of Laguna Pueblo Land Claims," in which several transcripts of oral versions of the Laguna story of emergence are published.

Conclusion: To San Simon and Back

1. Patricia Preciado Martin, "The Journey," *Days of Plenty, Days of Want,* 65.

2. For more on the TCE contamination of Tucson's southside Mexican American neighborhoods, see Keith Bagwell, "Pollution Affects Minorities Most, Census Shows," B1; and Keith Bagwell, "Plans to Put Southsiders on TCE Registry Will Be Discussed Tomorrow," B2.

3. See Keith Bagwell, "3rd Legal Team Will Seek Clients for Class-Action Case over TCE," B1.

Bibliography

Abbey, Edward. *Desert Solitaire: A Season in the Wilderness.* New York: Ballantine Books, 1968.

Alexie, Sherman. *The Lone Ranger and Tonto Fistfight in Heaven.* New York: Harper Perennial, 1994.

Anzaldúa, Gloria. *Making Face, Making Soul: Haciendo Caras: Creative and Critical Perspectives by Women of Color.* San Francisco: aunt lute foundation, 1990.

Aridjis, Homero. "Chiapas Revolt Rooted in Repressive History." *Arizona Daily Star,* 10 Jan. 1994, A13.

Associated Press. "Menchú Admits Inaccuracies in Her Book." On-line at www.seattletimes.com/news/nation-world/html98/guat_021299.html.

Awiakta, Marilou. *Selu: Seeking the Corn Mother's Wisdom.* Golden, Colo.: Fulcrum, 1993.

Bagwell, Keith. "Plans to Put Southsiders on TCE Registry Will Be Discussed Tomorrow." *Arizona Daily Star,* 11 Aug. 1994, B2.

———. "Pollution Affects Minorities Most, Census Shows." *Arizona Daily Star,* 29 Mar. 1992, B1.

———. "3rd Legal Team Will Seek Clients for Class-Action Case over TCE." *Arizona Daily Star,* 30 Oct. 1991, B1.

Bahre, Conrad. "Human Impacts on the Grasslands of Southeastern Arizona." In *The Desert Grassland,* edited by Mitchel P. McClaran and Thomas R. Van Devender, 230–64. Tucson: University of Arizona Press, 1995.

Baker, Houston, Jr. "Local Pedagogy; or, How I Redeemed My Spring Semester." *PMLA* 108, no. 3 (May 1993): 400–409.

Bakhtin, Mikhail. *The Dialogic Imagination: Four Essays.* Edited by Michael Holquist. Translated by Caryl Emerson and Michael Holquist. Austin: University of Texas Press, 1981.

Bardach, Ann Louise. "Mexico's Poet Rebel." *Vanity Fair* (July 1994): 68–74, 130–35.

Basso, Keith H. "'Stalking with Stories': Names, Places, and Moral Narratives among the Western Apache." In *Text, Play, and Story: The Construction and Reconstruction of Self and Society,* edited by Edward M. Bruner, 19–55. Washington, D.C.: American Ethnological Society, 1984.

"Black Mesa Decision." *Big Mountain Index.* On-line at http://www .planet-peace.org/archive/big_mountain/bigmt-3-96.html. 16 Feb. 1999.

Bonnetti, Kay. "An Interview with Louise Erdrich and Michael Dorris." *Missouri Review* 11 (spring 1988): 79–99.

Bruchac, Joseph. "Review of *Love Medicine.*" *North Dakota Quarterly* 53 (spring 1988): 79–99.

———. *Songs from This Earth on Turtle's Back.* Greenfield, N.Y.: Greenfield Review, 1987.

Buell, Lawrence. *The Environmental Imagination: Thoreau, Nature Writing, and the Formation of American Culture.* Cambridge, Mass.: Belknap, 1995.

Butler, Jon. "Magic, Astrology, and the Early American Religious Heritage, 1600–1760." *American Historical Review* 84, no. 2 (Apr. 1979): 317–46.

Christian, Barbara. "The Race for Theory." In *Making Face, Making Soul: Haciendo Caras: Creative and Critical Perspectives by Women of Color,* edited by Gloria Anzaldúa, 335–45. San Francisco: aunt lute foundation, 1990.

Coe, Michael D. *Breaking the Maya Code.* New York: Thames and Hudson, 1992.

Coltelli, Laura. *Winged Words: American Indian Writers Speak.* Lincoln and London: University of Nebraska Press, 1990.

Cronon, William. "The Trouble with Wilderness." In *Uncommon Ground: Rethinking the Human Place in Nature,* edited by William Cronon, 69–90. New York: W. W. Norton, 1996.

———, ed. *Uncommon Ground: Rethinking the Human Place in Nature.* New York: W. W. Norton, 1996.

Deitering, Cynthia. "The Postnatural Novel: Toxic Consciousness in Fiction of the 1980s." In *The Ecocriticism Reader: Landmarks in Literary Ecology,* edited by Cheryll Glotfelty and Harold Fromm, 196–203. Athens and London: University of Georgia Press, 1996.

Dewdney, Selwyn. *The Sacred Scrolls of the Southern Ojibway.* Calgary: University of Toronto Press, 1975.

Di Chiro, Giovanna. "Nature as Community: The Convergence of Environmental and Social Justice." In *Uncommon Ground: Rethinking the Human Place in Nature,* edited by William Cronon, 298–320. New York: W. W. Norton, 1996.

"Dinéh Alliance Press Statement." On-line at http://www.yvwiiusdinvnohii .net/news/Dinehopi.htm. 16 Feb. 1999.

Dombey, Daniel. "Chiapas Uprising Surprises a Mexico in Denial: History of Unrest Is Overlooked as Part of Government Snubbing." *Arizona Daily Star,* 1 Jan. 1994, A1, A16.

Dorson, Richard M. *Bloodstoppers and Bearwalkers: Tradition of the Upper Peninsula.* Cambridge, Mass.: Harvard University Press, 1952.

Douglas, Mary. *Purity and Danger: An Analysis of the Concepts of Pollution and Taboo.* London and New York: Ark Paperbacks, 1984.

Ebert, Teresa. "Ludic Feminism, the Body, Performance, and Labor: Bringing *Materialism* Back into Feminist Cultural Studies." *Cultural Critique* (winter 1992–93): 5–50.

Ellis, Florence H. "Anthropology of Laguna Pueblo Land Claims." In *Pueblo Indians,* 3: 9–120. Vols. 1–5 of *American Indian Ethnohistory: Indians of the Southwest,* edited by David Agee Horr. New York: Garland, 1974.

———. "Archaeological and Ethnological Data Pertaining to Acoma and Laguna Land Claims, 1957–59." In *Pueblo Indians,* 2: 9–330. Vols. 1–5 of *American Indian Ethnohistory: Indians of the Southwest,* edited by David Agee Horr. New York: Garland, 1974.

———. *The Hopi: Their History and Use of Lands.* New York: Garland, 1974.

Erdrich, Louise. *Love Medicine.* Toronto: Bantam, 1984.

———. *Tracks.* New York: Harper and Row, 1988.

Erickson, Jim. "The Man Who Ran the Biosphere." *Arizona Daily Star,* 17 July 1994, A1+.

Evers, Larry, ed. *The South Corner of Time: hopi navajo papago yaqui tribal literature.* Tucson: University of Arizona Press, 1980.

Finch, Robert, and John Elder, eds. *The Norton Book of Nature Writing.* New York: W. W. Norton, 1990.

Ganados, Hector Rosada. "Guatemala, Rebels Sign Rights Accords Aimed at Ending of 33 Years of Civil War." *Arizona Daily Star,* 30 Mar. 1994, A4.

Glotfelty, Cheryll, and Harold Fromm, eds. *The Ecocriticism Reader: Landmarks in Literary Ecology.* Athens and London: University of Georgia Press, 1996.

Golden, Tim. "Peasant Groups, Church Members Accused of Rebel Aid." *Arizona Daily Star,* 9 Jan. 1994, A16.

Gordon, G. B. Introduction to *The Book of Chilam Balam of Chumayel,* 3–11. Vol. 5 of *The Museum Anthropological Publications.* Philadelphia: University Museum, 1913.

Gossen, Gary H. "From Olmecs to Zapatistas: A Once and Future History of Souls." *American Anthropologist* 96, no. 3: 553–70.

Graulich, Melody, ed. *Leslie Marmon Silko's "Yellow Woman."* New Brunswick, N.J.: Rutgers University Press, 1993.

Griffith, James S. *Beliefs and Holy Places: A Spiritual Geography of the Pimería Alta.* Tucson: University of Arizona Press, 1992.

Hallowell, A. Irving. "Ojibwa Ontology, Behavior, and World View." In *Teachings from the American Earth: Indian Religion and Philosophy,* edited by Dennis Tedlock and Barbara Tedlock, 141–78. New York: Liveright, 1975.

Halpern, Daniel, ed. *On Nature: Nature, Landscape, and Natural History.* San Francisco: North Pointe, 1987.

Haraway, Donna J. "The Promises of Monsters: A Regenerative Politics for Inappropriate/d Others." In *Cultural Studies,* edited by Laurence Grossberg, Cory Nelson, and Paula Teichler, 295–337. New York: Routledge, 1992.

Harjo, Joy. *In Mad Love and War.* Middletown, Conn.: Wesleyan University Press, 1990.

——. Seminar for "Poetics and Politics: A Series of Readings by Native American Writers." University of Arizona, Tucson, 27 Apr. 1992. Unpublished transcript.

——. *She Had Some Horses.* New York: Thunder's Mouth, 1983.

Harjo, Joy, and Gloria Bird. *Reinventing the Enemy's Language.* New York: W. W. Norton, 1997.

Hartsock, Nancy. "Rethinking Modernism: Minority vs. Majority Theories." *Cultural Critique* (fall 1987): 187–206.

Harvey, David. *Justice, Nature, and the Geography of Difference.* New York: Blackwell, 1996.

Hecht, Susanna, and Alexander Cockburn. *The Fate of the Forest: Developers, Destroyers, and Defenders of the Amazon.* New York: Verso, 1989.

Hoebel, E. Adamson. "Zia Pueblo." In *Handbook of North American Indians,* edited by Alfonzo Ortiz, 407–17. Vol. 9 of *Southwest,* edited by William C. Sturtevant. Washington, D.C.: Smithsonian Institution, 1979.

Hogan, Linda. *Dwellings: A Spiritual History of the Living World.* New York: Touchstone, 1995.

Jackson, John Brinckerhoff. *Discovering the Vernacular Landscape.* New Haven, Conn.: Yale University Press, 1984.

Jenkins, Myra Ellen. "History of Laguna Pueblo Land Claims." In *Pueblo Indians,* 4: 9–204. Vols. 1–5 of *American Indian Ethnohistory: Indians of the Southwest,* edited by David Agee Horr. New York: Garland, 1974.

Jones, William. *Ojibwa Texts.* Edited by Truman Michelson. Vol. 7, part 1, of *Publications of the American Ethnological Society,* edited by Franz Boaz. New York: E. J. Brill, 1917.

Josephy, Alvin M., Jr. "The Murder of the Southwest." *Audubon* (July 1971): 50–67.

——, ed. *America in 1492: The World of the Indian Peoples Before the Arrival of Columbus.* New York: Knopf, 1992.

Kickingbird, Kirke, and Lynn Kickingbird. "A Short History of Indian Education, Part I." *American Indian Journal* (Aug. 1979): 13–16.

——. "A Short History of Indian Education, Part II." *American Indian Journal* (Sept. 1979): 17–21.

Kitteridge, William. *Owning It All.* Saint Paul, Minn.: Graywolf, 1987.

LaDuke, Winona, and Ward Churchill. "Native America: The Political Economy of Radioactive Colonialism." *Journal of Ethnic Studies* 13, no. 3 (fall 1985): 107–32.

Landes, Ruth. *Ojibwa Religion and the Midewiwin.* Madison: University of Wisconsin Press, 1968.

Lemonick, Michael. "Secrets of the Maya." *Time,* 9 Aug. 1993: 44–50.

Love, Glen. "Revaluing Nature: Toward an Ecological Criticism." In *The Ecocriticism Reader: Landmarks in Literary Ecology,* edited by Cheryl Glotfelty and Harold Fromm, 225–40. Athens: University of Georgia Press, 1996.

Lutwak, Leonard. *The Role of Place in Literature.* Syracuse, N.Y.: Syracuse University Press, 1984.

Lyon, Thomas J., ed. *This Incomparable Lande: A Book of American Nature Writing.* Boston: Houghton Mifflin, 1989.

Martin, Patricia Preciado. *Days of Plenty, Days of Want.* Tempe, Arizona: Bilingual, 1988.

Meeker, Joseph. *The Comedy of Survival: Studies in Literary Ecology.* New York: Charles Scribner's Sons, 1974.

Menchú, Rigoberta. *I, Rigoberta Menchú: An Indian Woman in Guatemala.* Edited by Elisabeth Burgos-Debray. Translated by Ann Wright. London: Verso, 1984.

Merchant, Carolyn. *The Death of Nature: Women, Ecology, and the Scientific Revolution.* San Francisco: Harper, 1980.

——. *Ecological Revolutions: Nature, Gender, and Science in New England.* Chapel Hill and London: University of North Carolina Press, 1989.

Murphy, Patrick D. *Literature, Nature, and Other: Ecofeminist Critiques.* Albany: State University of New York Press, 1995.

Nabhan, Gary. *Gathering the Desert.* Tucson: University of Arizona Press, 1997.

Ortiz, Simon. Seminar for "Poetics and Politics: A Series of Readings by Native American Writers." University of Arizona, Tucson, 3 Feb. 1992. Unpublished transcript.

——. "Towards a National Indian Literature: Cultural Authenticity in Nationalism." *MELUS: Multi-Ethnic Literatures of the United States.* 8, no. 2 (summer 1981): 7–12.

——. *Woven Stone.* Tucson: University of Arizona Press, 1992.

Pollan, Michael. *Second Nature: A Gardener's Education.* New York: Delta, 1991.

Poniewozik, James. "Rigoberta Menchú Meets the Press." *Salon.* On-line at www.salonmag.com/news/1999/02/12newsa.htm. 12 Feb. 1999.

Proctor, James. "Whose Nature?" In *Uncommon Grounds: Rethinking the Human Place in Nature,* edited by William Cronon, 269–97. New York: W. W. Norton, 1996.

Rands, Robert L. "Acoma Land Utilization: An Ethnohistorical Report." In *Pueblo Indians,* 3: 211–407. Vols. 1–5 of *American Indian Ethnohistory: Indians of the Southwest,* edited by David Agee Horr. New York: Garland, 1974.

———. "Laguna Land Utilization: An Ethnohistorical Report." In *Pueblo Indians,* 4: 205–396. Vols. 1–5 of *American Indian Ethnohistory: Indians of the Southwest,* edited by David Agee Horr. New York: Garland, 1974.

Relph, Edward. *Place and Placelessness.* London: Pion, 1976.

Rohter, Larry. "Rigoberta Menchú: Tarnished Laureate." *New York Times,* 15 Dec. 1998. On-line at www.frontpagemag.com/archives/academia/rohter12-17-98.htm.

Rueckert, William. "Literature and Ecology: An Experiment in Ecocriticism." In *The Ecocriticism Reader: Landmarks in Literary Ecology,* edited by Cheryll Glotfelty and Harold Fromm, 105–23. Athens and London: University of Georgia Press, 1996.

Ryan, Alan. "An Inept *Almanac of the Dead.*" Review of *Almanac of the Dead,* by Leslie Marmon Silko. *USA Today,* 21 Jan. 1992, D6.

Ryden, Kent C. "Landscape with Figures: Nature, Folk Culture, and the Human Ecology of American Environmental Writing." *Interdisciplinary Studies in Literature and the Environment* 4, no. 1 (spring 1997): 1–28.

———. *Mapping the Invisible Landscape: Folklore, Writing, and the Sense of Place.* Iowa City: University of Iowa Press, 1993.

Saville-Troike, Muriel. *The Ethnography of Communication: An Introduction.* Oxford: Blackwell, 1982.

Scheese, Don. *"Desert Solitaire."* In *The Ecocriticism Reader: Landmarks in Literary Ecology,* edited by Cheryll Glotfelty and Harold Fromm, 303–22. Athens and London: University of Georgia Press, 1996.

Silko, Leslie Marmon. *Almanac of the Dead.* New York: Simon and Schuster, 1991.

———. *Ceremony.* New York: Penguin, 1977.

———. "Interior and Exterior Landscapes: The Pueblo Migration Stories." In *Yellow Woman and a Beauty of the Spirit: Essays on Native American Life Today,* 25–47. New York: Touchstone, 1996.

———. Interview by Lupita Murillo. KVOA Nightly News at 10:00. Tucson, Arizona, 9 Jan. 1994.

——. "Landscape, History, and the Pueblo Imagination." *Anteus* 57 (1986): 92.

——. "Language and Literature from a Pueblo Indian Perspective." In *English Literature: Selected Papers from the English Institute, 1979,* edited by Leslie A. Fiedler and Houston A. Baker, 54–72. Baltimore and London: Johns Hopkins University Press, 1981.

——. Seminar for "Poetics and Politics: A Series of Readings by Native American Writers." University of Arizona, Tucson, 6 Apr. 1992. Unpublished transcript.

Simon, Joel. "Zapatistas Caution Against Election Fraud." *Arizona Daily Star,* 8 Aug. 1994, A11.

Skow, Jon. "People of the Monkey Wrench." Review of *Almanac of the Dead,* by Leslie Marmon Silko. *Time* (9 Dec. 1991): 86.

Slovic, Scott. "Ecocriticism: Storytelling, Values, Communication, Contact." Position paper presented at the Western Literature Association Conference, Salt Lake City, Oct. 1994.

——. *Seeking Awareness in American Nature Writing: Henry Thoreau, Annie Dillard, Edward Abbey, Wendell Berry, Barry Lopez.* Salt Lake City: University of Utah Press, 1992.

Stoll, David. *Rigoberta Menchú and the Story of All Poor Guatemalans.* Boulder, Colo.: Westview, 1999.

Stowell, Marion Barber. *Early American Almanacs: The Colonial Weekday Bible.* New York: Burt Franklin, 1977.

Tallent, Elizabeth. "Storytelling with a Vengeance." Review of *Almanac of the Dead,* by Leslie Marmon Silko. *New York Times Book Review,* 22 Dec. 1991, 6.

Tedlock, Dennis, trans. *Finding the Center: Narrative Poetry of the Zuni Indians.* From performances in the Zuni by Andrew Peynetsa and Walter Sanchez. Lincoln and London: University of Nebraska Press, 1972.

——. *The Spoken Word and the Work of Interpretation.* Philadelphia: University of Pennsylvania Press, 1983.

——, trans. *Popol Vuh: The Definitive Edition of the Mayan Book of the Dawn of Life and the Glories of Gods and Kings.* New York: Touchstone, 1985.

"Teen, 19, Receives 264 Years for Killings at Buddhist Temple." *Arizona Daily Star,* 16 July 1994, B1, B2.

Tuan, Yi Fu. *Space and Place: The Perspective of Experience.* Minneapolis: University of Minneapolis Press, 1977.

Tyler, Moses Coit. *A History of American Literature.* 2 vols. New York: G. P. Putnam's Sons, 1881.

Visvanathan, Shive. "From the Annals of the Laboratory State." *Alternatives* 12 (1987): 37–59.

Vizenor, Gerald. *The People Named the Chippewa: Narrative Histories.* Minneapolis: University of Minnesota Press, 1984.

White, Richard. "Are You an Environmentalist or Do You Work for a Living?" In *Uncommon Ground: Rethinking the Human Place in Nature,* edited by William Cronon, 171–85. New York: W. W. Norton, 1996.

Wild, Peter. "Edward Abbey: The Middle Class Maverick." *New Mexico Humanities Review* 6, no. 2 (summer 1983): 15–23.

Williams, Terry Tempest. "All That Is Hidden." In *An Unspoken Hunger: Stories from the Fields,* 115–24. New York: Pantheon, 1994.

———. *Refuge: An Unnatural History of Family and Place.* New York: Pantheon, 1991.

Wilson, Robin. "Anthropologist Challenges Veracity of Multicultural Icon." *Chronicle of Higher Education: Colloquy.* On-line at www.chronicle.com/colloquy/99/menchu/background.htm. 11 Jan. 1999.

Wright, Ronald. *Stolen Continents: The Americas Through Indian Eyes Since 1492.* Boston: Houghton Mifflin, 1992.

Zencey, Eric. *Virgin Forest: Meditations on History, Ecology, and Culture.* Athens and London: University of Georgia Press, 1998.

Zepeda, Ofelia. *Ocean Power.* Tucson: University of Arizona Press, 1995.

Index

About the Author

Joni Adamson is an assistant professor and the Program Head of English and Folklore at the University of Arizona, Sierra Vista, where she teaches American literature, Native American literature, environmental literature, and folklore.